Pour Your
Heart Into It

Pour Your Heart Into It

HOW STARBUCKS
BUILT A COMPANY
ONE CUP
AT A TIME

Howard Schultz

CHAIRMAN & CEO,
STARBUCKS COFFEE COMPANY

AND **Dori Jones Yang**

hachette
BOOKS

NEW YORK   BOSTON

Excerpt from "If" by Rudyard Kipling, reprinted by permission of A.P. Watt Ltd on behalf of The National Trust.

Hachette Books
Hachette Book Group
1290 Avenue of the Americas
New York, NY 10104
www.HachetteBookGroup.com

Printed in the United States of America

LSC-C

Originally published by Hyperion
First Hachette Books trade edition: December 2014

30

Hachette Books is a division of Hachette Book Group, Inc.
The Hachette Books name and logo are trademarks of Hachette Book Group, Inc.

The publisher is not responsible for websites (or their content) that are not owned by the publisher.

Book design by Christine Weathersbee

ISBN 978-0-7868-8356-1 (pbk.)

This book is dedicated with love to my wife, Sheri,
to my mother, to the memory of my father,
and to all my partners at Starbucks, especially
Mary Caitrin Mahoney, Aaron David Goodrich,
and Emory Allen Evans. You live on in our hearts.

CONTENTS

Pour Your
Heart Into It

PROLOGUE

Care more than others
think wise.

Risk more than others
think safe.

Dream more than others
think practical.

Expect more than others
think possible.

On a cold January day in 1961, my father broke his ankle at work.

I was seven years old at the time and in the midst of a snow-ball fight in the icy playground behind my school when my mother leaned out our seventh-floor apartment window and waved wildly in my direction. I raced home.

"Dad had an accident," she told me. "I have to go to the hospital."

My father, Fred Schultz, was stuck at home with his foot up for more than a month. I'd never seen a cast before, so it fascinated me at first. But the novelty quickly wore off. Like so many others of his station in life, when Dad didn't work, he didn't get paid.

His latest job had been as a truck driver, picking up and delivering diapers. For months, he had complained bitterly about the odor and the mess, saying it was the worst job in the world. But now that he had lost it, he seemed to want it back. My mom was seven months pregnant, so she couldn't work. Our family had no income, no health insurance, no worker's compensation, nothing to fall back on.

At the dinner table, my sister and I ate silently as my parents argued about how much money they would have to borrow, and from whom. Sometimes, in the evening, the phone would ring, and my mother would insist I answer it. If it was a bill collector, she instructed me to say my parents weren't at home.

My brother, Michael, was born in March; they had to borrow again to pay the hospital expenses.

Years later, that image of my father—slumped on the family couch, his leg in a cast, unable to work or earn money, and ground down by the world—is still burned into my mind. Looking back now, I have a lot of respect for my dad. He never finished high school, but he was an honest man who worked hard.

3

He sometimes had to take on two or three jobs just to put food on the table. He cared a lot about his three kids, and played ball with us on weekends. He loved the Yankees.

But he was a beaten man. In a series of blue-collar jobs—truck driver, factory worker, cab driver—he never made as much as $20,000 a year, never could afford to own his own home. I spent my childhood in the Projects, federally subsidized housing, in Canarsie, Brooklyn. By the time I was a teenager, I realized what a stigma that carried.

As I got older, I often clashed with my dad. I became bitter about his underachievement, his lack of responsibility. I thought he could have accomplished so much more, if he had only tried.

After he died, I realized I had judged him unfairly. He had tried to fit into the system, but the system had crushed him. With low self-esteem, he had never been able to climb out of the hole and improve his life.

The day he died, of lung cancer, in January 1988, was the saddest of my life. He had no savings, no pension. More important, he had never attained fulfillment and dignity from work he found meaningful.

As a kid, I never had any idea that I would one day head a company. But I knew in my heart that if I was ever in a position where I could make a difference, I wouldn't leave people behind.

My parents could not understand what it was that attracted me to Starbucks. I left a well-paying, prestigious job in 1982 to join what was then a small Seattle retailer with five stores. For my part, I saw Starbucks not for what it was, but for what it could be. It had immediately captivated me with its combination of passion and authenticity. If it could expand nationwide, romancing the Italian artistry of espresso-making as well as offering fresh-roasted coffee beans, I gradually realized, it could reinvent an age-old commodity and appeal to millions of people as strongly as it appealed to me.

PROLOGUE

I became CEO of Starbucks in 1987 because I went out, as an entrepreneur, and convinced investors to believe in my vision for the company. Over the next ten years, with a team of smart and experienced managers, we built Starbucks from a local business with 6 stores and less than 100 employees into a national one with more than 1,300 stores and 25,000 employees. Today we are in cities all over North America, as well as in Tokyo and Singapore. Starbucks has become a brand that's recognized nationally, a prominence than gives us license to experiment with innovative new products. Both sales and profits have grown by more than 50 percent a year for six consecutive years.

But the story of Starbucks is not just a record of growth and success. It's also about how a company can be built in a different way. It's about a company completely unlike the ones my father worked for. It's living proof that a company can lead with its heart and nurture its soul and still make money. It shows that a company can provide long-term value for shareholders without sacrificing its core belief in treating its employees with respect and dignity, both because we have a team of leaders who believe it's right and because it's the best way to do business.

Starbucks strikes an emotional chord with people. Some drive out of their way to get their morning coffee from our stores. We've become such a resonant symbol of contemporary American life that our familiar green siren logo shows up frequently on TV shows and in movies. We've introduced new words into the American vocabulary and new social rituals for the 1990s. In some communities, Starbucks stores have become a Third Place—a comfortable, sociable gathering spot away from home and work, like an extension of the front porch.

People connect with Starbucks because they relate to what we stand for. It's more than great coffee. It's the romance of the coffee experience, the feeling of warmth and community people get in Starbucks stores. That tone is set by our *baristas*, who custom-make each espresso drink and explain the origins of different coffees. Some of them come to Starbucks with no more skills than my father had, yet they're the ones who create the magic.

If there's one accomplishment I'm proudest of at Starbucks, it's the relationship of trust and confidence we've built with the people who work at the company. That's not just an empty phrase, as it is at so many companies. We've built it into such ground-breaking programs as a comprehensive health-care program, even for part-timers, and stock options that provide ownership for everyone. We treat warehouse workers and entry-level retail people with the kind of respect most companies show for only high executives.

These policies and attitudes run counter to conventional business wisdom. A company that is managed only for the benefit of shareholders treats its employees as a line item, a cost to be contained. Executives who cut jobs aggressively are often rewarded with a temporary run-up in their stock price. But in the long run, they are not only undermining morale but sacrificing the innovation, the entrepreneurial spirit, and the heartfelt commitment of the very people who could elevate the company to greater heights.

What many in business don't realize is that it's not a zero-sum game. Treating employees benevolently shouldn't be viewed as an added cost that cuts into profits, but as a powerful energizer that can grow the enterprise into something far greater than one leader could envision. With pride in their work, Starbucks people are less likely to leave. Our turnover rate is less than half the industry average, which not only saves money but strengthens our bond with customers.

But the benefits run even deeper. If people relate to the company they work for, if they form an emotional tie to it and buy into its dreams, they will pour their heart into making it better. When employees have self-esteem and self-respect they can contribute so much more: to their company, to their family, to the world.

Although I didn't consciously plan it that way, Starbucks has become a living legacy of my dad.

Because not everyone can take charge of his or her destiny, those who do rise to positions of authority have a responsibility to those whose daily work keeps the enterprise running, not only to steer the correct course but to make sure no one is left behind.

I never planned to write a book, at least not this early in my career. I firmly believe that the greatest part of Starbucks' achievement lies in the future, not the past. If Starbucks is a twenty-chapter book, we're only in Chapter Three.

But for several reasons, I decided that now was a good time to tell the Starbucks story.

First, I want to inspire people to pursue their dreams. I come from common roots, with no silver spoon, no pedigree, no early mentors. I dared to dream big dreams, and then I willed them to happen. I'm convinced that most people can achieve their dreams and beyond if they have the determination to keep trying.

Second, and more profoundly, I hope to inspire leaders of enterprises to aim high. Success is empty if you arrive at the finish line alone. The best reward is to get there surrounded by winners. The more winners you can bring with you—whether they're employees, customers, shareholders, or readers—the more gratifying the victory.

I'm not writing this book to make money. All my earnings from it will go to the newly formed Starbucks Foundation, which will allocate the proceeds to philanthropic work on behalf of Starbucks and its partners.

This is the story of Starbucks, but it is not a conventional business book. Its purpose is not to share my life's story, or to offer advice on how to fix broken companies, or to document a corporate history. It contains no executive summaries, no bulleted lists of action points, no theoretical framework for analyzing why some enterprises succeed and others fail.

Instead, it's the story of a team of people who built a successful enterprise based on values and guiding principles seldom encountered in corporate America. It tells how, along the way, we learned some important lessons about business and about life. These insights, I hope, will help others who are building a business or pursuing a life's dream.

My ultimate aim in writing *Pour Your Heart into It* is to reassure people to have the courage to persevere, to keep following their hearts even when others scoff. Don't be beaten down by naysayers. Don't let the odds scare you from even trying. What were the odds against me, a kid from the Projects?

A company can grow big without losing the passion and personality that built it, but only if it's driven not by profits but by values and by people.

The key is heart. I pour my heart into every cup of coffee, and so do my partners at Starbucks. When customers sense that, they respond in kind.

If you pour your heart into your work, or into any worthy enterprise, you can achieve dreams others may think impossible. That's what makes life rewarding.

There's a Jewish tradition called the *yahrzeit*. On the eve of the anniversary of a loved one's death, close relatives light a candle and keep it burning for twenty-four hours. I light that candle every year, for my father.

I just don't want that light to go out.

PART
ONE

Rediscovering Coffee

The Years up to 1987

I

IMAGINATION, DREAMS, AND HUMBLE ORIGINS

It is only with the heart that one can see rightly.
What is essential is invisible to the eye.

—Antoine de Saint-Exupéry,
The Little Prince

Starbucks, as it is today, is actually the child of two parents. One is the original Starbucks, founded in 1971, a company passionately committed to world-class coffee and dedicated to educating its customers, one on one, about what great coffee can be.

The other is the vision and values I brought to the company: the combination of competitive drive and a profound desire to make sure everyone in the organization could win together. I wanted to blend coffee with romance, to dare to achieve what others said was impossible, to defy the odds with innovative ideas, and to do all this with elegance and style.

In truth, Starbucks needed the influence of both parents to become what it is today.

Starbucks prospered for ten years before I discovered it. I learned of its early history from its founders, and I'll retell that story in

Chapter Two. In this book, I will relate the story the way I experienced it, starting with my early life, because many of the values that shaped the growth of the enterprise trace their roots back to a crowded apartment in Brooklyn, New York.

HUMBLE ORIGINS CAN INSTILL BOTH DRIVE AND COMPASSION

One thing I've noticed about romantics: They try to create a new and better world far from the drabness of everyday life. That is Starbucks' aim, too. We try to create, in our stores, an oasis, a little neighborhood spot where you can take a break, listen to some jazz, and ponder universal or personal or even whimsical questions over a cup of coffee.

What kind of person dreams up such a place?

From my personal experience, I'd say that the more uninspiring your origins, the more likely you are to use your imagination and invent worlds where everything seems possible.

That's certainly true of me.

I was three when my family moved out of my grandmother's apartment into the Bayview Projects in 1956. They were in the heart of Canarsie, on Jamaica Bay, fifteen minutes from the airport, fifteen minutes from Coney Island. Back then, the Projects were not a frightening place but a friendly, large, leafy compound with a dozen eight-story brick buildings, all brand-new. The elementary school, P.S. 272, was right on the grounds of the Projects, complete with playground, basketball courts, and paved school yard. Still, no one was proud of living in the Projects; our parents were all what we now call "the working poor."

Still, I had many happy moments during my childhood. Growing up in the Projects made for a well-balanced value system, as it forced me to get along with many different kinds of people. Our building alone housed about 150 families, and we all shared one tiny elevator. Each apartment was very small, and our family started off in a cramped two-bedroom unit.

Both my parents came from working-class families, residents of the East New York section of Brooklyn for two generations. My grandfather died young, so my dad had to quit school and start working as a teenager. During World War II, he was a medic in the Army in the South Pacific, in New Caledonia and Saipan, where he contracted yellow fever and malaria. As a result, his lungs were always weak, and he often got colds. After the war, he got a series of blue-collar jobs but never found himself, never had a plan for his life.

My mother was a strong-willed and powerful woman. Her name is Elaine, but she goes by the nickname Bobbie. Later, she worked as a receptionist, but when we were growing up, she took care of us three kids full time.

My sister, Ronnie, close to me in age, shared many of the same hard childhood experiences. But, to an extent, I was able to insulate my brother, Michael, from the economic hardship I felt and give him the kind of guidance my parents couldn't offer. He tagged along with me wherever I went. I used to call him "The Shadow." Despite the eight-year age gap, I developed an extremely close relationship with Michael, acting like a father to him when I could. I watched with pride as he became a good athlete, a strong student, and ultimately a success in his own business career.

I played sports with the neighborhood kids from dawn to dusk every day of my childhood. My dad joined us whenever he could, after work and on weekends. Each Saturday and Sunday morning, starting at 8 A.M., hundreds of us kids would gather in the school-yard. You had to be good there, because if you didn't win, you'd be out of the game, forced to watch for hours before you could get back in. So I played to win.

Luckily for me, I was a natural athlete. Whether it was baseball, basketball, or football, I jumped right in and played hard till I got good at it. I used to organize pickup games of baseball and basket-ball with whatever kids lived in the neighborhood—Jewish kids,

Italian kids, black kids. Nobody ever had to lecture us about diversity; we lived it.

It's always been a part of my personality to develop an unbridled passion about things that interest me. My first passion was for baseball. At that time in the boroughs of New York, every conversation started and ended with baseball. Connections and barriers with other people were made not by race or religion but by the team you rooted for. The Dodgers had just left for Los Angeles (they broke my father's heart, and he never forgave them), but we still had many of the baseball greats. I remember walking home and hearing play-by-play radio reports blaring out of open windows on every side of the courtyard.

I was a die-hard Yankees fan, and my dad took my brother and me to countless games. We never had good seats, but that didn't matter. It was the thrill of just being there. Mickey Mantle was my idol. I had his number, 7, on my shirts, sneakers, everything I owned. When I played baseball, I mimicked Mickey Mantle's stance and gestures.

When The Mick retired, the finality of it was hard to believe. How could he stop playing? My father took me to both Mickey Mantle Days at Yankee Stadium, September 18, 1968, and June 8, 1969. As I watched the tributes to him, and listened to the other players say good-bye, and heard him speak, I felt deeply sad. Baseball was never the same for me after that. The Mick was such an intense presence in our lives that years later, when he died, I got phone calls of consolation from childhood friends I hadn't heard from in decades.

Coffee was not a big part of my childhood. My mother drank instant coffee. When company came over, she'd buy some canned coffee and take out her old percolator. I remember listening to it grumble and watching that little glass cap until finally the coffee popped up into it like a jumping bean.

It was only as I grew older that I began to realize how tight the family finances were. On rare occasions we'd go to a Chinese restaurant, and my parents would discuss what dishes to order, based solely on how much cash my dad had in his wallet that day. I felt angry and ashamed when I realized that the sleepaway camp I attended in the summer was a subsidized program for underprivileged kids. After that, I refused to go back.

By the time I got to high school, I understood the stigma of living in the Projects. Canarsie High School was less than a mile away, but to get there I had to walk down streets lined with small single-family homes and duplexes. The people who lived there, I knew, looked down on us.

Once I asked out a girl from a different part of New York. I remember how her father's face dropped in stages as he asked:

"Where do you live?"

"We live in Brooklyn," I answered.

"Where?"

"Canarsie."

"Where?"

"Bayview Projects."

"Oh."

There was an unspoken judgment about me in his reaction, and it irked me to see it.

As the oldest of three children, I had to grow up quickly. I started earning money at an early age. At twelve, I had a paper route; later I worked behind the counter at the local luncheonette. At sixteen, I got an after-school job in the garment district of Manhattan, at a furrier, stretching animal skins. It was horrendous work, and left thick callouses on my thumbs. I spent one hot summer in a sweatshop, steaming yarn at a knitting factory. I always gave part of my earnings to my mother—not because she insisted but because I felt bad for the position my parents were in.

Still, in the 1950s and early 1960s, the American dream was vibrant, and we all felt entitled to a piece of it. My mother drummed that into us. She herself had never finished high school, and her biggest dream was a college education for all three of her kids. Wise and pragmatic in her blunt, opinionated way, she gave me tremendous confidence. Over and over, she would put powerful models in front of me, pointing out individuals who had made something of their lives and insisting that I, too, could achieve anything I set my heart on. She encouraged me to challenge myself, to place myself in situations that weren't comfortable, so that I could learn to overcome adversity. I don't know how she came to that knowledge, because she didn't live by those rules. But she willed us to succeed.

Years later, during one of her visits to Seattle, I showed my mother our new offices at Starbucks Center. As we walked around, passing departments and workstations, seeing people talking on the phone and typing on computers, I could tell her head was just spinning at the size and scope of the operation. Finally, she edged closer to me and whispered into my ear: "Who pays all these people?" It was beyond her imagination.

During my childhood, I never dreamed of working in business. The only entrepreneur I knew was my uncle, Bill Farber. He had a small paper factory in the Bronx, where he later hired my father as a foreman. I didn't know what work I would eventually do, but I knew I had to escape the struggle my parents lived with every day. I had to get out of the Projects, out of Brooklyn. I remember lying in bed at night and thinking: *What if I had a crystal ball and could see the future?* But I quickly shut out the thought, for I realized I would be too frightened to look into it.

I was aware of only one escape route: sports. Like the kids in the movie *Hoop Dreams*, my friends and I thought they were the ticket to a great life. In high school, I applied myself to schoolwork only when I had to, because what I learned in the classroom seemed irrelevant. Instead I spent hours and days playing football.

I'll never forget the day I made the team. As a symbol of that honor, I got my letter, the big blue C that identified me as an accomplished athlete. But my mother couldn't afford to pay $29 for the letter jacket, and asked me to wait a week or so till Dad got his paycheck. I was devastated. Everybody at school had been planning to wear those jackets on one agreed-upon day. I couldn't show up without a jacket, but I also didn't want to make my mother feel any worse. So I borrowed money from a friend to buy the jacket and wore it on the appointed day, but I hid it from my parents until they were able to afford it.

My biggest triumph in high school was becoming quarterback, which made me a Big Man on Campus among the 5,700 students of Canarsie High. The school was so poor that we didn't even have a football field, and all our games were away games. Our team was pretty bad, but I was one of the better players on it.

One day, a recruiter came to scout an opposing player at one of our games. I didn't know he was there. A few days later, though, I received a letter from what, in my frame of reference, sounded like another planet, Northern Michigan University. They were recruiting for the football team. Was I interested? I whooped and hollered. It felt as good as an invitation to the NFL draft.

Northern Michigan eventually offered me a football scholarship, the only offer I got. Without it, I don't know how I could have realized my mother's dream of going to college.

During spring break of my last year in high school, my parents drove me to see this unimaginable place. We drove nearly a thousand miles to Marquette, in the Upper Peninsula of Michigan. We had never been outside New York, and my parents were caught up in the adventure of it. We drove across wooded mountains, through vast stretches of flat fields, past huge lakes that looked like oceans. When we finally arrived, the campus looked like an America I had seen only in the movies, with budding trees, laughing students, flying frisbees.

I was out of Brooklyn at last.

By coincidence, Starbucks was founded that same year in Seattle, a city even farther beyond my imagination at that time.

I loved the freedom and the open space of college, although I felt lonely and out of place at first. I made some close friends my freshman year and ended up rooming with them for four years, on and off campus. Twice I sent for my brother and he flew out to visit. One year, for Mother's Day, I hitchhiked back to New York, surprising her.

It turned out I wasn't as good a football player as I thought, and I ended up not playing after all. To stay in school I took out loans and worked part-time and summer jobs to pay for my expenses. I had a night job as a bartender, and I even sold my blood sometimes. Still, those were mostly fun years, a time with little responsibility. With a draft number of 332, I didn't have to worry about going to Vietnam.

I majored in communications and took courses in public speaking and interpersonal communications. During senior year, I also picked up a few business classes, because I was starting to worry about what I would do after graduation. I maintained a B average, applying myself only when I had to take a test or make a presentation.

After four years, I became the first college graduate in my family. To my parents, I had attained the big prize: a diploma. But I had no direction. No one ever helped me see the value in the knowledge I was gaining. I've often joked since then: If someone had provided me with direction and guidance, I really could have been somebody.

It took years before I found my passion in life. Each step after that discovery was a quantum leap into something unknown, each move riskier than the last. But getting out of Brooklyn and earning a college degree gave me the courage to keep on dreaming.

For years I hid the fact that I grew up in the Projects. I didn't lie about it, but I just didn't bring it up, for it wasn't much of a credential. But however much I tried to deny them, those memories of my early experiences were imprinted indelibly in my mind. I could never forget what it's like to be on the other side, afraid to look into the crystal ball.

IMAGINATION, DREAMS, AND HUMBLE ORIGINS

In December 1994, a *New York Times* article about Starbucks' success mentioned that I had grown up in the Projects of Canarsie. After it appeared, I received letters from Bayview and other blighted neighborhoods. Most came from mothers, trying to guide their kids, who said that my story gave them hope.

The odds on my coming out of the environment in which I was raised and getting to where I am today are impossible to gauge. How did it happen?

The sun shone on me, it's true, as my brother, Michael, always tells me. But my story is as much one of perseverance and drive as it is of talent and luck. I willed it to happen. I took my life in my hands, learned from anyone I could, grabbed what opportunity I could, and molded my success step by step.

Fear of failure drove me at first, but as I tackled each challenge, my anxiety was replaced by a growing sense of optimism. Once you overcome seemingly insurmountable obstacles, other hurdles become less daunting. Most people can achieve beyond their dreams if they insist upon it. I'd encourage everyone to dream big, lay your foundations well, absorb information like a sponge, and not be afraid to defy conventional wisdom. Just because it hasn't been done before doesn't mean you shouldn't try.

I can't give you any secret recipe for success, any foolproof plan for making it in the world of business. But my own experience suggests that it *is* possible to start from nothing and achieve even beyond your dreams.

On a recent trip to New York I went back to Canarsie, to look around Bayview for the first time in nearly twenty years. It's not bad, really, except for the bullet hole in the entry door and the burn marks on the buzzer sheet. When I lived there, we didn't have iron gates on the windows, but then we didn't have air-conditioners either. I saw a group of kids playing basketball, just as I used to, and watched a young mother pushing a stroller. A tiny boy looked up at me, and I wondered: *Which of these kids will break out and achieve their dreams?*

I stopped by Canarsie High School, where the football team was practicing. In the warm autumn air, the blue uniforms and play calls brought the old exhilaration flooding back over me. I asked where the coach was. From the midst of the hefty backs and shoulder pads a small red-hooded figure emerged. To my surprise, I found myself face to face with Mike Camardese, a guy who had played on the team with me. He brought me up to date on the team, telling me how the school finally got its own football field. By coincidence, they were planning a ceremony that Saturday to name the field in honor of my old coach, Frank Morogiello. For the occasion, I decided to make a five-year commitment to help support the team. Without the support of Coach Morogiello, where would I be today? Maybe my gift will allow some Canarsie athlete, driven as I was, to rise above his roots and achieve something no one could ever imagine.

I've heard that some coaches face a curious dilemma. The world-class athletes on their teams—the players with the best skills and experience—sometimes falter when it comes to crunch time. Occasionally, though, there's a player on the team, a blue-collar guy whose skills and training are not quite world-class. Yet at crunch time, he's the one the coach sends out to the field. He's so driven and so hungry to win that he can outperform the top athletes when it really matters.

I can identify with that blue-collar athlete. I've always been driven and hungry, so at crunch time I get a spurt of adrenaline. Long after others have stopped to rest and recover, I'm still running, chasing after something nobody else could ever see.

ENOUGH IS NOT ENOUGH

Every experience prepares you for the next one. You just don't ever know what the next one is going to be.

After graduating from college in 1975, like a lot of kids, I didn't know what to do next. I wasn't ready to go back to New York, so I stayed in Michigan, working at a nearby ski lodge. I had no mentor, no role model, no special teacher to help me sort out my options. So I took some time to think, but still no inspiration came.

After a year, I went back to New York and got a job with Xerox, in the sales training program. It was a lucky break, since I was able to attend the best sales school in the country, Xerox's $100 million center in Leesburg, Virginia. I learned more there than in college about the worlds of work and business. They trained me in sales, marketing, and presentation skills, and I walked out with a healthy sense of self-esteem. Xerox was a blue-chip pedigree company, and I got a lot of respect when I told others who my employer was.

After completing the course, I spent six months making fifty cold calls a day. I knocked on doors of offices in midtown Manhattan, in a territory that ran from 42nd Street to 48th Street, from the East River to Fifth Avenue. It was a fantastic area, but I wasn't allowed to close sales, just drum up good prospects.

Cold-calling was great training for business. It taught me to think on my feet. So many doors slammed on me that I had to develop a thick skin and a concise sales pitch for a then-newfangled machine called a word processor. But the work fascinated me, and I kept my sense of humor and adventure. I thrived on the competition, trying to be the best, to be noticed, to provide the most leads to my salesmen. I wanted to win.

Finally, I succeeded: I became a full salesman in the same territory. I got to be pretty good at it, wearing a suit, closing sales, and earning good commissions for three years. I sold a lot of machines and outperformed many of my peers. As I proved myself, my confidence grew. Selling, I discovered, has a lot to do with self-esteem. But I can't say I ever developed a passion for word processors.

I paid off my college loans and rented an apartment in Greenwich Village with another guy. We were rolling, and having a great time. During one summer, eight of us rented a cottage in the

Hamptons for weekends, and it was there, on the beach, July Fourth weekend, 1978, that I met Sheri Kersch.

With her flash of long wavy blonde hair and unflagging energy, Sheri attracted me with her impeccable style and class. She was in graduate school studying interior design and also spent summer weekends with a group of friends at the beach. She was not only beautiful but well-grounded, with solid midwestern values, from a close and loving family. We were both starting our careers, without a care in the world. We began dating, and the more I got to know her, the more I realized what a fine human being she was.

By 1979, though, I was restless in my job. I wanted something more challenging. A friend told me that a Swedish company, Perstorp, was planning to set up a U.S. division for its Hammarplast housewares subsidiary. It seemed like an exciting opportunity to get in on the ground floor of a growing company. Perstorp hired me and sent me to Sweden for three months of training. I stayed in the charming little cobblestone town of Perstorp, near Malmö, and explored Copenhagen and Stockholm on weekends. Europe overwhelmed me, with its sense of history and joy of life.

The company initially placed me in a different division, one selling building supplies. They moved me to North Carolina and had me sell components for kitchens and furniture. I hated the product. Who could relate to plastic extruded parts? After ten months of misery, I couldn't take it anymore. I was ready to give up and go to acting school, anything to get back to New York and be with Sheri.

When I threatened to quit, Perstorp not only transferred me back to New York but also promoted me to vice president and general manager of Hammarplast. I was in charge of the U.S. operations, managing about twenty independent sales reps. They gave me not only a salary of $75,000 but also a company car, an expense account, and unlimited travel, which included trips to Sweden four times a year. Finally I was selling products I liked: a line of stylish Swedish-designed kitchen equipment and housewares. As a salesman myself, I knew how to motivate my team of salespeople. I quickly placed the products in high-end retail stores and built up sales volume.

I did that for three years and loved it. By age twenty-eight, I had it made. Sheri and I moved to Manhattan's Upper East Side, where we bought our apartment. Sheri was on the rise in her career, working for an Italian furniture maker as a designer and marketer. She painted our walls light salmon and began to use her professional skills to create a home in our loft-style space. We had a great life, going to the theater, dining at restaurants, inviting friends to dinner parties. We even rented a summer house in the Hamptons.

My parents couldn't believe I had come so far so fast. In only six years out of college I had achieved a successful career, a high salary, an apartment I owned. The life I was leading was beyond my parents' best dreams for me. Most people would be satisfied with it.

So no one—especially my parents—could understand why I was getting antsy. But I sensed that something was missing. I wanted to be in charge of my own destiny. It may be a weakness in me: I'm always wondering what I'll do next. Enough is never enough.

It wasn't until I discovered Starbucks that I realized what it means when your work truly captures your heart and your imagination.

2

A Strong Legacy Makes You Sustainable for the Future

A hundred times every day I remind myself
that my inner and outer life depend on the
labors of other men, living and dead, and
that I must exert myself in order to give in
the same measure as I have received.

—ALBERT EINSTEIN

Just as I didn't create Starbucks, Starbucks didn't introduce espresso and dark-roasted coffee to America. Instead, we became the respectful inheritors of a great tradition. Coffee and coffeehouses have been a meaningful part of community life for centuries, in Europe as well as in America. They have been associated with political upheaval, writers' movements, and intellectual debate in Venice, Vienna, Paris, and Berlin.

Starbucks resonates with people because it embraces this legacy. It draws strength from its own history and its ties to the more distant past. That's what makes it more than a hot growth company or a 1990s fad.

That's what makes it sustainable.

• • •

IF IT CAPTURES YOUR IMAGINATION, IT WILL CAPTIVATE OTHERS

In 1981, while working for Hammarplast, I noticed a strange phenomenon: A little retailer in Seattle was placing unusually large orders for a certain type of drip coffeemaker. It was a simple device, a plastic cone set on a thermos.

I investigated. Starbucks Coffee, Tea, and Spice had only four small stores then, yet it was buying this product in quantities larger than Macy's. Why should Seattle be so taken with this coffeemaker when the rest of the country was making its daily coffee in electric percolators or drip coffee machines?

So one day I said to Sheri, "I'm going to go see this company. I want to know what's going on out there."

In those days I traveled a lot, all over the country, but I had never been to Seattle. Who went to Seattle back then?

I arrived on a clear, pristine spring day, the air so clean it almost hurt my lungs. The cherry and crabapple trees were just beginning to blossom. From the downtown streets I could see snow-capped mountain ranges to the east and west and south of the city, etched cleanly against the blue sky.

Starbucks' retail merchandising manager, Linda Grossman, met me at my hotel and walked me to Starbucks' flagship store in the historic Pike Place Market district. Once there, we walked past the fresh salmon stalls where hawkers were shouting orders and tossing fish across customers' heads, past rows of freshly polished apples and neatly arranged cabbages, past a bakery with wonderful fresh bread smells wafting out. It was a showplace for the artistry of local growers and small independent vendors. I loved the Market at once, and still do. It's so handcrafted, so authentic, so Old World.

The original Starbucks store was a modest place, but full of character, a narrow storefront with a solo violinist playing Mozart at its entrance, his violin case open for donations. The minute the door opened, a heady aroma of coffee reached out and drew me in. I stepped inside and saw what looked like a temple for the worship of coffee. Behind a worn wooden counter stood bins containing coffees from all over the world: Sumatra, Kenya, Ethiopia, Costa Rica. Remember—this was a time when most people thought coffee came from a can, not a bean. Here was a shop that sold *only* whole-bean coffee. Along another wall was an entire shelf full of coffee-related merchandise, including a display of Hammarplast coffeemakers, in red, yellow, and black.

After introducing me to the guy behind the counter, Linda began to talk about why customers liked the thermos-and-cone sets. "Part of the enjoyment is the ritual," she explained. Starbucks recommended manual coffee brewing because with an electric coffeemaker, the coffee sits around and gets burned.

As we spoke, the counterman scooped out some Sumatra coffee beans, ground them, put the grounds in a filter in the cone, and poured hot water over them. Although the task took only a few minutes, he approached the work almost reverently, like an artisan.

When he handed me a porcelain mug filled with the freshly brewed coffee, the steam and the aroma seemed to envelop my entire face. There was no question of adding milk or sugar. I took a small, tentative sip.

Whoa. I threw my head back, and my eyes shot wide open. Even from a single sip, I could tell it was stronger than any coffee I had ever tasted.

Seeing my reaction, the Starbucks people laughed. "Is it too much for you?"

I grinned and shook my head. Then I took another sip. This time I could taste more of the full flavors as they slipped over my tongue.

By the third sip, I was hooked.

I felt as though I had discovered a whole new continent. By comparison, I realized, the coffee I had been drinking was swill. I was hungry to learn. I started asking questions about the company, about coffees from different regions of the world, about different ways of roasting coffee. Before we left the store, they ground more Sumatra beans and handed me a bag as a gift.

Linda then drove me to Starbucks' roasting plant to introduce me to the owners of the company, Gerald Baldwin and Gordon Bowker. They worked out of a narrow old industrial building with a metal loading door in front, next to a meat-packing plant on Airport Way.

The minute I walked in, I smelled the wonderful aroma of roasting coffee, which seemed to fill the place up to the high ceiling. At the center of the room stood a piece of equipment of thick silvery metal with a large flat tray in front. This, Linda told me, was the roasting machine, and I was surprised that so small a machine could supply four stores. A roaster wearing a red bandana waved cheerily at us. He pulled a metal scoop, called a "trier," out of the machine, examined the beans in it, sniffed them, and inserted it back in. He explained that he was checking the color and listening till the coffee beans had popped twice, to make sure they were roasted dark. Suddenly, with a whoosh and a dramatic crackling sound, he opened the machine's door and released a batch of hot, glistening beans into the tray for cooling. A metal arm began circling to cool the beans, and a whole new aroma washed over us—this one like the blackest, best coffee you ever tasted. It was so intense it made my head spin.

We walked upstairs and went past a few desks until we reached the offices in back, each with a high window of thick glass. Though Jerry Baldwin, the president, was wearing a tie under his sweater, the atmosphere was informal. A good-looking dark-haired man, Jerry smiled and took my hand. I liked him at once, finding him self-effacing and genuine, with a keen sense of humor. Clearly, coffee was his passion. He was on a mission to educate consumers about the joys of world-class coffee, roasted and brewed the way it should be.

"Here are some new beans that just came in from Java," he said.

"We just roasted up a batch. Let's try it." He brewed the coffee himself, using a glass pot he called a French press. As he gently pressed the plunger down over the grounds and carefully poured the first cup, I noticed someone standing at the door, a slender, bearded man with a shock of dark hair falling over his forehead and intense brown eyes. Jerry introduced him as Gordon Bowker, his partner at Starbucks, and asked him to join us.

I was curious about how these two men had come to devote their lives to the cause of coffee. Starbucks had been founded ten years earlier, and they now appeared to be in their late thirties. They had an easy camaraderie that dated back to their days as college roommates at the University of San Francisco in the early 1960s. But they seemed very different. Jerry was reserved and formal, while Gordon was offbeat and artsy, unlike anyone I'd ever met before. As they talked, I could tell they were both highly intelligent, well-traveled, and absolutely passionate about quality coffee.

Jerry was running Starbucks, while Gordon was dividing his time between Starbucks, his advertising and design firm, a weekly newspaper he had founded, and a microbrewery he was planning to start, called The Redhook Ale Brewery. I had to ask what a microbrewery was. It was clear that Gordon was far ahead of the rest of us, full of eccentric insights and brilliant ideas.

I was enamored. Here was a whole new culture before me, with knowledge to acquire and places to explore.

That afternoon I called Sheri from my hotel. "I'm in God's country!" I said. "I know where I want to live: Seattle, Washington. This summer I want you to come out here and see this place."

It was my Mecca. I had arrived.

HOW A PASSION FOR COFFEE BECAME A BUSINESS

Jerry invited me to dinner that night at a little Italian bistro on a sloping, stone-paved alley near Pike Place Market. As we ate, he told me the story of Starbucks' earliest days, and the legacy it drew upon.

The founders of Starbucks were far from typical businessmen. A literature major, Jerry had been an English teacher, Gordon was a writer, and their third partner, Zev Siegl, taught history. Zev, who sold out of the company in 1980, was the son of the concertmaster for the Seattle Symphony. They shared interests in producing films, writing, broadcasting, classical music, gourmet cooking, good wine, and great coffee.

None of them aspired to build a business empire. They founded Starbucks for one reason: They loved coffee and tea and wanted Seattle to have access to the best.

Gordon was from Seattle, and Jerry had moved there after graduation, looking for adventure. Jerry was originally from the Bay Area, and it was there, at Peet's Coffee and Tea in Berkeley in 1966, that he discovered the romance of coffee. It became a lifelong love affair.

The spiritual grandfather of Starbucks is Alfred Peet, a Dutchman who introduced America to dark-roasted coffees. Now in his seventies, Alfred Peet is gray-haired, stubborn, independent, and candid. He has no patience for hype or pretense, but will spend hours with anyone who has a genuine interest in learning about the world's great coffees and teas.

The son of an Amsterdam coffee trader, Alfred Peet grew up steeped in the exoticism of coffees from Indonesia and East Africa and the Caribbean. He remembers how his father used to come home with bags of coffee stuffed in the pockets of his overcoat. His mother would make three pots at a time, using different blends, and pronounce her opinion. As a teenager, Alfred worked as a trainee at one of the city's big coffee importers. Later, as a tea trader, he traveled the far seas to estates in Java and Sumatra, refining his palate until he could detect subtle differences in coffees from different countries and regions.

When Peet moved to the United States in 1955, he was

shocked. Here was the world's richest country, the undisputed leader of the Western world, yet its coffee was dreadful. Most of the coffee Americans drank was *robusta*, the inferior type that the coffee traders of London and Amsterdam treated as a cheap commodity. Very little of the fine *arabica* coffees ever got to North America; most went to Europe, where tastes were more discriminating.

Starting in San Francisco in the 1950s, Alfred Peet began importing arabica coffee into the States. But there was not much demand, for few Americans had ever heard of it. So in 1966, he opened a small store, Peet's Coffee and Tea, on Vine Street in Berkeley, which he ran until 1979. He even imported his own roaster, because he thought American companies didn't know how to roast small batches of fine arabica coffee.

What made Alfred Peet unique was that he roasted coffee dark, the European way, which he believed was necessary to bring out the full flavors of the beans he imported. He always analyzed each bag of beans and recommended a roast suited to that lot's particular characteristics.

At first only Europeans or sophisticated Americans visited his little shop. But gradually, one by one, Alfred Peet began educating a few discerning Americans about the fine distinctions in coffee. He sold whole-bean coffee and taught his customers how to grind and brew it at home. He treated coffee like wine, appraising it in terms of origins and estates and years and harvests. He created his own blends, the mark of a true connoisseur. Just as each of the Napa Valley winemakers believes his technique is best, Peet remained a firm proponent of the dark-roasted flavor—which in wine terms is like a big burgundy, with a strong, full body that fills your mouth.

Jerry and Gordon were early converts. They ordered Peet's coffee by mail from Berkeley, but they never seemed to have enough. Gordon discovered another store, in Vancouver, Canada, called Murchie's, which also carried good coffee, and he would regularly make the three-hour drive north to get bags of Murchie's beans.

One clear day in August 1970, on the way home from one of those coffee runs, Gordon had his own epiphany. Later he told the *Seattle Weekly* that he was "blinded, literally, like Saul of Tarsus, by the sun reflecting off Lake Samish. Right then it hit me: Open a coffee store in Seattle!" Jerry liked the idea right away. So did Zev, Gordon's next-door neighbor and a tea drinker. They each invested $1,350 and borrowed an additional $5,000 from a bank.

It was hardly a promising time to open a retail store in Seattle. From Day One, Starbucks was bucking the odds.

In 1971 the city was in the midst of a wrenching recession called the Boeing Bust. Starting in 1969, Boeing, Seattle's largest employer, had such a drastic downturn in orders that it had to cut its workforce from 100,000 to less than 38,000 in three years. Homes in beautiful neighborhoods like Capitol Hill sat empty and abandoned. So many people lost jobs and moved out of town that one billboard near the airport joked, "Will the last person leaving Seattle—turn out the lights?"

That famous message appeared in April 1971, the same month that Starbucks opened its first store. At that time, also, an urban renewal project was threatening to tear down the Pike Place Market. A group of developers wanted to build a commercial center with a hotel, convention hall, and parking lot in its place. In a referendum, Seattle's citizens voted to preserve Pike Place as it was.

Seattle in those days was just beginning to shed its image as an exotic, isolated corner of America. Only the adventurous moved here, thousands of miles from family in the East or Midwest or California, sometimes on their way to the mines and mountains and fishing grounds of Alaska. The city had not acquired the veneer and polish of the East Coast. Many of the leading families still had ties to the logging and lumber industries. Heavily influenced by the Norwegian and Swedish immigrants who came early in this century, Seattle people tended to be polite and unpretentious.

In the early 1970s, a few Americans, especially on the West Coast, were starting to turn away from prepackaged, flavor-added foods that were too often stale and tasteless. Instead, they chose to cook with fresh vegetables and fish, buy fresh-baked bread, and grind their own coffee beans. They rejected the artificial for the authentic, the processed for the natural, the mediocre for the high quality—all sentiments that resonated with Starbucks' founders.

A market study would have indicated it was a bad time to go into the coffee business. After reaching a peak of 3.1 cups a day in 1961, coffee consumption in America had begun a gradual decline, which lasted till the late 1980s.

But the founders of Starbucks were not studying market trends. They were filling a need—their own need—for quality coffee. In the 1960s, the large American coffee brands began competing on price. To cut costs, they added cheaper beans to their blends, sacrificing flavor. They also let coffee cans stay on supermarket shelves until the coffee got stale. Year after year, the quality of canned coffee got worse, even as advertising campaigns made claims for its great taste.

They fooled the American public, but they didn't fool Jerry and Gordon and Zev. The three friends were determined to go ahead and open their coffee store, even if it appealed only to a tiny niche of gourmet coffee lovers. Only a handful of American cities had such stores until well into the 1980s.

Gordon consulted with his creative partner, artist Terry Heckler, about a name for the new store. Gordon had pressed to call it *Pequod*, the name of the ship in Melville's *Moby Dick*. But Terry recalls protesting, "You're crazy! No one's going to drink a cup of Pee-quod!"

The partners agreed that they wanted something distinctive and tied to the Northwest. Terry researched names of turn-of-the-century mining camps on Mt. Rainier and came up with *Starbo*. In a brainstorming session, that turned into *Starbucks*. Ever the literature lover, Jerry made the connection back to *Moby Dick*: The first mate on the *Pequod* was, as it happened, named Starbuck. The name evoked the romance of the high seas and the seafaring tradition of the early coffee traders.

Terry also pored over old marine books until he came up with a logo based on an old sixteenth-century Norse woodcut: a two-tailed mermaid, or siren, encircled by the store's original name, Starbucks Coffee, Tea, and Spice. That early siren, bare-breasted and Rubenesque, was supposed to be as seductive as coffee itself.

Starbucks opened its doors with little fanfare in April 1971. The store was designed to look classically nautical, as though it had been there for decades. The fixtures were all built by hand. One long wall was covered with wooden shelving, while the other was devoted to whole-bean coffee, with up to thirty different varieties available. Starbucks did not then brew and sell coffee by the cup, but they did sometimes offer tasting samples, which were always served in porcelain cups, because the coffee tasted better that way. The cups also forced customers to stay a little longer to hear about the coffee.

Initially, Zev was the only paid employee. He wore a grocer's apron and scooped out beans for customers. The other two kept their day jobs but came by during their lunch hours or after work to help out. Zev became the retail expert, while Jerry, who had taken one college course in accounting, kept the books and developed an ever-growing knowledge of coffee. Gordon, in his words, was "the magic, mystery, and romance man." It must have been obvious to him from the start that a visit to Starbucks could evoke a brief escape to a distant world.

From the opening day, sales exceeded expectations. A favorable column in the *Seattle Times* brought in an overwhelming number of customers the following Saturday. The store's reputation grew mostly by word of mouth.

In those early months, each of the founders traveled to Berkeley to learn about coffee roasting at the feet of the master, Alfred Peet. They worked in his store and observed his interaction with customers. He never stopped stressing the importance of deepening their knowledge about coffee and tea.

In the beginning, Starbucks ordered its coffee from Peet's. But within a year, the partners bought a used roaster from Holland and installed it in a ramshackle building near Fisherman's Terminal, assembling it by hand with only a manual in German to guide them. In late 1972, they opened a second store, near the University of Washington campus. Gradually, they created a loyal clientele by sharing with their customers what they had learned about fine coffee. Seattle began to take on the coffee sophistication of the Bay Area.

To Starbucks' founders, quality was the whole point. Jerry, especially, imprinted his strong opinions and uncompromising pursuit of excellence on the young company. He and Gordon obviously understood their market, because Starbucks was profitable every year, despite the economy's ups and downs. They were coffee purists, and they never expected to appeal to more than a small group of customers with discriminating tastes.

"We don't manage the business to maximize anything except the quality of the coffee," Jerry Baldwin told me that evening at the restaurant. By then we had finished our main course and begun dessert. The waiter poured us each a strong cup of coffee, and Jerry proudly announced that it was Starbucks.

I had never heard anyone talk about a product the way Jerry talked about coffee. He wasn't calculating how to maximize sales; he was providing people with something he believed they ought to enjoy. It was an approach to business, and to selling, that was as fresh and novel to me as the Starbucks coffee we were drinking.

"Tell me about the roast," I said. "Why is it so important to roast it dark?"

That roast, Jerry told me, was what differentiated Starbucks. Alfred Peet had pounded into them a strong belief that the dark roast brought out the full flavors of coffee.

The best coffees are all arabicas, Jerry explained, especially those grown high in the mountains. The cheap robusta coffees used in supermarket blends cannot be subjected to the dark roasting process, which will just burn them. But the finest arabicas can withstand the heat, and the darker the beans are roasted, the fuller the flavor.

The packaged food companies prefer a light roast because it allows a higher yield. The longer coffee is roasted, the more weight it loses. The big roasters agonize over a tenth or a half of a percent difference in shrinkage. The lighter the roast, the more money they save. But Starbucks cares more about flavor than about yields.

From the beginning, Starbucks stayed exclusively with the dark roast. Jerry and Gordon tweaked Alfred Peet's roasting style and came up with a very similar version, which they called the Full City Roast (now called the Starbucks roast).

Jerry picked up a bottle of beer, a Guinness. Comparing the Full City Roast of coffee to your standard cup of canned supermarket coffee, he explained, is like comparing Guinness beer to Budweiser. Most Americans drink light beers like Budweiser. But once you learn to love dark, flavorful beers like Guinness, you can never go back to Bud.

Although Jerry didn't discuss marketing plans or sales strategies, I was beginning to realize he had a business philosophy the likes of which I had never encountered.

First, every company must stand for something. Starbucks stood not only for good coffee, but specifically for the dark-roasted flavor profile that the founders were passionate about. That's what differentiated it and made it authentic.

Second, you don't just give the customers what they ask for. If you offer them something they're not accustomed to, something so far superior that it takes a while to develop their palates, you can create a sense of discovery and excitement and loyalty that will bond them to you. It may take longer, but if you have a great product, you can educate your customers to like it rather than kowtowing to mass-market appeal.

Starbucks' founders understood a fundamental truth about

selling: To mean something to customers, you should assume intelligence and sophistication and inform those who are eager to learn. If you do, what may seem to be a niche market could very well appeal to far more people than you imagine.

I wasn't smart enough to comprehend all of this that first day I discovered Starbucks. It took years for these lessons to sink in.

Although Starbucks has grown enormously since those days, product quality is still at the top of the mission statement. But every so often, when executive decision making gets tough, when corporate bureaucratic thinking starts to prevail, I pay a visit to that first store in Pike Place Market. I run my hand over the worn wooden counters. I grab a fistful of dark-roasted beans and let them sift through my fingers, leaving a thin, fragrant coating of oil. I keep reminding myself and others around me that we have a responsibility to those who came before.

We can innovate, we can reinvent almost every aspect of the business except one: Starbucks will always sell the highest quality fresh-roasted whole-bean coffee. That's our legacy.

On the five-hour plane trip back to New York the next day, I couldn't stop thinking about Starbucks. It was like a shining jewel. I took one sip of the watery airline coffee and pushed it away. Reaching into my briefcase, I pulled out the bag of Sumatra beans, opened the top, and sniffed. I leaned back, and my mind started wandering.

I believe in destiny. In Yiddish, they call it *bashert*. At that moment, flying 35,000 feet above the earth, I could feel the tug of Starbucks. There was something magic about it, a passion and authenticity I had never experienced in business.

Maybe, just maybe, I could be part of that magic. Maybe I could help it grow. How would it feel to build a business, as Jerry and Gordon were doing? How would it feel to own equity, not just collect a paycheck? What could I bring to Starbucks that could make it even better than it was? The opportunities seemed as wide open as the land I was flying over.

By the time I landed at Kennedy Airport, I knew in my heart that this was it. I jumped into a taxi and went home to Sheri.

That was the way I met Starbucks, and neither of us has been the same since.

3

TO ITALIANS, ESPRESSO IS LIKE AN ARIA

Some men see things as they are and say "Why?"
I dream things that never were, and say "Why not?"

—GEORGE BERNARD SHAW,
OFTEN QUOTED BY ROBERT F. KENNEDY

IF YOU SAY YOU NEVER HAD A CHANCE, PERHAPS YOU NEVER TOOK A CHANCE

I couldn't stop thinking about Starbucks. Although it was much smaller than the multinationals I had been working for in New York, it was so much more intriguing, like a jazz tune you can't get out of your head. I could see so many ways I could contribute.

The next time Jerry Baldwin and his wife, Jane, were in New York, Sheri and I invited them out to dinner and the theater. We all hit it off. On a lark, I asked him: "Do you think there's any way I could fit into Starbucks?"

He was just beginning to ponder the need to hire trained professionals, so he was willing to think about it. We discussed ways I could help with sales and marketing and merchandising.

It took me a year to convince Jerry Baldwin to hire me. The idea appealed to him, but others in the company were nervous about bringing in someone they regarded as a high-powered New Yorker. It's always a risk to take on a manager who hasn't grown up with the values of the company.

Some days, I couldn't believe I was even entertaining the notion. Taking a job at Starbucks would mean giving up that $75,000 a year job, the prestige, the car, and the co-op, and for what? Moving 3,000 miles across the country to join a tiny outfit with 5 coffee stores didn't make sense to a lot of my friends and family. My mother was especially concerned.

"You're doing well, you have a future," she argued. "Don't give it up for a small company nobody's ever heard of."

Over the next year, I found reasons to get back to Seattle several times. I always made sure I had time to spend with Jerry. We got to be comfortable with each other, sharing thoughts about merchandise Starbucks might carry, products that should or shouldn't bear the brand name, ways to build up customer loyalty. On each visit, I came prepared with a long list of ideas, and listening to Jerry critique them helped me understand his vision for Starbucks.

Jerry confided in me about a notion he had that Starbucks could one day expand outside Seattle. He was considering opening a store in Portland, Oregon, the nearest big U.S. city. He knew the company could be bigger, but seemed ambivalent about the changes growth might bring. I told him it was a great opportunity.

The more I thought about it, the more promising an expansion seemed. Starbucks had such tremendous potential. All my friends in New York were wowed by the coffee once they tasted it. Why wouldn't people all over America have the same reaction? Surely, the market was bigger than just a few thousand coffee lovers in the Northwest. Jerry had such a missionary zeal; it made sense to spread Starbucks' excitement about coffee beans beyond Seattle. At that time, I knew of no other high-end coffee-bean stores in New York or any other city.

Although I wasn't bold enough to become an entrepreneur just yet, part of my fascination with Starbucks was the chance to take a hand in shaping a growing company. I was willing to take a salary cut if I could get a small piece of equity in a business with great promise. I had never owned a share of stock in anything, but I knew that if Jerry would give me even a small share in Starbucks, I would channel all my passion and energy into this job as I never had before.

Sheri liked the idea. We were ready to get married and settle down, and she could see how excited I was about Seattle and Starbucks. Even though it would mean a setback in her career as a designer, she, too, was ready to leave New York. As the daughter of an Ohio entrepreneur, she understood instinctively the value of taking risks and following your dreams.

As the months passed, I pursued Jerry more than he pursued me. We started talking about a job at Starbucks in which I would be head of marketing and oversee the retail stores. I told him I would want a small piece of equity, and he seemed receptive to the suggestion.

In the spring of 1982, Jerry and Gordon invited me to San Francisco to meet their silent partner, a shareholder and board member named Steve Donovan, over dinner. I was convinced that after all my lobbying, I had the job all but sewn up. I figured I would fly back to New York with an offer in hand.

This dinner, for me, was the capstone of a job courtship with Jerry that had lasted nearly a year, so I was determined it would go well. I dressed in one of my best suits and walked from my hotel to the restaurant, a high-end Italian place called Donatello's, uphill from the financial district.

I passed the restaurant and circled the block once, to pump up my confidence, despite a light rain. In a way, I had waited my whole career for this dinner. I knew Jerry had told them I had ideas for growing the company, and this dinner was a chance for Steve and Gordon to assess my capabilities and how well I might fit into the company.

Donatello's was an odd choice, more stuffy than I had expected, with white linen tablecloths and waiters in bow ties. I was waiting at the table when Jerry, Gordon, and Steve arrived. Steve was a tall, blond, classically handsome man. The three of them were wearing sports jackets, less formal than I was, but since they were all at least ten years older, I was glad I had dressed formally.

The dinner went well, exceptionally well. I liked Steve, an intellectual whose interests ranged from executive recruiting to research on meditation. Like Jerry and Gordon, he had traveled widely, read a great deal, and had a lot of interesting insights. Still, I was confident, as I talked, that I was impressing him. I kept glancing at Jerry, and I could see approval in his eyes. After four years of college in the Midwest, I knew how to tone down the New York in me, chatting easily about Italy and Sweden and San Francisco over appetizers and soup.

We ordered a bottle of Barolo and were soon conversing like long-time friends. When the main course came, though, I switched the subject to Starbucks. "You've got a real jewel," I said. I told them how I had served Starbucks coffee to my friends in New York, how enthused they had been by its dark, rich taste. New Yorkers would love Starbucks coffee. So would people in Chicago, Boston, Washington, everywhere.

Starbucks could be so much bigger, I argued. It could grow beyond the Northwest, up and down the West Coast. It could even, perhaps, become a national company. It could have dozens of stores, maybe even hundreds. The Starbucks name could become synonymous with great coffee—a brand that guaranteed world-class quality.

"Think of it," I said. "If Starbucks opened stores across the United States and Canada, you could share your knowledge and passion with so many more people. You could enrich so many lives."

By the end of the meal, I could tell I had charmed them with my youthful enthusiasm and energy. They smiled at one another and seemed inspired by my vision. We parted, shaking hands, and I nodded and congratulated myself as I walked back to the hotel. I called Sheri, waking her up. "It was fantastic," I told her. "I think everything is on track."

Even with the three-hour time difference, I had trouble sleeping that night. Every aspect of my life was about to change. I started envisioning how I would give notice, where Sheri and I would get married, how we'd move to Seattle. Perhaps we could buy a house with a yard. And Starbucks—even the name rang with magic. I was under its spell already.

Twenty-four hours later, I was back at my desk in New York, and when my secretary told me Jerry was on the line, I reached for the phone eagerly.

"I'm sorry, Howard. I have bad news." I couldn't believe the somber tone of his voice, or the words. The three of them had talked it over, and decided not to hire me.

"But why?"

"It's too risky, too much change." He paused, clearly pained at the message he was having to deliver. "Your plans sound great, but that's just not the vision we have for Starbucks."

Instead of charming them, I had spooked them. They feared that I would be disruptive. I wasn't going to fit. I felt like a bride, halfway down the aisle, watching her groom back out the side door.

I was too shell-shocked to think clearly. I saw my whole future flash in front of me and then crash and burn.

That night I went home and poured my despair out to Sheri. I still believed so much in the future of Starbucks that I couldn't accept "no" as a final answer. This was, I thought, a turning point in my life. It had to happen; I had to join Starbucks. I wanted to convey to Jerry what was in my heart.

The next day, I called Jerry back.

"Jerry, you're making a terrible mistake," I said. "After all this time, we owe it to each other to isolate the issues. What exactly is the reason?"

Very calmly, we talked it over. The concern was this: The partners did not want to give me license to change the company. They worried that by hiring me they would be committing themselves to a new direction for Starbucks. They also thought my style and energy would clash with the existing culture.

I drew upon all the passion I had about Starbucks, about coffee, about this opportunity, and spoke from my deepest convictions. I told him how much I could offer, from my professional sales and marketing skills to the broad perspective I had developed managing a national sales force for Hammarplast. I was used to playing on a larger playing field and could plan and execute whatever expansion strategy we mutually agreed upon.

"Jerry," I protested, "this isn't about me. It's about you. The destiny of Starbucks is at stake. We've talked so much about what Starbucks can be. It's your company. It's your vision. You're the only one who can achieve it. Somebody has to be courageous here, and it's you. Don't let them talk you out of something that you believe in your heart."

Jerry heard me out, then fell silent. "Let me sleep on it," he said. "I'll call you back tomorrow."

Perhaps he slept; I didn't.

The next morning, I picked up the phone on the first ring. "You were right," he said. "I'm sorry for the twenty-four-hour impasse. We're going forward. You have the job, Howard, and you have my commitment. When can you come?"

A whole new world had just opened up in front of my eyes, like the scene in *The Wizard of Oz* when everything changes from black and white to color. This barely imaginable dream was really going to happen.

Although I would have to take a steep cut in pay, Jerry agreed to give me a small equity share. I would own a tiny slice of Starbucks' future.

In the fifteen years since then, I've often wondered: *What would have happened had I just accepted his decision?* Most people, when turned down for a job, just go away.

Similar scenarios have subsequently played out in my life, in other settings and with other issues. So many times, I've been told it can't be done. Again and again, I've had to use every ounce of perseverance and persuasion I can summon to make things happen.

Life is a series of near misses. But a lot of what we ascribe to luck is not luck at all. It's seizing the day and accepting responsibility for your future. It's seeing what other people don't see, and pursuing that vision, no matter who tells you not to.

In daily life, you get so much pressure from friends and family and colleagues, urging you to take the easy way, to follow the prevailing wisdom, that it can be difficult not to simply accept the status quo and do what's expected of you. But when you really believe—in yourself, in your dream—you just have to do everything you possibly can to take control and make your vision a reality.

No great achievement happens by luck.

A BLACK CLOUD APPEARS

Now that I finally had the offer, I had to start planning for my move. My main concern, of course, was Sheri. "This is an opportunity I can't pass up," I told her. "I want you to go with me to Seattle for a visit. Before you say yes or no, you need to see the city and experience it for yourself."

We flew out for a weekend and once again, spring was at its peak, with the azaleas in full bloom and explosions of color bursting all over the city. Sheri liked Seattle, liked Starbucks, and was thrilled to see the Baldwins again, who were warm and generous with their time and advice. They knew volumes about food and wine, had interesting stories to tell of their world travels, and shared their knowledge about a wide range of subjects we were just beginning to explore. Sheri came back as certain as I was that this was the right thing to do.

Both of us recognized, though, that moving to Seattle would mean a career sacrifice for Sheri. New York was a world center for interior design, and Seattle far from it. But in the back of her mind she had always expected to move out of the city some day. She wanted to have children and raise them in a different environment. Few women would have willingly given up a promising career to move 3,000 miles, to a city where they didn't know a soul, because their husband wanted to join a small coffee company. But she didn't hesitate. She supported me 100 percent, as she's always done. That constant encouragement has been vital for me.

Although I was eager to start work at Starbucks, I decided to take some time off first. On a shoestring budget, we rented a small cottage for the summer in the Hamptons, where we had met. We were married in July and enjoyed the romantic interlude.

Our plan was to pack up our Audi and drive 3,000 miles across the country, with our golden retriever in the back seat. We were to leave in mid-August and would arrive in Seattle by Labor Day weekend.

We had already started loading the car to leave the following day when my mother called with terrible news: My father had lung cancer and was expected to live only a year. I was shaken to the core. He was only sixty years old, and my brother, Michael, was still in college. It would be a harsh struggle with a devastating disease. My mother had come to rely on my strength. How could she get through this period with me in Seattle?

It was one of those moments when you feel like you're being ripped into two jagged pieces. I had already committed to be in Seattle by the beginning of September. Yet how could I leave now? I discussed it with my family, and it seemed I had no choice. I had to go.

I went to see my dad in the hospital. I had to say good-bye to him, not knowing when or if I'd see him again. My mother sat at his bedside, crying. She was frightened, but she tried hard not to show it. It might have been the moment for a heart-to-heart with my father, but we had never developed that sort of relationship.

"Go to Seattle," my dad said. "You and Sheri have a new life to start there. We can handle things here."

As I sat with him, two emotions were warring in my heart—overwhelming sadness and unresolved bitterness. My father had never been a good provider for the family. He had stumbled through a series of mind-numbing jobs, always chafing against the system. And now his life might be ending, before he had taken control of it.

I squeezed his hand and said an awkward good-bye.

"I don't know how I'm going to do this," I said to my mother as we waited for the elevator.

"Howard, you have to go," she insisted.

I felt as if I were sinking, as all the strength and energy and optimism seeped out of my body.

When the elevator came, my mother gave me a hug and said firmly, "You must go."

I stepped inside, and as I turned, I saw my mother's puffy red face, bravely trying to smile. As soon as the doors clicked shut, I fell apart.

Sheri and I kept to our plan of driving to Seattle, but a cloud of worry and dread traveled with us. I called home at every stop. Gradually we learned that my father's prognosis was better than we thought. The tension eased, and we could throw our hearts into creating a new life together in this city we had barely started to explore.

IMMERSE YOURSELF IN THE CULTURE

We got to Seattle in the midst of a lively annual outdoor arts and music festival called Bumbershoot. The mood was upbeat and wild and adventurous.

We had picked out a house in the Capitol Hill part of Seattle with a big deck, but because it wasn't ready, we spent that first week with the Baldwins. They pampered us, cooking gourmet dinners every night, driving Sheri around the city. They even put up with Jonas, our 100-pound golden retriever, who took to swimming in their pool.

Although it took Sheri about a year to feel really at home in Seattle, it took me about twenty minutes. At Starbucks, I hit the ground running.

When I start something, I immerse myself totally in it. In those early months I spent all of my waking hours in the stores, working behind the counter, meeting the Starbucks people, tasting different kinds of coffee, and talking with customers. Jerry was committed to providing me with very strong training on the coffee side.

The last piece of my education—and definitely the highlight— was learning how to roast coffee. They didn't let me do that until December. I spent a week at the roaster, listening for the second pop, examining the color of the beans, learning to taste the subtle differences among various roasts. It was the fitting end of an intensive training. I felt as if I had been knighted.

I probably surprised the people at Starbucks with how impassioned I was about coffee. When I worked in the store behind the counter, they were constantly testing my knowledge and how much I believed. I always had a good palate at blind tastings. Word got out.

Not surprisingly, there was resentment from some members of the company that Jerry Baldwin had hired an outsider. I could sense that I had to prove myself—prove that I was worthy of the gestalt of Starbucks. I tried hard to blend in. For a tall, high-energy New Yorker in a quiet, understated city, that wasn't easy. I was used to dressing in expensive suits, and at Starbucks the informal dress code tended toward turtlenecks and Birkenstocks. It took a while to build trust. Still, I was hired to do a job, and I was overflowing with ideas for the company. I wanted to make a positive impact.

The atmosphere of Starbucks in those days was friendly and low-key, but we worked very hard. Christmas was our busiest season, and everybody in the office went to the stores to pitch in and help. One day I was working in the Pike Place store during the busy season. The store was packed, and I was in place behind the counter, ringing up sales, filling bags with coffee beans.

Suddenly, someone shouted, "Hey! That guy just headed out with some stuff!" Apparently, a customer had grabbed two expensive coffeemakers, one in each hand, and headed out the door.

I jumped over the counter and started running. Without stopping to wonder whether the guy had a gun, I chased him up a steep, cobblestone street, yelling "Drop that stuff! Drop it!"

The thief was so startled that he dropped both the pieces he had stolen and ran away. I picked them up and walked back into the store holding the coffeemakers up like trophies. Everybody applauded. That afternoon, I went back to the roasting plant, where my office was, and discovered that the staff had strung up a huge banner for me, which read: "Make my day."

The more I got to know the company, the more I appreciated the passion behind it. But I gradually noticed one weakness. While the coffee was unquestionably the best it could be, the service sometimes came across as a little arrogant. That attitude grew out of the high degree of pride Starbucks had in the superiority of our coffee. Customers who relished in discovering new tastes and blends enjoyed discussing their newfound knowledge with our people, but I noticed that first-time customers occasionally felt ignorant or slighted.

I wanted to bridge that gap. I identified so closely with Starbucks that any flaw in Starbucks felt like my own personal weakness. So I worked with employees on customer-friendly sales skills and developed materials that would make it easy for customers to learn about coffee. Still, I figured there must be a better way to make great coffee accessible to more than a small elite of gourmet coffee drinkers.

VISION IS WHAT THEY CALL IT WHEN
OTHERS CAN'T SEE WHAT YOU SEE

There's no better place to truly savor the romance of life than Italy. That's where I found the inspiration and vision that have driven my own life, and the course of Starbucks, from quiet Seattle to national prominence.

I discovered that inspiration in the spring of 1983, a time when I wasn't even particularly looking for it. I had been at Starbucks for a year, and the company had sent me to Milan to attend an international housewares show. I traveled alone and stayed at a low-budget hotel near the convention center.

The minute I stepped out the door and into the sunshine of a warm autumn day, the spirit of Italy washed over me. I didn't speak a word of Italian, but I felt I belonged.

Italians have an unparalleled appreciation for the fine pleasures of daily life. They have figured out how to live in perfect balance. They understand what it means to work, and equally what it means to relax and enjoy life. They embrace everything with passion. Nothing is mediocre. The infrastructure in Italy is appalling. Nothing works. But the food of Italy is absolutely incredible. The architecture is breathtaking. The fashion still defines elegance all over the world.

I especially love the light of Italy. It has a heady effect on me. It just brings me alive.

And what the light shines on is equally amazing. You can be walking down a drab street in an unremarkable residential neighborhood when suddenly, through a half-open door, you catch an unbelievably bright image of a woman hanging colorful clothing in a courtyard ringed with flowering plants. Or out of nowhere a merchant will roll up a metal door and reveal a gorgeous display of produce: freshly picked fruits and vegetables, arrayed in perfect gleaming rows.

Italians treat every detail of retail and food preparation with reverence and an insistence that nothing less than the best will do. In late summer and fall, for example, fresh figs are available at any ordinary produce stall. The merchant will ask: "White or black?" If the order is for half and half, the merchant will take a simple cardboard tray and cover it with three or four fig leaves, then pick each fig individually, squeezing it to ensure the perfect level of ripeness. He will arrange the fruit in four rows—three white, three black, three white, three black—and he will slide the tray carefully into a bag and hand it to you with the pride of an artisan.

The morning after I arrived, I decided to walk to the trade show, which was only fifteen minutes from my hotel. I love to walk, and Milan is a perfect place for walking.

Just as I started off, I noticed a little espresso bar. I ducked inside to look around. A cashier by the door smiled and nodded. Behind the counter, a tall, thin man greeted me cheerfully, "*Buon giorno!*" as he pressed down on a metal bar and a huge hiss of steam escaped. He handed a tiny porcelain demitasse of espresso to one of the three people who were standing elbow-to-elbow at the counter. Next came a handcrafted cappuccino, topped with a head of perfect white foam. The barista moved so gracefully that it looked as though he were grinding coffee beans, pulling shots of espresso, and steaming milk at the same time, all the while conversing merrily with his customers. It was great theater.

"Espresso?" he asked me, his dark eyes flashing as he held out a cup he had just made.

I couldn't resist. I reached for the espresso and took a sip. A strong, sensual flavor crossed my tongue. After three sips it was gone, but I could still feel its warmth and energy.

Half a block later, across a side street, I saw another espresso bar. This one was even more crowded. I noticed that the gray-haired man behind the counter greeted each customer by name. He appeared to be both owner and operator. He and his customers were laughing and talking and enjoying the moment. I could tell that the customers were regulars and the routines comfortable and familiar.

In the next few blocks, I saw two more espresso bars. I was fascinated.

It was on that day that I discovered the ritual and the romance of coffee bars in Italy. I saw how popular they were, and how vibrant. Each one had its own unique character, but there was one common thread: the camaraderie between the customers, who knew each other well, and the barista, who was performing with flair. At that time, there were 200,000 coffee bars in Italy, and 1,500 alone in the city of Milan, a city the size of Philadelphia. It seemed they were on every street corner, and all were packed.

My mind started churning.

That afternoon, after I finished my meetings at the trade show, I set off again, walking the streets of Milan to observe more espresso bars. I soon found myself at the center of the city, where the Piazza del Duomo is almost literally lined with them. As you walk through the piazza, you're surrounded by the smells of coffee and roasting chestnuts and the light banter of political debate and the chatter of kids in school uniforms. Some of the area's coffee bars are elegant and stylish, while others are bigger, workaday places.

In the morning, all are crowded, and all serve espresso, the pure essence of coffee in a cup. There are very few chairs, if any. All the customers stand up, as they do in a western bar. All the men, it seemed, smoke.

The energy pulses all around you. Italian opera is playing. You can hear the interplay of people meeting for the first time, as well as people greeting friends they see every day at the bar. These places, I saw, offered comfort, community, and a sense of extended family. Yet the customers probably don't know one another very well, except in the context of that coffee bar.

In the early afternoon, the pace slows down. I noticed mothers with children and retired folks lingering and chatting with the barista. Later in the afternoon, many espresso places put small tables on the sidewalk and served aperitifs. Each was a neighborhood gathering place, part of an established daily routine.

To the Italians, the coffee bar is not a diner, as coffee shops came to be in America in the 1950s and 1960s. It is an extension of the front porch, an extension of the home. Each morning they stop at their favorite coffee bar, where they're treated with a cup of espresso that they know is custom-made. In American terms, the person behind the counter is an unskilled worker, but he becomes an artist when he prepares a beautiful cup of coffee. The coffee baristas of Italy have a respected place in their neighborhoods.

As I watched, I had a revelation: Starbucks had missed the point—completely missed it. *This is so powerful!* I thought. *This is the link.* The connection to the people who loved coffee did not have to take place only in their homes, where they ground and brewed whole-bean coffee. What we had to do was unlock the romance and mystery of coffee, firsthand, in coffee bars. The Italians understood the personal relationship that people could have to coffee, its social aspect. I couldn't believe that Starbucks was in the coffee business, yet was overlooking so central an element of it.

It was like an epiphany. It was so immediate and physical that I was shaking.

It seemed so obvious. Starbucks sold great coffee beans, but we didn't serve coffee by the cup. We treated coffee as produce, something to be bagged and sent home with the groceries. We stayed one big step away from the heart and soul of what coffee has meant throughout the centuries.

Serving espresso drinks the Italian way could be the differentiating factor for Starbucks. If we could re-create in America the authentic Italian coffee bar culture, it might resonate with other Americans the way it did with me. Starbucks could be a great *experience*, and not just a great retail store.

I stayed in Milan about a week. I continued my walks through the city, getting lost every day. One morning I took a train ride to Verona. Although it's only a forty-minute ride from industrial

Milan, it felt as if it had stood still since the thirteenth century. Its coffee bars were much like Milan's, and in one, I mimicked someone and ordered a "caffè latte," my first taste of that drink. I had expected it to be just coffee with milk, but I watched as the barista made a shot of espresso, steamed a frothy pitcher of milk, and poured the two into a cup, with a dollop of foam on the top.

Here was the perfect balance between steamed milk and coffee, combining espresso, which is the noble essence of coffee, and milk made sweet by steaming rather than by adding sugar. It was the perfect drink. Of all the coffee experts I had met, none had ever mentioned this drink. *No one in America knows about this,* I thought. *I've got to take it back with me.*

Every night I would call Sheri back in Seattle and tell her what I was seeing and thinking. "These people are so passionate about coffee!" I told her. "They've elevated it to a whole new level."

On that day in the piazza in Milan, I couldn't foresee the success Starbucks is today. But I felt the unexpressed demand for romance and community. The Italians had turned the drinking of coffee into a symphony, and it felt right. Starbucks was playing in the same hall, but we were playing without a string section.

I brought that feeling back to Seattle and infused it in others around me, who re-created it for still others all over the country. Without the romance of Italian espresso, Starbucks would still be what it was, a beloved local coffee bean store in Seattle.

4

"Luck Is the Residue of Design"

Whenever you see a
successful business,
someone once made a
courageous decision.

—*Peter Drucker*

Branch Rickey, the Brooklyn Dodgers general manager who broke the color barrier by signing on Jackie Robinson, often remarked: "Luck is the residue of design."

People sometimes say the sun always shines on Starbucks, that our success was built on luck. It's true that we hit the front wave of what became a North American social phenomenon, the widespread popularity of cafés and espresso bars. I can't say that I predicted this wave, but I did perceive the romantic appeal of coffee by the cup, in Italy, and then spent three years brainstorming and laying the plans to translate it into an American context.

Whenever a company, or a person, emerges from the crowd and shines, others are quick to attribute that prominence to good fortune.

The achiever, of course, counters that it's the product of talent and hard work.

I agree with Branch Rickey. While bad luck, it's true, may come out of the blue, good luck, it seems, comes to those who plan for it.

GREAT IDEA, LET'S DO SOMETHING ELSE

Have you ever had a brilliant idea—one that blows you away— only to have the people who can make it a reality tell you it's not worth pursuing?

That's what happened to me on my return to Seattle from Italy. I thought I'd come upon a truly extraordinary insight, one that could serve as the foundation for a whole new industry and change the way Americans drank coffee. To my bosses, however, I was an overexcited marketing director.

Starbucks was a retailer—not a restaurant or a bar, they argued. Serving espresso drinks would put them in the beverage business, a move they feared would dilute the integrity of what they envisioned the mission of a coffee store to be. They also pointed to Starbucks' success. The company was small, closely held, private, and profitable every year. Why rock the boat?

But, as I was to learn, there was a more immediate reason my idea didn't appeal: Jerry was considering an opportunity that excited him far more.

The story of Starbucks has some unexpected twists and turns, but none so strange as the one that happened next. In 1984, Starbucks bought Peet's Coffee and Tea.

Just how that occurred is a part of Starbucks' history that isn't often told, since Peet's and Starbucks are now competitors in the San Francisco Bay area. Most customers don't know they were once intertwined.

It was like the son buying out the father. Starbucks' founders had, after all, drawn inspiration from Peet's and learned their roasting skills at the elbow of Alfred Peet. But Alfred Peet had sold the business in 1979, and by 1983 the new owner was ready to sell.

To Jerry Baldwin, it was the chance of a lifetime and a much more promising way of expanding than opening espresso bars. As a purist, he still regarded Peet's as the ultimate in coffee purveyors. It was the same size as Starbucks, with about 5 stores. But in Jerry's mind, Peet's would always be the real thing, the originator of dark-roasted coffee in America. The Seattle market, he thought, was already well-served, while San Francisco and northern California, a much larger area, offered plenty of room to grow.

To fund the acquisition, Starbucks went deeply into debt. The day we acquired Peet's, I recall, we had a debt-to-equity ratio of 6:1. Only in the go-go 1980s would the banks have made such a deal.

My heart sank when we took on that burden. It tied our hands and deprived us of the flexibility to try out new ideas. The company was now so heavily leveraged that there would be no money available for growth or innovation.

The task of consolidating Starbucks and Peet's proved more difficult than we had imagined. Despite a shared preference for dark-roasted coffee, our company cultures clashed. While Starbucks' people felt gratitude and respect for Peet's legacy, Peet's people feared an unknown Seattle upstart coming to swallow them up. What's more, the acquisition distracted management's attention. For most of 1984, the managers of Starbucks were flying back and forth between San Francisco and Seattle. I myself went there every other week to oversee Peet's marketing and retail operations.

Some Starbucks employees began to feel neglected. In one quarter, they didn't receive their usual bonus. They went to Jerry with a request for more equitable pay, for benefits, specifically for part-timers, and for a reinstatement of their bonuses. But his focus was elsewhere and he didn't respond. Angry employees from the plant eventually circulated a petition to invite the union in. Nobody in management realized how widespread and deep the discontent was. Retail employees seemed satisfied, and since they outnumbered plant workers, Jerry figured they would vote to keep the union out. But when the day came for the official tally, the union won by three votes.

Jerry was shocked. The company he had founded, the company he loved, no longer trusted him. In the months that followed, his heart seemed to go out of it. His hair grew grayer. The company lost its esprit de corps.

The incident taught me an important lesson: There is no more precious commodity than the relationship of trust and confidence a company has with its employees. If people believe management is not fairly sharing the rewards, they will feel alienated. Once they start distrusting management, the company's future is compromised.

Another important thing I learned during that difficult time was that taking on debt is not the best way to fund a company. Many entrepreneurs prefer borrowing money from banks because doing so allows them to keep control in their own hands. They fear that raising equity by selling shares will mean a loss of personal control over the operation. I believe that the best way for an entrepreneur to maintain control is by performing well and pleasing shareholders, even if his or her stake is below 50 percent. That risk is far preferable to the danger of heavy debt, which can limit the possibilities for future growth and innovation.

In hindsight I can say it was fortunate that I learned those lessons when I did. In those days, I had no idea I would ever head any company, let alone Starbucks. But because I saw what happens when trust breaks down between management and employees, I understood how vitally important it is to maintain it. And because I saw the harmful effects of debt, I later made the right choice to raise equity instead. These two approaches became critical factors in the future success of Starbucks.

You've Proved It Works, Now Let's Drop It

In many companies, mid-level managers and even entry-level employees become impassioned evangelists for risky, bold ideas. It's important that managers listen to those ideas and be willing to test them and implement them—even if the CEO is skeptical. I learned this truth first as an employee of Starbucks in 1984 and later as CEO. As boss, if you close your ears to new ideas, you may end up closing off great opportunities for your company.

It took me nearly a year to convince Jerry to test the idea of serving espresso. Preoccupied with the Peet's acquisition and concerned about changing the core nature of Starbucks, he didn't consider it a high priority. My frustration got more intense with each passing month.

Finally, Jerry agreed to test an espresso bar when Starbucks opened its sixth store, at the corner of Fourth and Spring in downtown Seattle, in April of 1984. This was the first Starbucks location designed to sell coffee as a beverage as well as coffee beans by the pound. It was also the company's first downtown location, in the heart of Seattle's business district. I was certain Seattle's office workers would fall in love with espresso bars the same way I had in Milan in 1983.

I asked for half the 1,500-square-foot space to set up a full Italian-style espresso bar, but I got only 300 square feet. My great experiment had to be crammed into a small corner, behind a stand-up bar, with no room for tables or chairs or lines, and only a tiny counter space to hold milk and sugar. Although I was forced to realize my dream on a far smaller scale than I had planned, I was sure that the results would bear out the soundness of my instincts.

We didn't plan any pre-opening marketing blitz, and didn't even put up a sign announcing Now Serving Espresso. We decided to just open our doors and see what happened.

On that April morning in 1984, unseasonably cool, there was drizzle in the air, but it wasn't raining hard. The plan was to open the store at 7 A.M., two hours earlier than usual. I arrived at around 6:30 and looked anxiously out the floor-to-ceiling windows at the streets. Only the most devoted office workers were striding up the steep slopes of downtown Seattle streets at this hour.

I began pacing around inside the store, and to keep myself occupied, helped with last-minute preparations and rearranging. On the left stood our usual whole-bean counter, stocked with bins of coffee. Behind it, a coffee expert in a brown Starbucks grocer's apron checked his metal scoop, his scale, and his grinding machine. He verified that each of the bin drawer labels correctly indicated its contents and readied a row of rubber stamps that would be used to mark each bag of coffee sold with its varietal name. He straightened the mugs and coffeemakers and tea canisters on their shelves along the wall, products already familiar to Seattle's Starbucks fans.

In the right rear corner of the store, my experiment was about to begin. Just like baristas in Milan, two enthusiastic employees were working a gleaming chrome machine pulling shots of espresso and practicing their newly acquired skill of steaming milk to a foam for cappuccinos.

At 7 A.M. sharp, we unlocked the door. One by one, curious people began walking in on their way to their offices. Many ordered a regular cup of coffee. Others asked about the unfamiliar espresso drinks listed on the Italian menu. The baristas were jazzed about the new drinks and enjoyed explaining what each contained. They recommended the drink I had discovered in Verona, one that many customers had never heard of: caffè latte, espresso with steamed milk. As far as I know, America was first introduced to caffè latte that morning.

I watched several people take their first sip. As I had, most opened their eyes wide, responding first to the unaccustomed burst of intense flavor. They hesitated, then sipped again, savoring the sweet warmth of the milk. I saw smiles as the full richness of the drink filled their mouths.

The pace quickened during the early morning rush, and then tapered off. It was awkward serving people in the cramped back corner of a store. Customers jammed into that small space on the right while the retail counter stood empty. If that store had been a ship, it would have capsized.

From the minute we opened, this much was clear to me: Starbucks had entered a different business. There could be no turning back.

By closing time, about 400 customers had passed through the door—a much higher tally than the average customer count of 250 at Starbucks' best-performing bean stores. More important, I could feel the first ripples of that same warm social interaction and engaging artistry that had captivated me in Italy. I went home that day as high as I've ever been.

As weeks went on, business grew, almost all on the beverage side. Within two months, the store was serving 800 customers a day. The baristas couldn't make espressos fast enough, and lines began snaking out the door onto the sidewalk. Whenever I stopped by to check on the progress of my experiment, customers came up to me, eager to share their enthusiasm. The response was overwhelming.

The Fourth and Spring store became a gathering place, and its atmosphere was electric. I thrived on it. So did the small cohort of Starbucks people who had supported the idea, people like Gay Niven, a merchandise buyer at Starbucks since 1979, and Deborah Tipp Hauck, whom I had hired in 1982 to manage a store.

Here were the test results I was looking for. With the success of the first espresso bar, I began to imagine many further possibilities. We could open coffee stores around the city, all dedicated to serving espresso drinks. These would become not only a catalyst but also a vehicle for introducing a new, broader base of customers to Starbucks coffee.

Surely, I thought, the popularity of Fourth and Spring would overcome any doubts Jerry Baldwin still had. He would see as vividly as I did the great opportunity that had arisen to take Starbucks to a whole new level.

Once again, my bubble burst.

To Jerry, the very success of that store felt wrong. Although I continue to have enormous respect for him, Jerry and I viewed the coffee business, and the world, differently. To him, espresso drinks were a distraction from the core business of selling exquisite arabica coffee beans at retail. He didn't want customers to think of Starbucks as a place to get a quick cup of coffee to go.

To me, espresso was the heart and soul of the coffee experience. The point of a coffee store was not just to teach customers about fine coffee but to show them *how* to enjoy it.

I must have seemed a real nuisance to Jerry during the months following the Fourth and Spring opening. Each day I would rush into his office, showing him the sales figures and the customer counts. He couldn't deny that the venture was succeeding, but he still didn't want to go forward with it.

Jerry and I never had an argument, throughout the entire course of our professional relationship. But we both recognized that we had reached an impasse, that our disagreement was not over merely a new twist on business, but over what could potentially represent a sea change for the company. Shrewd as he was, he knew there was a fire burning inside me, a fire there was no way to put out.

After weeks of trying to convince him, I strode into Jerry's office one day, resolved to have a conclusive discussion about the issue.

"The customers are telling us something," I said. "This is a big idea. We've got to keep moving on it."

"We're coffee roasters. I don't want to be in the restaurant business," he said, wearily, realizing we were going to have yet another run-through of this topic.

"It's not the restaurant business!" I insisted. "We're giving people a chance to enjoy our coffee the way it's supposed to be prepared."

"Howard, listen to me. It's just not the right thing to do. If we focus too much on serving coffee, we'll become just another restaurant or cafeteria. It may seem reasonable, each step of the way, but in the end, we'll lose our coffee roots."

"But we're reconnecting with our coffee roots!" I argued. "This will bring more people into our stores."

Seeing my determination, Jerry sat silently at his desk for a few minutes, his arms folded in front of him, until he finally offered:

"Maybe we can put espresso machines in the back of one or two other stores."

"It could be so much bigger than that," I repeated, knowing that if I accepted that concession, it would be the farthest I would ever be able to take the company.

"Starbucks doesn't need to be any bigger than it is. If you get too many customers in and out, you can't get to know them the way we always have."

"In Italy, the baristas know their customers," I answered.

"Besides, we're too deeply in debt to consider pursuing this idea. Even if we wanted to, we couldn't afford to." He stood up and prepared to leave for home, but seeing my reluctance to end the conversation, added firmly: "I'm sorry, Howard. We aren't going to do it. You'll have to live with that."

I was depressed for months, paralyzed by uncertainty. I felt torn in two by conflicting feelings: loyalty to Starbucks and confidence in my vision for Italian-style espresso bars.

I was busy enough with my everyday work, flying back and forth to San Francisco and finding ways to consolidate the operations of the two companies, that I could have distracted myself and just dropped the idea. But I refused to let it die. The espresso business felt too right, and my instincts about it ran too deep to let it go.

One weekend, around that time, when I went to a downtown athletic club for my usual game of Sunday basketball, I was paired up with a wiry, muscular blond guy, about my age. He was two inches taller than my own six feet two, and a good player.

When the game was over, we started talking, and he introduced himself as Scott Greenburg. He told me he was a lawyer with a big firm in town. After he learned what I did, he said he loved Starbucks coffee. So I began to bring a pound of coffee to the games for him every now and then. We met occasionally for beers, and over time, I found myself sharing some of my frustrations with him.

Scott, as it happened, was a corporate lawyer, whose job it was to advise companies on many matters, including private placements and public stock offerings. When I told him I was thinking of going independent and opening espresso bars, he said he thought investors might be interested.

Gradually, in talking over my ideas with Scott and Sheri, I realized what I had to do. *This is my moment,* I thought. *If I don't seize the opportunity, if I don't step out of my comfort zone and risk it all, if I let too much time tick on, my moment will pass.* I knew that if I didn't take advantage of this opportunity, I would replay it in my mind for my whole life, wondering: *What if? Why didn't I?* This was my shot. Even if it didn't work out, I still had to try it.

I made up my mind to leave Starbucks and start my own company. My idea was to open stores that would serve coffee by the cup and espresso drinks, concentrating on high-traffic downtown locations. I wanted to re-create the romance and artistry and community I had seen in Italy.

It took several months of planning, but I finally made the move. Knowing how frustrated I had become, Jerry and Gordon supported the idea. They let me stay on in my job and at my office until I was ready to move, in late 1985.

In some respects, leaving to start my own company took a lot of courage. Just as I made up my mind, we found out that Sheri was pregnant. Without my salary, we would have to live on her income until I could get the new company up and running. She was willing to go back to work soon after the baby was born in January, but I hated the fact that, because of my decision, she had no choice.

But at some level, I felt I'd been preparing for this step my entire life. Ironically, it ran counter to the values my parents had taught me. From my dad, I learned that quitting a job causes instability and disruption in the family. My mother's constant refrain was: "You have a good job. Why quit?"

But I saw the move as consistent with my life's dream, my earliest desires to do something for myself and for my family, to achieve something unique, to be in control of my own destiny. The insecurity, the desire for respect, the burning need to rise far above the circumstances of my parents' struggles all came together in that defining moment.

My close friend Kenny G later told me about a similar experience in his life. In the 1980s he was in an established band, with a secure position and income. (This was long before he became famous as a jazz saxophonist.) But he realized that he would have to leave the band if he was ever to find his own sound. Musically speaking, he went out and did exactly that. If he hadn't, today he'd just be a saxophone player in some little-known band.

What distinguishes the talented person who makes it from the person who has even more talent but doesn't get ahead? Look at the aspiring actors waiting tables in New York, as an example: Many of them are probably no less gifted than stars like Robert DeNiro and Susan Sarandon.

Part of what constitutes success is timing and chance. But most of us have to create our own opportunities and be prepared to jump when we see a big one others can't see.

It's one thing to dream, but when the moment is right, you've got to be willing to leave what's familiar and go out to find your own sound. That's what I did in 1985. If I hadn't, Starbucks wouldn't be what it is today.

5

NAYSAYERS NEVER BUILT
A GREAT ENTERPRISE

*We judge ourselves by what
we feel capable of doing,
while others judge us by
what we have already done.*

—HENRY WADSWORTH LONGFELLOW,
Kavanagh, *1849*

 It's a classic American tale, every entrepreneur's dream: to start with a great idea, attract some investors, and build a business that is profitable and sustainable.

Trouble is, you usually have to start as the underdog.

If you want to know how underdogs feel, try to raise money for a new enterprise. People will shut you out. They'll regard you with suspicion. They'll undermine your self-confidence. They'll offer you every reason imaginable why your idea simply won't work.

Being an underdog has a flip side, though, for facing such adversity can be invigorating. In my case, part of me relished the fact that so many people said my plan couldn't be done. No matter how many times people put me down, I believed strongly that I could pull it off. I was so confident of winning that I enjoyed being in a position where people's expectations were so low that I knew I could beat them.

Nobody ever accomplished anything by believing the naysayers. And few have done so by sticking to proven ideas in proven fields.

It's those who follow the road less traveled who create new industries, invent new products, build long-lasting enterprises, and inspire those around them to push their abilities to the highest levels of achievement.

If you stop being the scrappy underdog, fighting against the odds, you risk the worst fate of all: mediocrity.

"NO" IN ITALIAN DOESN'T SOUND AS BAD

Jerry Baldwin surprised me. When I was drawing up the documents to form my new company and planning how to approach investors to raise money for it, he called me into his office and offered to invest $150,000 of Starbucks money into my coffee-bar enterprise.

"This isn't a business we want to go into ourselves," he explained, "but we'll support you."

With those words, ironically, Starbucks became my first investor, committing a huge sum of money for a company so deeply in debt. Jerry also agreed to serve as a director, and Gordon promised to be a part-time consultant for six months. That stamp of approval eased my transition enormously.

Perhaps Jerry hoped to prevent me from becoming a competitor or perhaps he wanted to ensure that I would use Starbucks coffee, although it would have been my first choice anyway. It was clear to me, though, that Jerry also simply wanted to be supportive, and I was grateful.

Gordon was as pumped up about the venture as I was, and he put his creative mind to work, helping refine my idea. "This is not about the ordinary," Gordon told me. "You need to elevate the expectation of the customers. Everything about the new store—the name, the setting, the presentation, the care taken to create the coffee—everything should lead the customer to expect something better."

It was Gordon who proposed that I should call the company Il Giornale. While best known as the name of the largest newspaper in Italy, *giornale* also has the more basic meaning of *daily*. You've got your daily paper, your daily pastry, your daily cup of coffee. If we served great coffee with Italian elegance and style, we hoped people would come back daily.

With Jerry and Gordon's support, I thought, naively, I could attract all the investment funds I needed within six months.

There's nothing sweeter to a freshly minted entrepreneur than the taste of success after raising that initial dollar of investment. But when the first "no" comes, it's like a slap in the face. I had to experience that in, of all places, Italy.

In December, just as I left Starbucks, Gordon and I set off on an adventure, flying to Italy to research coffee bars. Over the previous three years, I had grown fond of him and enjoyed his eclecticism. I expected to come back with $1 million in investment financing.

Our big prospect was Faema, a producer of espresso machines in Milan. I had pitched my idea by phone to them, and they had sounded very interested. On our first full day in Milan, I made my initial presentation, and I was proud of it. I explained to them how we would re-create the Italian espresso bar experience in the United States, eventually expanding to fifty stores. I spoke as eloquently as I could about the potential scope of the opportunity and stressed the appeal of Italian-style coffee, which was little known in America. For a company that sold commercial espresso machines, I figured, the venture would appear an obvious winner.

But after a surprisingly short discussion, they turned us down. Americans, they insisted, could never enjoy espresso the way Italians do.

Although I realized I had probably been too optimistic about the prospects of a major foreign corporation's taking a financial stake in a small and untested American company, I couldn't help feeling deflated. Faema's rejection meant that I would have to go door-to-door to individual investors to raise the $1.7 million I needed. I knew how hard that would be.

But as always, Italy made it impossible to be unhappy for long. Gordon and I visited nearly 500 espresso bars in Milan and Verona. We took notes, snapped photographs, and videotaped baristas in action. We observed local habits, menus, decor, espresso-making techniques. We drank a lot of coffee, tasted a lot of Italian wine, and ate some fantastic meals. We sat at outdoor cafés in that intense Italian light and sketched out different design schemes, figuring out how we could replicate an authentic, Italian-style coffee bar.

By the time we got back to Seattle, we were as high on the idea as when we had left, and I was renewed in my determination to raise as much money as it took to get Il Giornale under way.

I had no funds of my own to invest, and I knew nothing of venture capital. It didn't seem right to approach friends or family for money. If the idea was sound, I reasoned, experienced investors would want a piece of it. If it was unworkable, they would let me know.

They let me know, and then some.

I didn't realize, until much later, the long-term implications of raising equity. Unlike knowledge-based companies like Microsoft, retail businesses are highly capital intensive; when they expand rapidly with company-owned stores, they require repeated injections of funds for such expenses as build-out costs, inventory, and rents. Each time more money is raised, the founder's stake diminishes. I could never have retained 50 percent ownership, as some software company executives did. I wish, today, that I could have kept a larger stake in the company. But at the time, it seemed I had no choice. And if I had, Starbucks could not have grown large as rapidly and smoothly as it did.

After my return from Italy, my friend Scott Greenburg and I sat down at my kitchen table and drafted a new private placement plan for Il Giornale. We were both young and fascinated by the possibilities, and we complemented each other well: I had the vision, and he knew what information and projections were needed to attract private investors and how to outline the opportunities and risks.

Since we were introducing something new to Seattle, I figured I had to open at least one store, to show people the practical operations and artistic appeal of an Italian-style coffee bar. To do so, however, I needed to raise an initial $400,000 in seed capital. After that, I calculated, I would need another $1.25 million to launch at least eight espresso bars and prove the idea would work on an extended scale both in and outside Seattle. From its inception, Il Giornale was intended to be a major enterprise, not just a single store.

SOMETIMES SINCERITY SELLS
BETTER THAN BUSINESS PLANS

Il Giornale's first outside investor was Ron Margolis—in some respects, the unlikeliest investor you could imagine. Ron was a physician who had put some of his savings into the stock market and the rest into small, risky start-ups, mostly businesses begun by people he got to know and trust.

When I approached him for money, Ron and I were total strangers. Sheri knew his wife, Carol, through professional contacts. One fall day, the three of them were walking their dogs through the fallen leaves in a Seattle park. Carol had an infant, Sheri was pregnant, and Ron was an obstetrician, so most of the talk revolved around babies. But when Sheri mentioned that I was looking to start my own company, Ron told her: "If Howard ever starts a business, I'm sure he'll succeed, so I want to know about it." Not long afterwards, Sheri arranged for me to meet with them. Carol invited us over.

At this early stage, I was still too excited about my idea to be nervous. I brought along the business plan Scott and I had spent hours writing. We had prepared the standard financial projections: how much money I needed to raise, how long it would take to open the first store, how long before we'd be profitable, how investors would get a return on their capital. I had even had an architect's blueprint drawn up for my first store.

Ron never gave me a chance to show them off.

When we got to the Margolises' home, we sat down at their dining table. "Tell me about this new business you're starting up," said Ron, after some small talk.

I jumped in eagerly. I told him about the inspiration I had had during my trip to Italy, about how a quick stop at an espresso bar is a daily routine for Italians. I described the flair and artistry the barista brought to the preparation of every espresso drink. I discussed my idea for displaying newspapers on racks for customers to read, in keeping with the name *Il Giornale*. If the espresso culture could thrive in Italy, I argued, it could in Seattle, too—and anywhere else, for that matter.

The more I talked, the more enthusiastic I grew, until suddenly, Ron interrupted me. "How much do you need?" he said.

"I'm looking for seed capital now," I replied, as I started unraveling my papers. "Let me show you the financial projections."

"Don't do that," he said, waving the documents away. "I wouldn't understand them. How much do you need? Will $100,000 be enough?" Ron pulled out his checkbook and pen and wrote the check on the spot.

I wish all my fund-raising had been so easy.

Ron doesn't invest based on financial projections but looks instead for honesty and sincerity and passion. He looks, in short, for someone he can trust. It was a risky move he made that day. It was four years before the company started to make any money. Ron and Carol had no assurance they'd get their investment back at all, let alone any return on it. But once the company went public, and the profits and stock price started climbing, they were rewarded: The shares they bought for $100,000 grew to be worth more than $10 million.

Passion alone is no guarantee of remarkable returns. Ron himself will tell you that many of his other investments, made based on the same instincts, didn't pay back so handsomely. Some entrepreneurs fail because their idea ultimately isn't sound. Others remain short-sighted and unwilling to give up control. Some refuse to bring in more money. Any number of different factors can knock a company off its course in the period between its founder's initial enthusiasm and the eventual returns. But passion is, and will always be, a necessary ingredient. Even the world's best business plan won't produce any return if it is not backed with passion and integrity.

The irony of Ron's vote of confidence in Il Giornale is that he is not even a coffee drinker. He invested in me, not in my idea. He's a doctor, not a businessman. But his advice is worth remembering:

"It appears to me that people who succeed have an incredible drive to do something," observes Ron. "They spend the energy to take the gamble. In this world, relatively few people are willing to take a large gamble."

If you find someone who is, listen carefully; you may end up helping achieve a dream of amazing proportions.

HOW THE WORLD LOOKS TO AN UNDERDOG

By the time my son was born, in January, I had raised the entire amount of seed money, $400,000, at 92 cents a share. (Because of two stock splits since, that's the equivalent of 23 cents a share today.) The bulk was provided by Starbucks and Ron Margolis; the rest came from Arnie Prentice and his clients.

Arnie Prentice, co-chairman of a financial services firm who knew both Starbucks and Italian espresso, was one of the first to believe strongly in what I was trying to accomplish. He organized breakfasts and lunches for me to present my idea to his clients, putting his reputation on the line to validate mine. He joined the board of Il Giornale and still sits on the Starbucks board today.

The seed capital enabled me to secure a lease and start building the first Il Giornale store, in a new office building that became the highest skyscraper in Seattle, Columbia Center. It was at this point that Dave Olsen joined me (I'll talk more about him in the next chapter). The two of us began working together to get the store running by April 1986.

But the bulk of my energy and time still went toward raising the next $1.25 million. We rented a tiny office on First Avenue, and I started pounding the pavement. I spent every minute of my day asking for money, racing from one meeting to another and trying to keep my pitch sounding fresh. I was on the phone constantly, before and after the first store opened, approaching every potential investor I could find.

I wasn't just an underdog during that year; I was an *under-underdog*. It was the roughest period of my life. I felt as if I were being kicked and beaten every time I scratched on another door.

At the time, I was thirty-two years old and had been in Seattle for only three years. I had experience in sales and marketing, but had never run my own company. I hadn't had any exposure to the moneyed elite of Seattle.

I knew nothing about raising money, and I was so naive I would talk to anybody. There's a legal definition for an "accredited investor," someone who has a net worth large enough to assume the risk of investing in a small start-up. Whenever I could find anyone who fit this description, I would approach him or her. I suspect that half the time I was talking to people who couldn't have invested if they wanted to. I had to lower the price three times.

I was often turned away with a great deal of arrogance. When I was in high school, I worked one summer as a waiter in a bungalow colony at a restaurant in the Catskill Mountains. I remember how terribly rude some of the guests were to me. They would be brusque and demanding, and I'd run around and do my best to please them, and when they departed, they would leave only a meager tip. As a poor kid from Brooklyn, I figured this is what the rich were like. I remember saying to myself: *If I'm ever wealthy enough to vacation in a place like this, I'm always going to be a big tipper. I'm always going to be generous.*

I had some of the same feelings during that year when I was raising capital, and I swore to myself that if I was ever in a position of being successful and approached by entrepreneurs asking me to invest, even if I thought they had the worst concocted concept, I would always be respectful of the entrepreneurial spirit.

Many of the investors I approached told me bluntly that they thought I was selling a crazy idea.

"Il Giornale? You can't pronounce the name."

"How could you leave Starbucks? What a stupid move."

"Why on earth do you think this is going to work? Americans are never going to spend a dollar and a half for coffee!"

"You're out of your mind. This is insane. You should just go get a job."

In the course of the year I spent trying to raise money, I spoke to 242 people, and 217 of them said "no." Try to imagine how disheartening it can be to hear that many times why your idea is not worth investing in. Some would listen to my hour-long presentation and not call me back. I'd phone them but they wouldn't take my call. When I finally got through, they would tell me why they weren't interested. It was a very humbling time.

The hardest part was maintaining an upbeat attitude. You don't want to pay a visit to a prospective investor and not display the full measure of passion and enthusiasm about what you're proposing to do. You can't be dejected when you meet with a landlord to begin negotiations about leasing a location. But if you've had three or four fruitless meetings that week, how do you whip yourself up? You really have to be a chameleon. Here you are in front of somebody else. You're depressed as hell, but you have to sound as fresh and confident as you were at your first meeting.

Still, I never once believed, *not ever*, that my plan wasn't going to work. I was truly convinced that the essence of the Italian espresso experience—the sense of community and artistry and the daily relationship with customers—was the key to getting Americans to learn to appreciate great coffee.

There's a fine line between self-doubt and self-confidence, and it's even possible to feel both emotions simultaneously. Back then, and often enough today, I could be overwhelmed with insecurities, and at the same time have an abundance of self-assurance and faith.

Frankly, when I started, I don't think I was all that good at raising money, because it took me so long to meet my goals. With practice, though, I got better at making my presentation and at anticipating objections and concerns.

In the meantime, I was eating up my seed capital. In April, when we opened the first Il Giornale store, it was exciting to watch as Seattlites discovered the pleasures of handcrafted espresso drinks on their way to work. From the first day, sales exceeded our expectations, and the atmosphere was just as we had envisioned it. But it would be a long time before we could expect any profits, and in the meantime I had to pay rent and hire people, spending funds I didn't yet have.

As each month passed, we worried about how we were going to continue in business because the money wasn't coming in as I had planned. At times we weren't sure we could meet payroll or pay the rent. Dave Olsen and I would sit together and ask each other: "Who do you want to pay this week?" In fact, we never did miss a payroll, but we came frighteningly close.

For some reason, the people around me never doubted that I was going to get them through it, that I would figure out some way to work things out. Somehow, their confidence strengthened my resolve. The odds against our pulling it off were so slim. Investors had to have a pretty strong stomach to bet on our success.

I continued to get commitments, but I couldn't use any of the money until I reached what's called an "impound number." The impound number is the minimum amount of money an entrepreneur must raise to gain access to the original cash commitments. In my case, I couldn't use any of the money I raised until I had guaranteed investments totalling $900,000.

A key turning point for Il Giornale came in June, when, to my relief, I was finally able to meet my impound number. An investor named Harold Gorlick gave us more than $200,000, the biggest single check I'd ever received. I stared at it for a long time, wondering what magic mixture of timing and inclination it takes to make any given investor believe. Gorlick was a client of Arnie Prentice's. He was an unusual guy, a self-made man who had made his fortune in the heating and plumbing businesses. He was rough around the edges, but I became very fond of him.

A few years later, Harold introduced me to his nephew, a rising jazz saxophonist known as Kenny G. We were two young men, each aspiring to make a mark in different fields, and our friendship grew as we faced similar kinds of challenges. Kenny eventually invested in the business, too, and even played at employee events and performed benefit concerts at our plant and market openings. His music became a part of the culture of the company.

With the impound number, I was able to collect on earlier commitments, easing our immediate financial crisis. But the goal of $1.25 million still seemed far off. There were not many doors left to knock on.

YES, YOU CAN REINVENT A COMMODITY

The tension grew as the summer progressed. The biggest barrier I continued to face was the apparent improbability of my own idea at a time when investors had so many other, more attractive industries in which to put their money.

One of the groups I approached was called Capital Resource Corp., a small business investment corporation, in which fifteen to twenty partners pooled their money to back promising start-ups. By now, the success of the first store was visible and my pitch had grown more ambitious. Il Giornale Coffee Company, I figured, would open and run as many as 50 Italian-style espresso bars, starting in Seattle but eventually spreading to other cities.

The member who did due diligence, Jack Rodgers, recommended a sizable investment, but the group declined. According to their charter, they were committed to investing in high-technology start-ups. There's nothing high-tech about coffee.

Conventional business wisdom tells you that the most attractive business start-ups have a proprietary idea or technology—something to offer that no one else has. Notable examples are Apple's computers, Intel's chips, and Microsoft's operating system. If you hold a patent to your product, so much the better. It's less risky if you can erect some barrier to entry, to prevent a dozen competitors from popping up and grabbing your market away from you before you can establish yourself. And the most promising ideas are those in the industries of the future, such as biotechnology, software, or telecommunications.

Il Giornale didn't fit any of these paradigms—nor does Starbucks today. We had no lock on the world's supply of fine coffee, no patent on the dark roast, no claim to the words *caffè latte* apart from the fact that we popularized the drink in America. You could start up a neighborhood espresso bar and compete against us tomorrow, if you haven't done so already.

I heard all the arguments about why coffee could never be a growth industry. It was the second most widely traded commodity in the world, after oil. Consumption of coffee had been falling in America since the mid-1960s, as soft drinks surpassed it as the country's favorite beverage. Coffee shops have been around since time immemorial.

I explained, again and again, the rising interest in specialty coffee. In cities like Seattle and San Francisco, a growing niche of people had learned to drink high-quality coffee at home and at restaurants. But they had little or no opportunity to experience good coffee in the workplace. And while in more and more cities, small neighborhood places were starting to sell quality whole-bean coffee, espresso was available mostly in restaurants as an after-dinner drink. Although a few espresso bars did exist, no one offered high-quality, quick-service espresso to go in urban areas.

What we proposed to do at Il Giornale, I told them, was to rein-vent a commodity. We would take something old and tired and common—coffee—and weave a sense of romance and community around it. We would rediscover the mystique and charm that had swirled around coffee throughout the centuries. We would enchant customers with an atmosphere of sophistication and style and knowledge.

Nike is the only other company I know of that did something comparable. Sneakers were certainly a commodity—cheap and standard and practical and generally not very good. Nike's strategy was first to design world-class running shoes and then to create an atmosphere of top-flight athletic performance and witty irrever-ence around them. That spirit caught on so widely that it inspired myriads of nonathletes to lace up Nike shoes as well. Back in the 1970s, good sneakers cost $20 a pair. Who would have thought anyone would pay $140 for a pair of basketball shoes?

How, then, should you evaluate a good investment opportunity? How do you identify a good entrepreneurial idea? What were peo-ple missing when they turned down the chance to invest in Il Giornale?

The answer's not easy, but it has a lot to do with instinct. The best ideas are those that create a new mind-set or sense a need before others do, and it takes an astute investor to recognize an idea that not only is ahead of its time but also has long-term prospects. Back in 1985, although Capital Resource Corp. turned me down, Jack Rodgers and several other individuals who were part of that group invested in Il Giornale on their own. They didn't let conventional business wisdom stop them. I've often wondered if their high-tech investments paid off as well.

BREAKTHROUGHS AREN'T CHEAP

By August, I felt as if I were in the twelfth inning. The store had been open four months, and business was good. But I still had raised only half as much as I needed. I had already signed a lease for a second store, and I didn't know how I would pay for it. I had to score the winning run soon.

There was one big powerhouse I hadn't tapped. Three of Seattle's most prominent business leaders had not yet heard my pitch. This was the triumvirate of Jack Benaroya, Herman Sarkowsky, and Sam Stroum. Locally, they were titans who had developed some of the tallest buildings, most successful residential complexes, and sturdiest businesses in Seattle. Active in the Jewish community, and generous philanthropists, the three were friends and sometimes invested together.

Herman's son, Steve, is about my age. One day he brought his father into the Il Giornale store and introduced me, and Herman agreed to let me make a presentation to the three of them. It was my last chance. If these three big investors turned me down, I didn't know who else to go to in Seattle. It had to work.

By now, I had made my pitch almost a hundred times, but I practiced it again and again before that crucial meeting. I didn't want to step on stage until I was absolutely prepared. Even if they invested only a little, their commitment would be an invaluable endorsement, and I could count on others in the higher-echelon business community to follow their lead.

The meeting was to take place on the top floor of one of Seattle's tallest office buildings. I had to walk around the block three times to calm myself. My presentation went well, and they appeared ready to invest a lot of money. But the group made some stiff demands. They wanted a lower price, and options, and board seats. It took two weeks to work out the details. Then they decided, as a group, to invest $750,000. That took me over the top. I had made it.

I ended up raising $1.65 million from about thirty investors, including the seed capital. The biggest chunk came from the Big Three. Along with Arnie Prentice, Harold Gorlick, and Jack Rodgers, Steve Sarkowsky became a director and strongly supported me during some tense and difficult times later. If you ask any of those investors today why they took the risk, almost all of them will tell you that they invested in me, not in my idea. They believed because I believed, and they prospered because they trusted someone in whom nobody else had confidence.

Il Giornale has faded into history, remembered by only a few of its old customers. But those initial investors ended up earning a one hundred-to-one return on their investment. How that happened involved some strange twists of fate.

6

THE IMPRINTING OF THE COMPANY'S VALUES

*The ultimate measure of a man is not where he stands
in moments of comfort and convenience, but where
he stands at times of challenge and controversy.*

—MARTIN LUTHER KING, JR.

A couple with a newborn child doesn't usually sit down and think: *What is our mission as parents? What values do we want to give this child?* Most new parents are preoccupied with merely wondering how to get through the night.

Similarly, most entrepreneurs can't afford to be that farsighted, either. They're too absorbed with the problems directly in front of their noses to have the luxury of pondering values. I know I certainly was.

But as a parent, or as an entrepreneur, you begin imprinting your beliefs from Day One, whether you realize it or not. Once the children, or the people of the company, have absorbed those values, you can't suddenly change their world view with a lecture on ethics.

It's difficult, if not impossible, to reinvent a company's culture. If you have made the mistake of doing business one way for five years, you can't suddenly impose a layer of different values upon it. By then, the water's already in the well, and you have to drink it.

Whatever your culture, your values, your guiding principles, you have to take steps to inculcate them in the organization early in its life so that they can guide every decision, every hire, every strategic objective you set. Whether you are the CEO or a lower level employee, the single most important thing you do at work each day is communicate your values to others, especially new hires. Establishing the right tone at the inception of an enterprise, whatever its size, is vital to its long-term success.

SHARING THE MISSION

I won't mislead you. When I began planning for Il Giornale, I didn't draft a mission statement or list the values I wanted the company to embody. I had some pretty good notions, though, based on what I had seen go right and wrong at Starbucks, about what kind of company I wanted to create.

What's almost inconceivable to me today is how the ideal person came to me, just when I needed him most, to help articulate our common values and grow the company. Perhaps it was destiny.

One day, late in 1985, I was sitting at my desk, absorbed in planning the details of the Il Giornale launch. I had already left Starbucks but was still using my office there, and its floor was littered with drafts of menus, graphics, layouts, and designs.

I answered the phone and was greeted by a man I had met only a few times and knew mainly by reputation: Dave Olsen. People at Starbucks spoke of Dave with respect bordering on awe, so knowledgeable was he about coffee. A tall, broad-shouldered Montanan with longish wavy hair and intense eyes that sparkle from behind small oval glasses, he ran a small, funky establishment in the University District called Café Allegro. Students and professors would hang out there, studying philosophy or debating U.S. foreign policy or simply drinking cappuccinos. In a sense, Café Allegro was a prototype for what Starbucks later became, a neighborhood gathering place, although its style was more bohemian and it did not sell coffee beans and merchandise or cater to an early morning, urban, coffee-to-go clientele. It was more in the European café tradition than the Italian stand-up espresso bars I had seen in Milan.

"I hear you are putting a plan together to open some coffee bars downtown," Dave said. "I've been thinking about looking for a location or two downtown myself. Maybe we could talk."

"Great, come on down," I told him, and we made an appointment to meet in a few days.

I hung up and turned to Dawn Pinaud, who had been helping me get Il Giornale started. "Dawn," I said, "do you have any idea who that was?"

She stopped and looked at me expectantly.

"*Dave Olsen!* He might want to work with us!" It was such a remarkable stroke of good fortune. Although he jokes about it now, protesting that he was just a guy in jeans, running a little café and having fun, I knew that having Dave on my team would lend Il Giornale an authenticity and coffee expertise far beyond what I had been able to develop in three years. With his humble manner, precise speech, deep thoughts, and strong laugh, I also knew he'd be a lot of fun to work with.

On the day of our meeting, Dave and I sat on my office floor and I started spreading the plans and blueprints out and talking about my idea. Dave got it right away. He had spent ten years in an apron, behind a counter, serving espresso drinks. He had experienced firsthand the excitement people can develop about espresso, both in his café and in Italy. I didn't have to convince him that this idea had big potential. He just knew it in his bones.

The synergy was too good to be true. My strength was looking outward: communicating the vision, inspiring investors, raising money, finding real estate, designing the stores, building the brand, and planning for future growth. Dave understood the inner workings: the nuts and bolts of operating a retail café, hiring and training baristas, ensuring the best quality coffee.

It never occurred to us to become competitors. Although Dave had been looking for ways to move forward and grow, when he saw what I was planning, he thought it would be more fun to join forces. He agreed to work with me to get Il Giornale off the ground.

Because I still had very little cash, Dave agreed to work twenty hours a week for a paltry salary of $12,000 a year. In fact, he committed himself full time and then some from the start. He later was rewarded generously as his stock options gained in value. But Dave wasn't in it for the money. He joined our team because he believed. He was intrigued by the Italian coffee bar approach, and he wanted to make sure we served the best coffee and espresso possible. He became the coffee conscience of the company.

Even today, as Starbucks' senior vice president for coffee, Dave explains that he doesn't view himself as either an employee or an executive or a founder, but rather as "a willing and eager and very fortunate participant." "It's like a mountain climbing expedition," says Dave. "Yeah, I get a paycheck fortunately. I wouldn't do everything I do if I didn't. But I probably would do a lot of it anyway."

If every business has a memory, then Dave Olsen is right at the heart of the memory of Starbucks, where the core purpose and values come together. Just seeing him in the office centers me.

If you're building an organization, you realize quickly that you can't do it alone. You'll build a much stronger company if you can find a colleague you trust absolutely, someone who brings different strengths to the mix but who still shares your values. Dave gets exhilarated at the top of Mt. Kilimanjaro. I get energized by the excitement at a basketball game. He can rhapsodize over a flavorful coffee from Sulawesi; I can fire up a roomful of people because of my heartfelt commitment to the future of the company.

Dave Olsen and I came from different worlds. He grew up in a quiet Montana town, and in his Levis, T-shirts, and Birkenstocks, was already running a little café while I was making sales calls in midtown Manhattan skyscrapers for Xerox. Dave's love affair with coffee started in 1970, during a visit to a friend in Berkeley. While on a walk he came upon Peet's, then an offbeat coffee store on Vine Street. He bought a little stovetop espresso maker and half a pound of dark Italian roast from the Dutchman himself and started fiddling. The espresso he brewed that day captivated him so much that he began regularly experimenting with the taste to get it just right.

The Army moved him to Seattle, where he worked as a carpenter. One day in 1974 he quit his job, loaded up his bicycle, and pedaled to San Francisco, nearly a thousand miles. There, he discovered the cafés of North Beach, Italian restaurants with atmospheres that were operatic, bohemian, noisy, eclectic, and stimulating. They treated espresso-making as one of many fine Italian arts. Dave began parking his bike against the windows of a number of restaurants and talking to their owners about food and wine and coffee.

Lots of people dream about opening a coffee house. Few actually do. But that's precisely what Dave Olsen did when he got back to Seattle in the fall of 1974. He rented a space in Seattle's University District, in the garage of a former mortuary, on an alley just opposite the busiest entrance to campus.

Café Allegro became a shrine to espresso, with a shiny espresso machine front and center. Few Americans knew the term *caffè latte* in those days. He made a similar drink and called it *café au lait*. Dave searched Seattle for the best coffee beans and quickly found Starbucks, then selling only coffee by the pound. He got to know the founders and the roasters, and tasted coffee with them. He worked with them to co-develop a custom espresso roast that suited his palate, just a shade darker than most of Starbucks' other coffees, but a shade lighter than the darkest coffees they offered.

That espresso roast, developed for Café Allegro, is still sold in Starbucks stores today, and it's used in every espresso drink we serve. That's how closely integrated Dave Olsen is to the legacy of Starbucks.

As different as our backgrounds were, when Dave and I started Il Giornale in 1985, we had one undeniable connection: our passion for coffee and for what we wanted to accomplish in serving it. We took on different roles, but no matter whom we talked to or what situation we were involved in, we broadcast exactly the same message, each in a way that reflected our individual styles. There were two voices, but one point of view. The linkage, the alignment, and the common purpose that Dave and I have had is as rare in business as it is in life.

When I first met him, Dave owned only one sports coat, and that was because his wife worked for an airline that required a coat and tie for employees' relatives flying on free airline passes. Today, he is as amazed as anyone that he is an executive in a $1 billion company, though he retains the spirit of an artist or inventor.

Starbucks would not be what it is today if Dave Olsen hadn't been part of my team back at Il Giornale. He helped shape its values, bringing a strong, romantic love for coffee, unshakable integrity, disarming honesty, and an insistence on authenticity in every aspect of the business. He shared a vision with me of an organization where people left their egos at the door and worked together as an inspired team. He freed me up to build the business, for I knew I never had to worry about the quality of the coffee. Dave is a rock, part of the foundation of the company.

When you're starting a new enterprise, you don't recognize how critical those early decisions are not only in the formulation of the business itself but in laying the groundwork for its future. As you build, you never know which decisions will end up being the cornerstones. Each one adds so much value later on, and you're not cognizant of it at the time.

Don't underestimate the importance of the early signals you send out in the course of building your enterprise and imprinting your values upon it. When you take on a partner, and when you select employees, be sure to choose people who share your passion and commitment and goals. If you share your mission with like-minded souls, it will have a far greater impact.

EVERYTHING MATTERS

At the time, our plans seemed impossibly ambitious. Even then, when nobody had heard of Il Giornale, I had a dream of building the largest coffee company in North America, with stores in every major city. I hired someone who knew how to run a spreadsheet on a personal computer to do some projections, and originally asked him to build a model based on opening 75 stores over five years. But when I looked at the numbers, I told him to scale the plan back to 50 stores, as I figured nobody would believe 75 was achievable. In fact, five years later, we did reach that goal.

The tiny office I rented had space for only three desks, jammed close together, and there was a little conference room in an adjoining loft. When we started selling *panini* sandwiches, Dave used to slice the meats in the office, about ten yards away from my desk. I'd be on the phone, talking to potential investors, with the smell of those cured meats wafting up under my nose. Dave delivered the meat to the stores in his beat-up, old red truck.

The day the first Il Giornale store opened, April 8, 1986, I came in early, just as I had for the first Starbucks coffee bar. At 6:30 A.M., the first customer was waiting outside the door. She came right in and paid for a cup of coffee.

Somebody actually bought something! I thought with relief.

I stayed the entire day, and because I was too nervous to work behind the counter, I just paced and watched. A lot of Starbucks people came down that day to see what my store looked like. By closing time, we had nearly 300 customers, mostly in the morning. They asked a lot of questions about the menu, and we started educating them about Italian-style espresso. It was a gratifying start, and I was pleased.

In those first weeks, I checked on the quality, the speed of service, the cleanliness. I refused to let anything slip. This was my dream, and everything had to be executed perfectly. Everything mattered.

Dave worked behind the counter, from opening through the morning rush. Then he would come to the office. Dave and I would always go back to the store for lunch. We paid full price, doing everything we could to keep the sales up, drinking and eating lots of food and coffee to make sure potential investors saw strong sales numbers. It's a custom we continue; we still pay full price at every Starbucks store we visit.

We made a lot of mistakes. In that first store, we were determined to re-create a true Italian-style coffee bar. Our primary mission was to be authentic. We didn't want to do anything to dilute the integrity of the espresso and the Italian coffee bar experience in Seattle. For music, we played only Italian opera. The baristas wore white shirts and bow ties. All service was stand-up, with no seating. We hung national and international newspapers on rods on the wall. The menu was covered with Italian words. Even the decor was Italian.

Bit by bit, we realized many of those details weren't appropriate for Seattle. People started complaining about the incessant opera. The bow ties proved impractical. Customers who weren't in a hurry wanted chairs. Some of the Italian foods and drinks needed to be translated.

We gradually accepted the fact that we had to adapt the store to our customers' needs. We quickly fixed a lot of the mistakes, adding chairs, varying the music. But we were careful, even early on, not to make so many compromises that we would sacrifice our style and elegance. We even debated whether we should have paper cups for the to-go business, which we knew would constitute a large part of our revenues. Although espresso tastes better in ceramic cups, we didn't really have a choice: If we didn't offer coffee to go, business would have been minimal.

Still, the core idea worked. Within six months, we built up to serving more than 1,000 customers a day. Our tiny 700-square-foot store, near the main entrance of Seattle's tallest building, became a gathering place. We were filling a void in people's lives. The regulars learned to pronounce the name, Il Giornale (*il jor-nahl´-ee*), and even took pride in the way they said it, as if they were part of a club. That first store was a little jewel, definitely ahead of its time.

Speed, we realized, was a competitive advantage. Our customers, most of whom worked in the busy downtown office buildings nearby, were always in a hurry. Hap Hewitt, an innovative engineer who had set up the conveyor belts in Starbucks' factory, also invented a proprietary system for serving three kinds of drip coffee simultaneously, modeled after a beer tap.

Our logo reflected the emphasis on speed. The Il Giornale name was inscribed in a green circle that surrounded a head of Mercury, the swift messenger god. Later, we created a portable backpack tap system and sent employees out with a tray and cups to sell coffee in offices. We called them the Mercury men.

Still, the key to success, we figured, was in the hands of the people we hired. Dave trained them in coffeemaking; I taught them selling and managing techniques. More important, we infused them with a desire to achieve the Big Dream, the spirit that together, we could accomplish great things.

Dawn Pinaud was Il Giornale's first employee. She helped me start the company and she managed the Columbia Center store. Jennifer Ames-Karreman came on in March and worked as a barista from Day One. She had been an advertising account executive and hoped to grow with the company.

In their enthusiasm, Dawn and Jennifer created systems that, while far too sophisticated for a single store, helped us get an accurate picture of our business. We kept careful accounts of our coffee, our pastries, our cash, our spoilage. We tracked a lot of product categories to see what was selling best. We always knew what we needed to do to make our budget. With all this information, we were able to set definite goals as we began our rollout.

In November, I hired Christine Day as my assistant. She had just ended a maternity leave and had a business degree as well as first-hand experience at a financial company. She wound up doing nearly everything: administration, finance, computers, payroll, human resources, purchasing, banking, and typing. At first, she even prepared the profit and loss statements, balance sheets, and inventory and sales audits. She did all the bookkeeping by hand. Like Dave and me, Christine immediately started working twelve-hour days, so quickly was she caught up in our passion and our conviction.

One day, Christine was negotiating with Solo, the huge paper cup supplier, trying to get a lower price. As we were hardly a major client, they saw no reason to give us a break. "We'll be your biggest customer someday," Christine told them. I doubt they believed it, but I'm sure she did. We all had such faith in the enterprise that none of us ever questioned our ability to become a world-class company.

We were, in many respects, like a family. I used to invite everyone to my house for pizza, and they watched as my son learned to crawl and walk. On my thirty-third birthday, they ordered a cake and presented it to me as a surprise in the store. The customers gathered around and joined the baristas in singing "Happy Birthday," embarrassing me, but filling me with gratitude that with all of our hard work, we were still able to create some fun for each other.

We opened a second store just six months after the first, in another downtown high-rise, the Seattle Trust Tower at Second and Madison. For the third store, however, we went international, and picked a site in Vancouver, British Columbia, in the SeaBus Terminal, which opened in April 1987. That might have seemed an illogical choice for a venture with only two stores. But I figured that, given my desire to grow to 50 stores and given my investors' doubts about my ability to expand outside Seattle, I needed to demonstrate quickly and decisively that my plan was feasible. I couldn't afford to wait till the tenth store to make my move. I had to do it soon.

We had no idea of the complexities of exchange rates and customs and different labor practices. We never considered the intricacies of operating in a foreign country, such as the need for a separate bank account, separate statements for the Canadian government, and foreign exchange adjustments in our accounting —all for one small coffee bar.

Dave went north to open the Vancouver store and to train its staff. When Dave is involved in a project, you know not only that it's going to be done properly but also that it's going to be done fastidiously. Although he had a young family in Seattle, he spent nearly a month in Canada, living in a budget hotel, just to make sure our Il Giornale coffee bar there would be a mirror image of the service and authenticity of our Columbia Center store in Seattle.

All three of the Il Giornale stores quickly caught on with customers. By mid-1987, our sales were around $500,000 a year for each store. Although we were still losing money, we were on track to reach our ambitious goals, and as a team we were elated about what we were creating. Our customers were delighted. My vision was becoming a reality.

WHEN YOU SEE THE OPPORTUNITY OF A LIFETIME, MOVE QUICKLY

In March of 1987, something happened that changed the course of my life, and that of Starbucks: Jerry Baldwin and Gordon Bowker decided to sell the Seattle stores, the roasting plant, and the name Starbucks, keeping only the Peet's assets. Gordon wanted to cash out to take a break from the coffee business to focus on other enterprises, while Jerry, who was dividing his time between Seattle and Berkeley, wanted to concentrate on Peet's.

They had kept their idea quiet, but it was not completely unexpected to those who knew them. I was aware of some of their troubles and the tension between the two parts of the company. As soon as I heard, I knew I had to buy Starbucks. It seemed like my destiny. Again, *bashert*.

At that time, Starbucks was much bigger than we were, with 6 stores to Il Giornale's 3. My company hadn't yet completed a full year of operations, so Starbucks had annual sales many times the size of ours. It would be like a case of salmon swallowing the whale—or, as Dave put it, "the child is father to the man." But to me, the fit seemed natural and logical: Not only would Il Giornale soon need its own roasting plant, but Starbucks' whole-bean business and Il Giornale's beverage business complemented each other perfectly. More important, I understood and valued what Starbucks stood for.

I had only recently exhausted nearly every resource in raising $1.25 million. Now I needed to find nearly $4 million to buy the Starbucks' assets. However daunting that task appeared, I was confident I could do it. My original supporters were impressed with the progress Il Giornale had made in a short time, and I was sure some of them would agree to increase their stake. And other investors, who had said no the first time, were sure to jump in for this round, now that it involved buying Starbucks. If we managed it well, all the investors would benefit.

Quickly, we pulled together the numbers. I had just hired Ron Lawrence, who had years of experience in the restaurant business, to handle finance and accounting and to design a point-of-sale system for the company.

"Ron," I said, "we need a pro forma and a complete private-placement package to go out to our investors. We need to get all the financials on Starbucks. Can you do it in a week or two?"

He was game, and we set to work figuring how to raise enough to buy the company and have some expansion capital as well. After arranging a line of credit with local banks, we prepared an offering circular to distribute to all the Il Giornale investors and a few others I had come to know.

I went to my board and ran the plan past them. It seemed like a sure win.

WHAT TO DO WHEN THEY
TRY TO GRAB IT FROM YOU

Then, one day, it nearly fell apart. I almost lost Starbucks before I ever had it.

While we were structuring the deal, I heard that one of my investors was preparing a separate plan to buy Starbucks. His arrangement would not evenly distribute the ownership among Il Giornale shareholders, but would ensure a disproportionate share for himself and some of his firends. I was certain that this man intended to reduce me from a founder and major shareholder to an employee with a much smaller, diluted position, running Starbucks at the will of a new board he controlled. I also thought his plan would have unfairly treated some of my other early investors, people who had trusted me with their money for Il Giornale.

The pressure on me was almost unbearble. This man was a business leader in Seattle, and I thought he had already lined up support from the city's other leading lights. I feared all my influential backers would defect to this new arrangement, leaving me with no options. I went to Scott Greenburg, and we approached one of his senior partners, Bill Gates, father of Microsoft's founder, who at six feet, seven inches, was a towering figure in town. We prepared a new strategy and arranged to meet with the investor. Bill Gates agreed to go with me.

The day of our meeting was one of the toughest, most painful of my life. I had no idea how it would turn out, and my life's work was at stake. As I walked in, I felt like the Cowardly Lion, shaking on my way to an audience with the Great Oz. My opponent sat at the head of a conference table, larger than life, in full command of the room. Without even waiting to hear me out, he began blasting me.

"We've given you the chance of a lifetime," I remember him shouting. "We invested in you when you were nothing. You're still nothing. Now you have an opportunity to buy Starbucks. But it's our money. It's our idea. It's our business. This is how we're going to do it, with or without you." He sat back before delivering the ultimatum: "If you don't take this deal, you'll never work again in this town. You'll never raise another dollar. You'll be dog meat."

I was appalled, but I was also angry. Was I just supposed to roll over and take this? "Listen," I said, my voice shaking. "This is the chance of a lifetime. It's *my* idea! I brought it to you, and you're not taking it away. We *will* raise the money, with or without you."

"We have nothing to discuss with you," he said. Others in the room sat quietly or supported him.

When the meeting ended, I walked out and started to cry, right there in the lobby. Bill Gates tried to reassure me that everything would turn out all right, but he was aghast about the outburst at the meeting. I'm certain he had never seen anything quite like it before.

That night, when I got home, I felt as though my life had ended. "There's no hope," I told Sheri. "I don't know how I'm going to raise the money. I don't know what we're going to do."

This was a turning point in my life. If I had agreed to the terms that investor demanded, he would have taken my dream from me. He could have fired me at whim and dictated the atmosphere and values of Starbucks. The passion, the commitment, and the dedication that made it thrive would have all disappeared.

Two days later, with the support of Steve Sarkowsky, I met with some of my other investors and presented my proposal: Every investor in Il Giornale would have a chance to invest in the purchase of Starbucks. The plan would be fair to all of them, and it would be fair to me. They saw that, and they told me they admired my integrity for refusing to agree to a plan that benefited big investors at the expense of smaller ones. They backed me, as did almost all my other investors. Within weeks, we managed to raise the $3.8 million we needed to buy Starbucks, and life has not been the same since.

Many of us face critical moments like that in our lives, when our dreams seem ready to shatter. You can never prepare for such events, but how you react to them is crucial. It is important to remember your values: Be bold, but be fair. Don't give in. If others around you have integrity, too, you can prevail.

It's during such vulnerable times, when the unexpected curve balls hit you hard on the head, that an opportunity can be lost. It's also the time when your strength is tested most tellingly.

I can't say that I've made the right choice in every business interaction of my life. But no matter how much I achieve, no matter how many people report to me, I cannot even imagine treating anyone as I was treated that day. Skeptics smirk when they hear me talk about "treating people with respect and dignity," a line we later used in the Starbucks Mission Statement. They think it's empty talk, or a truism that is self-evident. But some people don't live by that rule. If I sense that a person lacks integrity or principles, I cut off any dealings with him. In the long run, it's not worth it.

Those original investors, who put their faith in me, were well rewarded. They've stood by me through tough times and trusted in my integrity. I have tried to never violate that trust.

By August of 1987, Starbucks was mine. It was electrifying but also frightening.

I woke up early one morning that month and took a long run. By now, the enormity of the task, and the responsibility, was starting to sink in. I had a chance to accomplish my dreams, but I also had the hopes and fears of nearly a hundred people resting on my shoulders. As I jogged through the lush arboretum, I saw a long, winding road stretching out ahead of me, disappearing just over the crest of the next hill, into the heavy mist.

The Starbucks Corporation of today is actually Il Giornale. Founded in 1985, it acquired the assets of Starbucks in 1987 and changed its name to Starbucks Corporation. The company Jerry and Gordon founded was called Starbucks Coffee Company, and they sold us the rights to that name. Their company is now known as Peet's.

At thirty-four, I was at the beginning of a great adventure. What would keep me on track was not the size of my holdings but my heartfelt values and my commitment to building long-term value for our shareholders. Every step of the way, I made it a point to underpromise and overdeliver. In the long run, that's the only way to ensure security in any job.

PART
TWO

Reinventing the
Coffee Experience

The Private Years,
1987-1992

7

ACT YOUR DREAMS
WITH OPEN EYES

*Those who dream by night in the
dusty recesses of their minds
Awake to find that all was vanity;
But the dreamers of day are dangerous men,
That they may act their dreams with open
eyes to make it possible.*

— *T. E. LAWRENCE (OF ARABIA)*

It was a sunny Friday afternoon in August that greeted me when I walked out of the lawyers' offices after closing the deal to acquire Starbucks. People were rushing around the streets as if it were an ordinary day, but I felt light-headed. Jerry and Gordon had signed, I had signed, paper after paper. A check had been passed across the table. I had shaken hands with everyone and accepted their congratulations. Now Starbucks was mine.

Automatically, Scott Greenburg and I strode across the street to Columbia Center, to that first Il Giornale store. At 2 P.M. on a summer afternoon, there was only one other customer, a woman standing at the window, deep in thought. I greeted the baristas, who had no idea of the transaction we had just completed. They made me a *doppio macchiato*—two shots of espresso, marked with a dash of milk foam in a demitasse cup—and a cappuccino for Scott. We sat on barstools near the window.

Here we were, two guys in our early thirties, who a few years earlier had met each other on a basketball court and had just now concluded a $4 million deal. It was a highly visible, career-making move for Scott as an attorney, and it propelled me to the presidency of a company I had joined as an employee.

Scott placed on the table between us the business plan, a hundred-page confidential document we had used for the private placement. On its cover were the two logos of Il Giornale and Starbucks. We had written it with meticulous care, spelling out clearly everything I intended to do with Starbucks once Il Giornale bought it. The plan had been our bible for months, and now it had come to life. It was a thrilling moment, the kind you can't believe you're living through. Scott lifted his coffee cup in a toast, his eyes sparkling. "We did it," we said at the same time.

Coming Home to Starbucks

The following Monday morning, August 18, 1987, the modern Starbucks was born.

I stepped through the front door of the old roasting plant again, as I had so many times before, but now as the new owner and CEO. I headed straight to the roasting machines. The roaster greeted me with a smile and a thump on the back and then turned to attend to the cooling tray, which was swirling with freshly roasted beans. I dipped my hands into the warm, fragrant beans and lifted out a handful, rubbing them slowly between my fingers. Touching the beans grounded me to what Starbucks was all about, and it became a daily tradition.

As I walked through the plant, people grinned and hugged me

and welcomed me. It was like coming home; the aromas, the sounds, the faces were all familiar. Gay Niven was there, with her bright red hair, and Deborah Tipp Hauck, who now oversaw five stores. I was happy to see Dave Seymour and Tom Walters, a roaster. But despite their good wishes, I knew, some Starbucks people felt nervous. Their lives had just been changed, and they had had no say in the decision. They knew Starbucks would change, but they didn't know how. Would I lower the quality of the coffee? Would I ease some people out, or fail to recognize how others had grown in their jobs? Were my fast-growth plans really feasible?

At 10 A.M., I called everyone together for a big meeting on the roasting plant floor. It was the first of many.

I was more excited than nervous. I had written just a few points down on a 5-by-7 note card, to remember as I addressed the group. They were:

1. Speak from my heart.

2. Put myself in their shoes.

3. Share the Big Dream with them.

Once I started talking, though, I found I didn't need to look at my notes.

"It feels so good to be back," I began. The tension in the room started to ease. "Five years ago, I changed my life for this company. I did it because I recognized in it your passion. All my life I have wanted to be part of a company and a group of people who share a common vision. I saw that here in you, and I admired it.

"I'm here today because I love this company. I love what it represents." Working together, I told them, we could take everything that Starbucks means to the people of Seattle and multiply it on a national scale. We could share our coffee mission so much more widely.

"I know you're scared. I know you're concerned," I said. "Some of you may even be angry. But if you would just meet me halfway, I

POUR YOUR HEART INTO IT

promise you I will not let you down. I promise you I will not leave anyone behind.

"I want to assure you that I'm not here to do anything to dilute the integrity of the company."

It was easy for me to be able to talk like that because I had been one of them.

My goal, I announced, was to build a national company whose values and guiding principles we all could be proud of. I discussed my vision of the growth of the company and promised to bring it about in a way that would add value to Starbucks, not diminish it. I explained how I wanted to include people in the decision-making process, to be open and honest with them.

"In five years," I told them, "I want you to look back at this day and say, 'I was there when it started. I helped build this company into something great.'"

Most important, I assured them that no matter which investors owned how many shares, Starbucks was their company and would remain so. Spiritually and psychically, it belonged to them. Starbucks' best days, I told them, were yet to come.

I watched their faces as I spoke. Some of them seemed to want to believe what I was saying, but were guarded. Others had that smug look of doubters who had already decided not to buy into this dream—at least not yet.

Coming back to a company I knew inside and out gave me an incredible advantage. I knew the organization, both its weaknesses and its strengths. With that insight, I could predict what would be possible, what wouldn't be possible, and how fast we could go.

But in the few days after that, I learned that there was one serious gap in my knowledge: Morale at Starbucks was terrible. In the twenty months since I had left, divisions had grown within the company. People were cynical and wary, beaten down and unappreciated. They felt abandoned by previous management and anxious about me. The fabric of trust and common vision that Starbucks had had when I first joined had frayed badly.

As the weeks went on, I learned the full extent of the damage. It quickly became obvious to me that my number-one priority would have to be to build a new relationship of mutual respect between employees and management. All my goals, all my dreams would amount to nothing unless I could achieve that.

This realization was a great lesson to me. A business plan is only a piece of paper, and even the greatest business plan of all will prove worthless unless the people of a company buy into it. It can not be sustainable, or even implemented properly, unless the people are committed to it with the same heartfelt urgency as their leader. And they will not accept it unless they both trust the leader's judgment and understand that their efforts will be recognized and valued.

I had seen, with the small Il Giornale team, how much a few people can accomplish if they believe in what they're doing, with fervor. Starbucks could be so much more, I knew, if its people were motivated with the same zeal.

The only way to win the confidence of Starbucks' employees was to be honest with them, to share my plans and excitement with them, and then to follow through and keep my word, delivering exactly what I promised—if not more. No one would follow me until I showed them with my own actions that my promises were not empty.

It would take time.

EMBARKING ON THE FAST TRACK

"Lack of experienced management" was one of the risk factors I had noted in my acquisition document. That was an understatement. I had served for less than two years as president of a company of any size. Dave Olsen had run only a single café for eleven years. Ron Lawrence, our controller, had worked as an accountant and controller for several organizations. Christine Day was adept at handling everything we threw at her, but she had never worked as a manager.

The four of us now had to figure out not only how to merge Il Giornale and Starbucks but also how to open 125 new stores in five years, as we had promised investors. We figured that as our expertise increased, we should be able to open 15 the first year, 20 the second, 25 the third, 30 the fourth, and 35 the fifth. No problem. Sales would grow to $60 million, and profits would grow in tandem. The plan looked great on paper.

I had never attempted anything remotely similar, and in order to do so, I knew I needed to learn quickly, hire experienced managers, and take steps immediately to win over the support and enthusiasm of Starbucks' people.

But realizing what was necessary hardly prepared me for the enormity of the undertaking. Within days, I felt as if I were in a wind tunnel, going in the wrong direction. Urgent issues and problems of a complexity I had never faced before came rushing at me. Any one of them might knock my head off.

That first Monday morning, I was informed that a key Starbucks coffee roaster and buyer had decided to resign. His departure left us with not a single experienced buyer and only a handful of junior roasters. Literally overnight, Dave Olsen had to master the incredibly complex skills of buying and roasting coffee. Luckily, he jumped in with gusto.

That opportunity turned out to be a godsend for Dave. It gave him, in his field, the same chance I was getting: the chance to grow into a new job. He began to travel around the world to the leading coffee-producing countries, to get to know producers, and to learn about the agriculture and economics of coffee. He had always been our most-valued "nose" for coffee, with the discrimination of the finest winemaker. Now, as he explored different sources and blends, the range of coffees Starbucks offered got even better.

We all got used to doing the impossible. In the first two months, Ron Lawrence had to close the offering, merge the financial records of Starbucks and Il Giornale, put a new computer system in place, switch accounting systems, and conduct a fiscal year-end audit. "Okay," he said, after taking stock of his tasks, "what else?"

My own urgent list kept getting longer as well. I knew I needed someone to help me run Starbucks, someone who had experience as a corporate executive. I turned to a man I had met through mutual friends, Lawrence Maltz. Lawrence was fifteen years older than I and had twenty years experience in business, including eight years as president of a profitable public beverage company.

Lawrence invested in Starbucks and joined the company as executive vice president in November 1987. I put him in charge of operations, finance, and human resources, while I handled expansion, real estate, design, marketing, merchandising, and investor relations.

Our little management team didn't examine our motives for wanting to grow fast. We set out to be champions, and speed was part of the equation. When I looked into the future, I saw a bold, vividly painted landscape—not a still life in subtle muted colors.

Now that we had merged with Starbucks, our Il Giornale goal of opening 50 stores in five years no longer seemed so farfetched. That's why I promised investors in 1987 that Starbucks would open 125 stores in five years. We would go public, someday. Customers would respect our brand so much that they would talk of "a cup of Starbucks." Long lines would form out the doors of newly opened stores in cities far from Seattle. Perhaps we could change the way Americans drank coffee.

It was a stretch, and plenty of people told me it was impossible. But that was part of the appeal, for me and for many other people at Starbucks. Defying conventional wisdom, achieving against the odds, offers a thrill that's hard to top.

But my view of a successful business wasn't just measured in number of stores. I wanted to create a brand name respected for the best in coffee and a well-run company admired for its corporate responsibility. I wanted to elevate the enterprise to a higher standard, to make our people proud of working for a company that cared for them and gave back to their community.

In those early days, as I worked to build trust, I began to envision the kind of company I ultimately wanted to create. Fostering an atmosphere in which people were treated with respect wasn't something I considered an intriguing option; it was essential to the mission of Starbucks. We could never accomplish our aims unless we shared a common vision. To attain that ideal, we needed to create a business that valued its people, that inspired them, that shared its rewards with those who worked with us to create long-term value.

I wanted to build a company that would thrive for years because its competitive advantage was based on its values and guiding principles. I wanted to attract and hire individuals who worked together with a single purpose, who avoided political infighting and loved reaching for goals others thought impossible. I wanted to create a culture in which the endgame was not only personal gratification but a respected and admired enterprise.

Instead of a small dream, I dreamed big.

If you want to build a great enterprise, you have to have the courage to dream great dreams. If you dream small dreams, you may succeed in building something small. For many people, that is enough. But if you want to achieve widespread impact and lasting value, be bold.

Who wants a dream that's near-fetched?

CHOOSING AN IDENTITY

After the acquisition, I had to make a critical decision about our identity: Should we keep the Il Giornale name, or should we consolidate under the name Starbucks?

For most entrepreneurs who have founded their first company, giving up its name is like throwing away their baby. I certainly felt attached to Il Giornale, which I had created out of nothing. But the

Starbucks name was so much better known, and I knew in my heart that it was the right choice. Still, I owed it to the original Il Giornale team to carefully weigh the pros and cons.

To confirm my instincts, I went back to Terry Heckler, who had helped name Starbucks years before. He has since named several other successful products in Seattle, including Cinnabon, Encarta, and Visio software. I decided to hold two meetings—one with major investors and another with employees—to debate the issue. I asked Terry to present his recommendations at both meetings.

His opinion was unequivocal. The name Il Giornale, he said, is hard to write, spell, and pronounce. People find it obscure. After less than two years of operation, it was too new to have widespread recognition. Italians were really the only ones with a legitimate claim to espresso, and none of us was Italian.

The name Starbucks, in contrast, has magic. It piques curiosity. Around Seattle, it already had an undeniable aura and magnetism, and, thanks to mail order, it was beginning to be known across America, too. Starbucks connoted a product that was unique and mystical, yet purely American.

The hardest part was convincing the original Il Giornale employees, who loved the Italian name because it captured the romance of the authentic espresso experience. The small Il Giornale team had grown as tight-knit as a family and was afraid of losing what they had worked so hard to build, swallowed up by what they perceived to be a giant with a fifteen-year tradition.

After much soul-searching, we finally opted to take the Il Giornale name down from the espresso bars and replace it with Starbucks. Throughout the process, I knew I had to leave my ego at the door. I wanted everyone involved to make the best choice for the long-term value of the business and select the name that would best differentiate us from the competition. Having a name that people could recognize and remember, a name people could relate to, would provide enormous equity. That name, clearly, was Starbucks, not Il Giornale.

To symbolize the melding of the two companies and two cultures, Terry came up with a design that merged the two logos. We kept the Starbucks siren with her starred crown, but made her more contemporary. We dropped the tradition-bound brown, and changed the logo's color to Il Giornale's more affirming green.

One by one, we also transformed the look of the original Starbucks stores, from brown to green, from Old World traditional to Italian elegance. In the process, we also remodeled and remerchandised them so that all were equipped to sell both whole-bean coffee and espresso drinks. That combination created a new type of store, more than retail but not restaurant, that has been Starbucks' signature pattern ever since.

It's a marriage that has lasted.

A VITAL SHOW OF CONFIDENCE

By December 1987, as new stores prepared to open in Chicago and Vancouver and the quality of the coffee remained high, initial doubts some employees had about my intentions began to fade. Trust began to build.

I wanted people to feel proud of working at Starbucks, to believe in their hearts that management trusted them and treated them with respect. I was convinced that under my leadership, employees would come to realize that I would listen to their concerns. If they had faith in me and my motives, they wouldn't need a union.

Fortunately, one employee in a retail store also questioned the need for the union. As a college student, Daryl Moore had started at Starbucks in 1981 as a part-time clerk in our Bellevue store. He later worked for six months in the warehouse and voted against unionization in 1985. Although he comes from a blue-collar family, Daryl didn't see the need for a union as long as Starbucks managers were responsive to employee concerns. He had left Starbucks to try his hand at starting a business but returned in late 1987 to work as a barista in our Pike Place store. When he saw the changes I was making, he began philosophical debates with his colleagues and with the union representative, whom he knew. He did some research on his own and began an effort to decertify the union. He wrote a letter and carried it to many stores in person to get signatures of people who no longer wished to be represented by the union. When he had a majority, he presented the letter to the National Labor Relations Board in January. As a result of Daryl's efforts, the union no longer represented our store employees, although it did continue to represent our warehouse and roasting plant workers until 1992.

When so many of our people supported decertification, it was a sign to me that they were beginning to believe I would do what I had promised. Their distrust was beginning to dissipate and their morale was rising. Once I had their full support, I knew I could count on them to work as a team and imbue them with the enthusiasm they would need to spread the word about Starbucks coffee around the country.

8

IF IT CAPTURES YOUR IMAGINATION, IT WILL CAPTIVATE OTHERS

Whatever you can do,
or dream you can, . . . begin it.
Boldness has genius,
power and magic in it.

—*GOETHE*

For five years, from 1987 to 1992, Starbucks remained a privately held company. I was able to learn my job and grow into it outside the glaring spotlight that is cast on publicly traded companies. With the support and approval of my investors, and ultimately the confidence of employees, we pushed ahead on many fronts at once: national expansion, employee benefits, investing in the future, and management development.

The following chapters describe what we accomplished on each of these fronts and recount the important lessons we learned during Starbucks' formative years, when our culture was being shaped. It was a time of many debates, of honing our core values, of standing firm on some issues and learning to compromise on others.

• • •

SPECIALTY COFFEE IN A
MEAT-AND-POTATOES TOWN

Perhaps the gutsiest, and possibly the riskiest, move we made during this period was our entry into the Chicago market. In hindsight, it's hard to believe we took on such a challenge so early in the development of Starbucks.

The idea had actually originated at Il Giornale, even before the marriage to Starbucks. Even though at that point we had only two coffee bars in Seattle and one in Vancouver, British Columbia, I was eager to prove the idea could work in cities across North America. A crucial test would be to see if people in other cities would be receptive to the taste of Starbucks coffee, which was stronger, richer, and more robust than they were used to. Would our retail stores become daily gathering places like those I had seen in Italy? If this combination was going to catch on nationwide, we were going to have to test the idea far from home, and the sooner the better.

It probably would have been more prudent to delay the expansion when the Starbucks acquisition opportunity came up. But even when I was absorbed in raising money for that deal, I refused to drop the Chicago plan. Once Starbucks and Il Giornale merged, it would be even more critical to establish that growth would be feasible outside Seattle. My objective was a national company, and I needed to know what the barriers were to attaining it.

A number of business experts made various arguments against opening stores in Chicago. Tiny Il Giornale didn't have the infrastructure to support such a major move. As Chicago was 2,000 miles away, it was logistically hard to supply with a perishable product like fresh-roasted coffee. And how could we guarantee the appeal of top-quality coffee in the heartland of Folger's and Maxwell House? Chicagoans, I was told, would never drink dark-roasted coffee. For take-out, they preferred the coffee they got at the White Hen Pantry, the local convenience store chain.

If I had listened to the prevailing wisdom, I would have waited till the acquisition was complete, built up a strong home base in Seattle, and then gradually expanded to nearby cities, specifically Portland and Vancouver, where there was a demonstrated appetite for specialty coffee.

But I wanted to go to Chicago. It's a city with a cold climate, great for hot coffee. The downtown area is much bigger than Seattle's. It's a city of neighborhoods, which usually welcome local gathering places. Before 1971 Seattlites didn't know anything about dark-roasted coffee, either. Why couldn't Chicagoans learn to love it even more quickly?

As it happened, an enthusiastic real estate broker in Chicago had three or four locations to show us, and Jack Rodgers and I went to check them out. An early investor in Il Giornale, Jack was a veteran in the franchising and restaurant business, and also a native Chicagoan. With his fatherly affection and sentimental heart, he had become a friend and adviser, a consultant we could pay only in what seemed to be worthless stock. He was an early member of the Il Giornale board of directors and became an executive of the company when we purchased Starbucks. He remained a valued member of our executive management team for ten years.

Because Il Giornale had little money, Jack and I shared a hotel room. We had not yet completed the Starbucks acquisition. The next day, as we made our way through Chicago's crowded streets on our way to look at sites, I said, "Jack, five years from now, every one of these people is going to be walking around holding a Starbucks cup."

He looked at me and said, laughing, "You're crazy."

But I could just see it.

We eventually signed a lease for a prime downtown location, near the corner of West Jackson and Van Buren, one block from Sears Tower. I asked Christine Day to take care of the logistics. She opened the Yellow Pages and started looking up freight companies.

We didn't know it couldn't be done, so we just did it.

We opened that first store, as Starbucks, in October of 1987—the very day the stock market crashed. But it was a disaster for other reasons. I didn't realize that to be successful in Chicago's Loop we needed to open into a lobby. Because the winters are so cold and windy, no one wants to walk outside to get a cup of coffee. Our store faced the street. A few years later, we closed it down, one of the few times we've made an error in site selection. Yet in hindsight, I think shutting it down probably was the real mistake. If we had had the patience, today that site would have proven a winner.

We jumped feet first into Chicago, so in love with our product that we couldn't imagine that everybody else wouldn't love it, too. Over the next six months, we opened three more stores in the area. But by the time the long winter was over, we realized that Chicagoans were not exactly breaking down our doors to buy our coffee. And there were other problems. Costs of goods were higher there. Many of the early employees weren't buying into either our coffee or our dream. And many customers just didn't get it.

Over the next two years, we lost tens of thousands of dollars in Chicago. Starbucks' directors began asking some tough questions, and at first I didn't really have good answers. I knew the stores would eventually work, but how could I convince them?

When we tried to attract venture capitalists in late 1989, some potential investors saw us floundering in Chicago and challenged the whole premise of my growth plan. They wondered if Starbucks was at the front of a long-term trend or if it was a fad; until we succeeded in Chicago, we couldn't prove that our idea was transportable throughout North America. We did manage to raise the money we needed, but at a far lower price per share than we had hoped for.

It wasn't until 1990, after we hired Howard Behar to run our retail operations, that Chicago began to turn the corner. The solution included hiring experienced managers and raising the prices we charged to reflect higher rents and labor costs. What really solved the problem, though, was simply time. In Chicago, loyal customers were saying the same thing as in Seattle; there just weren't enough of them. By 1990, though, a critical mass of customers had caught on to our taste profile. Many switched from our drip coffee, which was stronger than they were used to, to cappuccinos and caffè lattes, which tend to appeal more often on first taste. As they got to know us, many Chicagoans gradually learned to love dark-roasted coffee.

Today, Starbucks has become so much a part of the landscape and culture of Chicago that a lot of residents think it's a local company.

DISPROVING THE DOUBTERS

As time went on and we reached each goal, our self-confidence grew. We accelerated the pace of store openings, aiming to outdo ourselves each year. On a base of 11 stores, we opened 15 new stores in fiscal 1988. For the following year, we figured we could open 20 more. When we realized our targets weren't as hard to hit as they looked, we challenged ourselves to harder ones. We started opening more stores annually than in the original plan: 30 in fiscal 1990, 32 in 1991, 53 in 1992—all company-owned. Each time we achieved a big dream, we were already planning for a bigger one.

Yet this self-assurance was always counterbalanced by a measure of fear. With our greater visibility, I became increasingly afraid of waking up the sleeping giants, the big packaged food companies. If they had begun to sell specialty coffee early on, they could have wiped us out. But with every passing month, quarter, and year, with every new market we entered, I gained confidence that it was going to get harder and harder for them to displace us. With a business based on the next price discount and no retail store experience, they weren't equipped to establish the same sort of close relationship with the customer that we had.

I also worried about competition from other specialty coffee companies. While many were poor operators or franchisers, others roasted good coffee, owned their own stores, and enjoyed a strong reputation in their local regions. If one of them had developed a hunger to go national and obtained the capital to do so, it could have presented a serious challenge to us. But by the time any of them decided to grow, it was too late.

Our competitive strategy was to win customers by offering the best coffee and customer service and an inviting atmosphere. We tried to be first in each market if we could, but then to succeed by playing fair, with integrity and high principles.

Until 1991, we confined our expansion to Chicago and the Pacific Northwest, from Portland through Seattle to Vancouver. Our strategy was to gain a foothold in each market and create a strong presence there before we moved to another city.

But even with this regional concentration, we found ourselves beginning to gain a national following through the medium of mail order. Starbucks had started serving customers by mail in the mid-1970s, mostly travelers who had visited one of the stores or people who had recently moved away from Seattle. At first, we just mailed out a simple brochure listing our products. In 1988, we developed our first catalogue and began expanding our mail-order base to targeted demographic groups. In 1990, we invested in a small phone and computer system to set up our 800 number. That allowed us to extend our one-on-one discussions to some of our most knowledgeable customers. Before we had national retail distribution, mail order was a wonderful vehicle to nurture loyal customers and to build awareness of Starbucks across America. Since they had to make a special effort to obtain our coffee, mail-order buyers were often the most loyal customers, and it made sense to open stores in cities and neighborhoods where they were clustered.

By 1991, we were ready for the next big market entry, which, we agreed, had to be California. With its host of neighborhood centers and openness to high-quality, innovative food, it was an attractive opportunity. Although it's a huge state with diverse regions, we viewed it as one market. Given the size of its population, we could achieve economies of scale if we opened many stores at once. In addition, it was close to Seattle and therefore relatively easy for us to reach and supply.

Still, we debated the best way to make our entry into California. Some wanted to start with San Diego; I voted for Los Angeles. But L.A. is too sprawling and complex, I was warned. People don't walk, they drive. That will hurt us. Others questioned whether Starbucks could even succeed in a warm climate. Would people there really choose to drink hot coffee?

Despite the reasonable arguments made against the move, I finally put a stake in the ground and said: "We're going to L.A."

In the building of a retail brand, you have to create awareness and attract people's favorable attention. You have to become in vogue. You need opinion leaders who naturally endorse your product. With its status as a trendsetter and its cultural ties to the rest of the country, Los Angeles was the perfect place for Starbucks. If we could become the coffee brand of choice in Hollywood, it would not only help our expansion into the rest of California but also serve as a jumping-off point to other markets around the country.

Thanks to careful planning and a bit of luck, that is exactly what happened. L.A. embraced us immediately. Before we opened our first store, the *Los Angeles Times* named us the best coffee in America. Unlike our experience in Chicago, we never had to struggle with a learning curve. Almost overnight, Starbucks became chic. Word of mouth, we discovered, is far more powerful than advertising.

San Francisco was a harder market to enter. Under the terms of our acquisition of Starbucks in August 1987, we had agreed not to open stores in northern California for four years, to avoid competing with Peet's. I wrote an impassioned letter to Jerry Baldwin, who still owned Peet's, asking if we couldn't explore a way to join forces and cooperate rather than compete. But he said no.

By early 1992, we were ready to enter San Francisco but faced another problem: That city had a moratorium on converting stores to restaurant-related uses in certain prime urban neighborhoods.

We could sell coffee beverages and pastries for our customers to consume at stand-up counters but could not offer seating in locations that had formerly been used by general retailers. We took a risk, opting to open stores in visible locations on prime shopping streets. Arthur Rubinfeld, then an outside real estate broker, along with other café owners, convinced the City Council to add a new classification to the zoning code to allow "beverage houses" with tables and chairs. Once the code was changed, many cafés opened, reenergizing the neighborhood street life in several communities in the city of San Francisco.

As our growth became more visible, our biggest doubters were others in the specialty coffee business. Many of them assured us that our plans were unworkable. Even Alfred Peet, a longtime admirer of Starbucks, predicted that the excellence of our coffee would suffer if we attempted to sell it nationwide.

One reason they doubted us was the conventional wisdom that the whole-bean coffee business would always have to remain local, with stores close to the roasting plant. If you shipped fresh-roasted coffee beans to stores half a continent away, most people believed, they would lose their freshness and flavor.

In 1989, we figured out an answer to what seemed an impossible conundrum. We began using FlavorLock bags, a kind of vacuum packaging with a one-way valve to allow carbon dioxide gases to escape without allowing harmful air and moisture in. This device, used by Starbucks in the early 1980s for wholesale customers only, enabled us to preserve freshness by putting coffee in five-pound silver bags right after roasting and sealing in the flavor before shipping. Once the bag is opened, the fresh flavor begins to decline, so the coffee must be sold within seven days or we donate it to charity.

In retrospect, the reintroduction of FlavorLock bags was a key decision that made our expansion strategy feasible. It allowed us to sell and serve coffee with the highest freshness standards even in stores thousands of miles from our roasting plant. It meant we did not need to build a roasting plant in every city we entered. Even our Seattle stores, which are only minutes from the roasting plant, receive fresher-tasting coffee because of these bags.

Every time we open in a new city, someone predicts we'll fail. So far, they've been mistaken.

For me, the thrill of business is in the climb. Everything we try to achieve is like climbing a steep slope, one that very few people have managed to scale. The more difficult the climb, the more gratifying the effort put into the ascent and the greater the satisfaction upon reaching the summit. But, like all dedicated mountain climbers, we're always seeking a higher peak.

THE THIRD PLACE

I like to think of myself as a visionary, but I have to admit that the whole specialty coffee phenomenon grew a lot bigger and a lot faster than I had ever imagined.

Nobody believed that espresso would jump out of its narrow niche and become so popular and widely accepted a drink.

Nobody foresaw that coffee bars and espresso carts would appear on street corners and in office lobbies all across America, with more opening every month.

Nobody imagined that even fast-food places and gas-station convenience stores would hang big "espresso" signs in their windows to lure in customers.

When an innovative idea for a retail store makes history by creating a whole new paradigm, it's rewarding for anyone who's had the foresight to recognize its merits early on. When it creates a new social phenomenon, when it gives rise to a new vocabulary that finds its way onto TV talk shows and sitcoms, and ultimately becomes part of the American lexicon, when it becomes a defining element of the culture and a decade, it's gone far beyond being simply the timely brainstorm of a single entrepreneur or a small team.

Starbucks' success in so many different types of cities eventually forced me to ponder: What is it that people are responding to? Why did Starbucks, and similar cafés, strike a chord in so many disparate places? What need are we really fulfilling? Why do so many customers willingly wait in long lines at Starbucks stores? Why do so many linger afterward, even with a to-go cup in their hands?

At first, we figured it was simply because of the coffee.

But as time went on, we realized that our stores had a deeper resonance and were offering benefits as seductive as the coffee itself:

A taste of romance. At Starbucks stores, people get a five- or ten-minute break that takes them far from the routine of their daily lives. Where else can you go to get a whiff of Sumatra or Kenya or Costa Rica? Where else can you get a taste of Verona or Milan? Just having the chance to order a drink as exotic as an *espresso macchiato* adds a spark of romance to an otherwise unremarkable day.

An affordable luxury. In our stores you may see a policeman or a utility worker standing in line in front of a wealthy surgeon. The blue-collar man may not be able to afford the Mercedes the surgeon just drove up in, but he can order the same $2.00 cappuccino. They're both giving themselves a reward and enjoying something world class.

An oasis. In an increasingly fractured society, our stores offer a quiet moment to gather your thoughts and center yourself. Starbucks people smile at you, serve you quickly, don't harass you. A visit to Starbucks can be a small escape during a day when so many other things are beating you down. We've become a breath of fresh air.

Casual social interaction. One of the advertising agencies that pitched for our business interviewed Los Angeles–area customers in focus groups. The common thread among their comments was this: "Starbucks is so social. We go to Starbucks stores because of a social feeling."

Yet, strangely, the agency discovered that fewer than 10 percent of the people they observed in our stores at any given time actually ever talked to anybody. Most customers waited silently in line and spoke only to the cashier to order a drink. But somehow, just being in a Starbucks store, they felt they were out in the world, in a safe place yet away from the familiar faces they saw every day.

In America, we are in danger of losing the kind of casual social interaction that is part of the daily routine for many Europeans. In the 1990s, coffee bars became a central component of the American social scene in part because they fulfilled the need for a nonthreatening gathering spot, a "third place" outside of work and home. Ray Oldenburg, a Florida sociology professor, wrote most eloquently of this need in his book, *The Great Good Place* (1989).

Oldenburg's thesis is that people need informal public places where they can gather, put aside the concerns of work and home, relax, and talk. Germany's beer gardens, England's pubs, and French and Viennese cafés created this outlet in people's lives, providing a neutral ground where all are equal and conversation is the main activity. America once had such spots, in its taverns, barber shops, and beauty parlors. But with suburbanization, they are vanishing, replaced by the self-containment of suburban homes. As Oldenburg observes:

> *Without such places, the urban area fails to nourish the kinds of relationships and the diversity of human contact that are the essence of the city. Deprived of these settings, people remain lonely within their crowds.*

However well they seem to have stepped into the role, though, Starbucks stores are not yet the ideal Third Place. We don't have a lot of seating, and customers don't often get to know people they meet there. Most just grab their coffee and depart. Still, Americans are so hungry for a community that some of our customers began gathering in our stores, making appointments with friends, holding meetings, striking up conversations with other regulars. Once we understood the powerful need for a Third Place, we were able to respond by building larger stores, with more seating. In some stores, we hire a jazz band to play on weekend nights.

While my original idea was to provide a quick, stand-up, to-go service in downtown office locations, Starbucks' fastest growing stores today are in urban or suburban residential neighborhoods. People don't just drop by to pick up a half-pound of decaf on their way to the supermarket, as we first anticipated. They come for the atmosphere and the camaraderie.

The generation of people in their twenties figured this out before the sociologists. As teenagers, they had no safe place to hang out except shopping malls. Now that they are older, some find that bars are too noisy and raucous and threatening for companionship. So they hang out in cafés and coffee bars. The music is quiet enough to allow conversation. The places are well-lit. No one is carded, and no one is drunk. Sometimes a group will gather at a Starbucks before heading off to a movie or other entertainment; sometimes they just meet to talk.

The atmosphere obviously works for romance, as well. We've received dozens of letters from couples who met at Starbucks, whether during the morning rush or in the lazy evening hours. One couple even wanted to get married at a Starbucks store.

Other trends of the 1990s also nourish the growth of such gathering places. More and more people are working from home offices, telecommuting by phone and fax and modem with distant offices. They go to coffee stores for the human interaction they need on a regular basis. As the Internet becomes increasingly widely used, people spend more time sitting in front of their computers. There's no interactive relationship with anything but that box. Is it mere coincidence that coffee bars became popular at the same time as the Internet was growing? Many cities, like Seattle, have cybercafés, gathering places for people who love coffee, computers, and socializing.

Back in 1987, none of us could foresee these social trends, and how our stores would accommodate them. What we did, though, was to appeal to the sophistication and wisdom and better nature of our potential customers, providing them the kind of music and atmosphere that we liked for ourselves.

People didn't know they needed a safe, comfortable, neighborhood gathering place. They didn't know they would like Italian espresso drinks. But when we gave it to them, the fervor of their response overwhelmed us.

That's why our expansion—gutsy as it was—succeeded even better than we imagined.

Big opportunities lie in the creation of something new. But that innovation has to be relevant and inspiring, or it will burst into color and fade away as quickly as fireworks.

9

PEOPLE ARE NOT A LINE ITEM

*Wealth is the means and people are the
ends. All our material riches will avail us
little if we do not use them to expand
the opportunities of our people.*

—*JOHN F. KENNEDY, STATE OF THE UNION,
JANUARY 1962*

A LESSON OF LOSS

Throughout 1987 my father's lung cancer grew worse. I
kept in frequent touch by phone and flew back to New
York whenever I could. My mother was by now spending every
day with him in the hospital, having given up her job as a receptionist, and relied on the support of my brother, sister, and me.

Then one day, in early January 1988, I received an urgent call
from my mother. I had been expecting it for five years, but you can
never be prepared for the tenseness of heart that clamps you at a
moment like that. I took the first plane to New York and, fortunately, arrived in time to see my dad the day before he died. I sat
next to his hospital bed, my hand on his, and tried to think of the
way we were twenty years earlier, when he taught me to hit a baseball or throw a football.

So many emotions were battling in my head at that time that I couldn't think straight. The regrets I had always had about my dad's life struggles were now mixed with grief and loss; the fantasies I'd had of how he might have lived his life clashed with the dreams of my own that were coming true; the anguished look in his eyes helped me comprehend the significance of all the years he had worked for us and all the lives that now depended on me. On that last day, nothing in my life mattered in comparison to the pain he was suffering.

One of the terrible tragedies, for me, was the fact that my father passed away before he could witness what I achieved. On his last visit to Seattle, I had taken him to the first Il Giornale store, when it was still under construction. But now I could never show him the growing, thriving enterprise that was Starbucks. If he could have watched the company grow, he wouldn't have believed it.

Soon after his death, I spent some time with a good friend who has known me since childhood. He was then working in Germany, where I had gone for a trade show. We talked for hours one night over beers, and I discussed my confused feelings about my father.

"If your dad had been successful," he said, "maybe you wouldn't have had as much drive as you have."

My friend was probably right. Part of what has always driven me is fear of failure, for I know too well the face of self-defeat.

I finally came to terms with my bitterness and learned to respect the memory of what my dad was, instead of regretting what he was not. He did the best he could. He passed away before I was able to tell him I understood that. That's one of the great losses of my life. It was wrong of me to blame him for failing to overcome circum-stances beyond his control. But it was also wrong that in America, land of dreams, a hard-working man like him couldn't find a niche where he would be treated with dignity.

It was a strange but fitting coincidence that during my dad's final months, my major preoccupation at work was building trust with the employees of Starbucks. I saw on some of their faces the same doubts about the intentions of management that my father had expressed so often to me. People felt undervalued and uncertain about their future, and at times they directed their anger at me, as he had.

But I was no longer a helpless kid. I was in a position to do something about the insecurity and lack of respect that seemed to be becoming far too commonplace in much of American business.

Within a year, I did.

THE PAYOFF OF A COSTLY HEALTH PLAN

It's an ironic fact that, while retail and restaurant businesses live or die on customer service, their employees have among the lowest pay and worst benefits of any industry. These people are not only the heart and soul but also the public face of the company. Every dollar earned passes through their hands.

In a store or restaurant, the customer's experience is vital: One bad encounter, and you've lost a customer for life. If the fate of your business is in the hands of a twenty-year-old part-time worker who goes to college or pursues acting on the side, can you afford to treat him or her as expendable?

From the beginning of my management of Starbucks, I wanted it to be the employer of choice, the company everybody wanted to work for. By paying more than the going wage in restaurants and retail stores, and by offering benefits that weren't available elsewhere, I hoped that Starbucks would attract people who were well-educated and eager to communicate our passion for coffee. To my thinking, a generous benefits package was a key competitive advantage. So many service-oriented companies have the opposite view, regarding benefits for entry-level people as a cost to be minimized, not an opportunity to attract and reward good people.

I wanted to win the race. But I also wanted to make sure that when we got to the finish line, no one was left behind. If a small group of white-collar managers and shareholders won at the expense of employees, that wouldn't be a victory at all. We had to be in a position where we all reached the tape together.

After my dad died, I wanted to make a gesture to Starbucks' employees that would cement the trust we were building. Ideally, I would have liked to be able to make them all owners of the company, but I knew that, in the short term, we would be losing money while we invested in the future. For a few years, at least, there would be no profits to share.

So I needed to come up with another way to reward them. One of the requests employees had made to the original owners had been health benefits for part-time workers. They were turned down. The symbolism wasn't lost on me.

I decided to recommend to the board of directors that we expand our health-care coverage to include part-timers who worked as little as twenty hours a week.

In the late 1980s, employer generosity was hopelessly out of fashion. Corporate raiders and soaring health-care costs had forced many American executives to reduce benefits. Under the prevailing mantra of "maximizing shareholder value," CEOs were applauded by Wall Street if they cut costs and laid off thousands. Companies that did value their employees above shareholders were mocked as paternalistic and uncompetitive. They were encouraged to become more hard-nosed, to cut bloated payrolls, and to become lean and mean. White-collar workers, too, were learning the hard way that loyalty didn't pay.

At the same time, health-care bills were soaring to unmanageable heights. The cost of medical care rose far faster than the consumer price index, especially during the late 1980s. Few companies covered part-time workers at all, and those who did restricted benefits to those working at least thirty hours a week. Most executives were actively looking for ways to contain their medical insurance expenses.

Starbucks went the other direction: Instead of cutting health-care benefits, we found a way to increase ours.

I saw my plan not as a generous optional benefit but as a core strategy: Treat people like family, and they will be loyal and give their all. Stand by people, and they will stand by you. It's the oldest formula in business, one that is second nature to many family-run firms. Yet by the late 1980s, it seemed to be forgotten.

When I first presented this plan, Starbucks' directors were skeptical. I was proposing to raise expenses at a time when Starbucks was struggling to stay afloat. How could we afford to expand health-care coverage when we couldn't even make a profit?

At that time, our board members were all big individual investors, or their representatives, and few of them had experience managing and motivating large numbers of people. "How can you be so extravagant toward employees—with our money?" they asked. "How can you possibly justify the cost?"

But I argued passionately that it was the right thing to do. On the surface, I acknowledged, it will seem more expensive. But if it reduces turnover, I pointed out, it will cut our costs of recruiting and training. Starbucks provides at least twenty-four hours of training for every retail employee, so each person we hire represents a significant investment. At that time, it cost $1,500 a year to provide an employee with full benefits, compared with $3,000 to train a new hire. Many retailers encourage turnover, either consciously or unconsciously, in the belief that it keeps down wages and benefits. But high turnover also affects customer loyalty. Some of our customers are such regulars that the minute they walk into the store, a barista recalls their favorite drink. If that barista leaves, that strong connection is broken.

Part-timers, I argued, are vital to Starbucks. In fact, they represented two-thirds of our workforce. Our stores have to open early—sometimes at 5:30 or 6 A.M.—and often don't close until 9 P.M. or later. We depend on people willing to work short shifts on a steady basis. In many cases, part-timers are students or individuals who are juggling other obligations. They want health-care benefits as much as the full-time employee does, and I argued strongly that we should honor and value their contribution to the company.

The board approved, and we began offering full health benefits to all part-timers in late 1988. To my knowledge, we became the only private company—and later the only public company—to do so.

It turned out to be one of the best decisions we have ever made.

It's true, our health insurance program is costly. Over the years, we've added coverage far more generous than most companies our size, with coverage for preventative care, crisis counseling, mental health, chemical dependency, vision, and dental. Starbucks subsidizes 75 percent of coverage; each employee pays only 25 percent. We also offer coverage for unmarried partners in a committed relationship. Since our employees tend to be young and healthy, our rates stay within reason, allowing us to afford broader coverage while keeping monthly payments relatively low.

But Starbucks gets back plenty for its investment. The most obvious effect is lower attrition. Nationwide, most retailers and fast-food chains have a turnover rate ranging from 150 percent to as high as 400 percent a year. At Starbucks, turnover at the barista level averages 60 percent to 65 percent. For store managers, our turnover is only about 25 percent, while at other retailers, it's about 50 percent. Better benefits attract good people and keep them longer.

More significantly, I found that the health plan made a huge difference in the attitudes of our people. When a company shows generosity toward them, employees show a more positive outlook in everything they do.

The true value of our health-care program struck me most deeply in 1991, when we lost one of our earliest and most devoted partners, Jim Kerrigan, to AIDS. Jim started as a barista behind the counter of our second Il Giornale store, in 1986, and he quickly rose to the position of store manager. Jim was a fantastic advocate of Il Giornale and later of Starbucks. He loved it.

Then one day, Jim came into my office and told me he had AIDS. It took incredible courage. I had known he was gay but had no idea he was sick. His disease had entered a new phase, he explained, and he wouldn't be able to work any longer. We sat together and cried, for I could not find meaningful words to console him. I couldn't compose myself. I hugged him.

At that point, Starbucks had no provision for employees with AIDS. We had to make a policy decision. Because of Jim, we decided to offer health-care coverage to all employees who have terminal illnesses, paying medical costs in full from the time they are not able to work until they are covered by government programs, usually twenty-nine months.

After his visit to me, I spoke with Jim often and visited him at the hospice. Within a year, he was gone. I received a letter from his family afterward, telling me how much they appreciated our benefit plan. Without it, Jim wouldn't have had money to take care of himself, and he was grateful for that one less worry during his last few months.

Even today, there are scarcely any companies of our size that offer full health-care benefits to all employees, including part-timers. That fact was brought home to me memorably in April 1994, when President Clinton invited me to Washington, D.C., for a one-on-one meeting in the Oval Office, to tell him about Starbucks' health-care program.

Others have been to the White House many times, but to me, born in the Projects of Brooklyn and working in Seattle, the thought of a chat in the Oval Office was overwhelming.

When I arrived at 1600 Pennsylvania that day, I tried to act nonchalant, but I could feel my heart thumping in my chest. Someone met me at the back door and took me in through a basement corridor, past pictures of great presidents, Washington, Jefferson, Wilson. These are the same halls, I thought, where Lincoln walked, and Roosevelt, and Kennedy. And what got me here was not some extraordinary feat, not walking on the moon or finding the cure for cancer. All I had done was provide health care to the people of my company, all of them, something any employer could do.

I was taken upstairs and shown to a chair outside the Oval Office.

"The president will be with you in three minutes," a woman said. I straightened my tie and took in every detail around me. Phones were ringing, thick documents were stacked on the desk, and somber faces from history looked down from portraits on the walls.

"The president will be with you in one minute," the woman said. I tugged on my cuffs and straightened my tie again. I watched the second hand go around the clock, and the door didn't open. I fidgeted in my chair. Finally, the door burst open, and the president's hand was in my face. He ushered me in. I had seen the Oval Office so many times in movies that now it seemed surreal. On his desk, I noticed immediately, was a green-and-white Starbucks cup, filled with hot coffee.

I don't know why I said it, but the first words out of my mouth were: "Don't you ever get intimidated, walking around here?"

He laughed and said "All the time." He put me at ease and we talked for about fifteen minutes.

When the meeting was over, he led me across the hall to the Roosevelt Room for a small press conference. After speaking to the reporters, we attended a private luncheon with other CEOs. It was a heady experience.

At one point, with a few minutes between events, I asked to use a phone. How many guys like me do this kind of thing? I called my mother in Brooklyn, saying, "Mom, I just want you to know, I'm callin' you from the White House."

"Howard," she said, "it doesn't get any better than this!"

I wish my dad could have been there. In a sense, he was.

• • •

MEANINGFUL MISSION
STATEMENTS HAVE TEETH

From the beginning, I wanted employees to identify with the mission of the company and to have the sense of accomplishment that goes with being part of a successful team. That meant defining a strong sense of purpose and listening to input from people at all levels of the enterprise.

Early in 1990, we as a senior executive team carefully examined our values and beliefs and then drafted a Mission Statement at an off-site retreat. Our aim was to articulate a powerful message of purpose and translate that into a set of guidelines to help us gauge the appropriateness of each decision we make, at all levels of the company. We submitted a draft to everyone else at Starbucks for review and made changes based on these comments. The Mission Statement that emerged from that process puts people first and profits last. It's not a trophy to decorate our office walls, but an organic body of beliefs, not a list of aspirations but a foundation of guiding principles we hold in common. (For Mission Statement, see page 139.)

Drafting the Mission Statement was just the first step in a strategic planning process that lasted three months and involved more than fifty employees. We wanted to make sure we in management were hearing the views of our co-workers—and to ensure we had a long-term plan that our people had helped shape. At the urging of the board of directors, we invited in a Portland consulting firm called the Mt. Hood Group and assembled several teams, each composed of nonexecutive members from the stores, offices, and plant They met frequently that summer of 1990, away from the workplace, to discuss problems and make suggestions to management about decision-making, market expansion, and "people growth." We implemented almost all their recommendations.

The "people growth" team had some of the most far-reaching

ideas. They recommended that Starbucks implement a long-term stock option plan, a dream I had harbored almost since the beginning. And they insisted that writing and posting a Mission Statement wasn't enough. Starbucks needed a way to make sure we were living up to it. So they suggested a "Mission Review" team. Every employee in each store and other location would be given a postcard-sized comment card and encouraged to report to the Mission Review team if they saw a decision that did not support our Mission Statement.

Most executives would feel threatened by such a setup. I sure did. The day of their presentation to management in September 1990, the "people growth" team members were tense. They had practiced several times, and they wondered if it might be confrontational. As I listened, I thought: *Do I want a team of employees monitoring management like this, holding us to our own high standards?* If I turned it down, what would that say about the sincerity of management toward the Mission Statement? We listened respectfully and asked a few questions. After a few days of consideration, we approved the idea.

Within a few months, the Mission Review system was set up. It's still in place today. Any employee, anywhere, can make a suggestion or report an action that seems contradictory to our purpose, and we promise that a relevant manager will respond within two weeks, either by phone or by letter. Printed comment cards are given to each new employee upon hire and are also kept in common areas along with other company forms. Hundreds are submitted each year. People also have the option of not including their name. They don't get a response, but their comment appears with others in a report I review carefully every month.

As the company has grown, Mission Review has become a vital link to the concerns of our large and scattered workforce. Every quarter, a team of people from different parts of the company meets to go over top employee concerns, seek solutions, and provide a report at our quarterly Open Forums. Not only does this process help keep the Mission Statement alive, it provides an important avenue for open communications with our people. Many great suggestions have been implemented.

WHY HAVE EMPLOYEES IF EVERYONE CAN BE A PARTNER?

By October 1990, I could report to the board that we had achieved our first profitable year. Comfortably in the black, I could now undertake a venture that had a profound, long-term effect on the success of Starbucks.

If I hang my hat on one thing that makes Starbucks stand out above other companies it would be the introduction of Bean Stock. That's the name we gave to our stock option plan. With its introduction, we turned every employee of Starbucks into a partner.

I wanted to find a way to share both the ownership of the company and the rewards of financial success with the people of Starbucks. But I wasn't sure how best to do that. In January of 1991, a woman in our human resources department, Bradley Honeycutt, researched various alternatives for introducing such a plan. In conversations with consultants and surveys of other companies, she found a lot of different models but none that did what we wanted to do. Most plans were available only for public companies, such as outright stock grants and stock purchase programs, or for top executives, such as stock options. Privately held companies, like ours, didn't grant stock or options because there was no market for them; their only alternative was to set up an Employee Stock Ownership Plan (ESOP). But that plan was mainly a way of raising capital.

We had a different aim. My goal was to link shareholder value with long-term rewards for our employees. I wanted them to have a chance to share in the benefits of growth, and to make clear the connection between their contributions and the growing value of the company.

Finally, we decided to do something novel. Even though we were a private company, we would grant stock options to every employee, company-wide, from the top managers to the baristas, in proportion to the level of base pay. If they, through their efforts, could help make Starbucks more successful every year, and if Starbucks someday went public, their options could eventually be worth a good sum of money. We had, in effect, given them a chance to create their own value.

Several of us had been tossing around names for the plan, trying to be creative. Bradley came up with the name *Bean Stock* one Sunday, when she was out jogging with her husband. It's not only a playful reference to the coffee beans we sell, but it also evokes Jack's beanstalk, which grew to the sky. So, eventually, did ours.

In May 1991, we formally presented the idea to the board of directors. All spring, I had been busy crusading with board members, in groups and one-on-one, explaining why I was convinced this proposal would work. Their main worry was that it would dilute the shareholdings of investors who had taken a risk with hard cash.

I had anticipated just that objection, and countered it by arguing that granting stock options would give the company a strong backbone that would help it achieve its objectives, in terms of both sales and profits. Investors might own a slightly smaller percentage of the company, but the value of their holdings would grow faster and more surely. If we linked everyone in Starbucks to the performance of the company as a whole, I told them, every employee would bring the same attitude to work as the CEO who is himself a shareholder. In the end, the stock plan would add value in several respects—to the performance of the business as a whole, to the bottom line, and to the morale and spirit of the workplace.

When Bean Stock came up for a vote in May, the board approved it unanimously. They were as excited about the possibilities as I was.

As far as I know, no other company has attempted a stock option plan as widespread and ambitious as Bean Stock. We granted stock

PEOPLE ARE NOT A LINE ITEM

options to over 700 employees when we were still private. To do so, we had to obtain a special exemption from the Securities and Exchange Commission. (The SEC considers a company public if it has more than 500 registered shareholders.) Even today, you'd be hard-pressed to find another company, especially a retailer, that gives stock options to all its employees. Software and other high-tech companies routinely offer stock options, but normally just to developers and other highly skilled technical employees. In retail, it's unheard of.

In August 1991, we introduced the plan to the employees, and in early September, we held a big meeting to roll it out. I spoke about how this program fulfilled a long-held dream, and Orin Smith, then chief financial officer, gave a slide presentation to explain the way stock options worked—a complex matter even public company employees might have a hard time understanding. Every employee was presented a packet tied with a blue ribbon, and inside was a brochure explaining Bean Stock. We celebrated with cookies and sparkling cider and toasted to being "Partners . . . in Growth," the line we used to describe Bean Stock.

From that day on, we stopped using the word "employee." We now call all our people "partners," because everyone is eligible for stock options as soon as he or she has been with Starbucks for six months. Even part-timers who work as little as twenty hours a week qualify.

The first grant was made on October 1, 1991, just after the end of the fiscal year. Each partner was awarded stock options worth 12 percent of his or her annual base pay. A partner earning $20,000, for example, would be given $2,400 worth of stock options. He or she could cash in one-fifth of the amount each year after that, simultaneously buying at the first year's low price and selling at the current price, keeping the difference. Every October since then, good profits have allowed us to raise the grant to 14 percent of base pay. So each year the partner remains with Starbucks, he or she receives another 14 percent of his or her salary, awarded at the

stock price prevailing at the start of the new fiscal year. As the stock price goes up every year, the options become more valuable.

We granted those first Bean Stock options at $6 per share. By the time they were fully vested, on September 30, 1996, our share price was $33; but since our stock had split twice, each of those original options became four shares, worth $132. To illustrate the value, an employee making $20,000 a year in 1991 would have been able to cash in his 1991 options alone for more than $50,000 five years later.

Even with no guarantee that the options would ever be worth anything, Bean Stock began to affect people's attitudes and performance immediately. I started hearing comments like "I'm Bean-Stocking it" when someone figured out a way to save the company money—say, by traveling with a Saturday night stay-over to reduce airfare. People started coming up with innovative ideas about how to cut costs, to increase sales, to create value. They could speak to our customers from the heart, as partners in the business.

By educating our people on the importance of creating value and profits for our company, we linked them to shareholder value. Every quarter, to this day, we explain our results to them in Open Forums, allowing time for questions and answers. Sometimes they resent the fact that, as a public company, we have to focus so much on numbers. But at the end of the day, they appreciate the need to balance their individual concerns with the company's overall performance.

How do you measure the benefits of listening to your people and sharing ownership with them? You can't. But the benefits can run deeper than you think. One member of the "people growth" team was Martin Shaughnessy, a tall, talkative, pony-tailed man who worked in receiving, unloading heavy burlap bags of green coffee at the plant. He was amazed and thrilled to be invited to off-site meetings with office workers, asked for his input, and given the opportunity to present ideas to management. Months later he came into my office and told me we needed a professional distribution manager—in effect, asking us to hire him a boss. I asked him to write up a proposal and make a presentation to the executive board. He did, and within six months, we acted on his suggestion.

One day in early 1992, Martin came into the human resources department, bearing a letter, signed by an overwhelming majority of the warehouse and roasting plant employees, indicating they no longer wished to be represented by the union. "You included us in the running of this business," he said. "Whenever we complained, you fixed the problem. You trusted us, and now we trust you."

For me, working at Starbucks has provided no greater reward than the pride I feel whenever I receive a letter from a partner about Bean Stock, thanking me. I was especially moved by one from Jani Daubenspeck, who joined Starbucks in 1989 as an assistant to Dave Olsen and rose to become a production scheduler at our Seattle roasting plant. In 1994, she bought her first home, a one-story bungalow in Seattle's Seward Park neighborhood with a "great garden." She had been living with her sister and was finally able to afford her own place, thanks to cashing in some of her early Starbucks stock options to make the down payment of $10,000.

I get letters and messages like that all the time. Martin Shaughnessy bought a brand-new Harley-Davidson motorcycle when he sold his Bean Stock shares. Another partner purchased a vacation home. Another got an antique car. Yet another cashed in her options and took the family to visit her husband's relatives, whom she had never met. Several have cashed in options to pay for college tuition.

Stories like this crystallize for me the true importance of the work we do and the truth that Starbucks stands for something special beyond buying and roasting coffee and satisfying customers.

• • •

If you treat your employees as interchangeable cogs in a wheel, they will view you with the same affection.

But they're not cogs. Every one of them is an individual who needs both a sense of self-worth and the financial means to provide for personal and family needs.

I tried to make Starbucks the kind of company I wish my dad had worked for. Without even a high school diploma, he probably could never have been an executive. But if he had landed a job in one of our stores or roasting plants, he wouldn't have quit in frustration because the company didn't value him. He would have had good health benefits, stock options, and an atmosphere in which his suggestions or complaints would receive a prompt, respectful response.

The bigger Starbucks grows, the more chance that some employee, somewhere, isn't getting the respect he or she deserves. If we can't attend to that problem, we are facing a failure worse than any shortcomings Wall Street can detect.

Ultimately, Starbucks can't flourish and win customers' hearts without the passionate devotion of our employees. In business, that passion comes from ownership, trust, and loyalty. If you undermine any of those, employees will view their work as just another job.

Sometimes we lose sight of that at Starbucks, especially as we get larger and a distance develops between me and the newest hire in the newest store. But I know, in my heart, if we treat people as a line item under expenses, we're not living up to our goals and our values.

Their passion and devotion is our number-one competitive advantage. Lose it, and we've lost the game.

STARBUCKS MISSION STATEMENT

Establish Starbucks as the premier purveyor of the finest coffee in the world while maintaining our uncompromising principles as we grow. The following six guiding principles will help us measure the appropriateness of our decisions:

Provide a great work environment and treat each other with respect and dignity.

Embrace diversity as an essential component in the way we do business.

Apply the highest standards of excellence to the purchasing, roasting, and fresh delivery of our coffee.

Develop enthusiastically satisfied customers all of the time.

Contribute positively to our communities and our environment.

Recognize that profitability is essential to our future success.

10

A HUNDRED-STORY BUILDING FIRST
NEEDS A STRONG FOUNDATION

The builders of visionary companies . . .

concentrate primarily on building an organization—

building a ticking clock—rather than on hitting a

market just right with a visionary product idea.

— JAMES C. COLLINS AND JERRY I. PORRAS,
BUILT TO LAST

Sometimes losing money is healthy.

Now there's a novel thought.

Losing money is scary—that I know from experience. It's a danger sign for most businesses, especially mature, established ones. But for a young entrepreneurial company, full of promise, losing money could be a healthy sign that it's investing ahead of the growth curve.

If you aspire to fast growth, you need to create an infrastructure for the larger enterprise you are planning to create.

You can't build a hundred-story skyscraper on a foundation designed for a two-story house.

• • •

The Importance of Investors
with Strong Stomachs

Starbucks was profitable until I took over. It didn't take long for me to realize that we couldn't both sustain that level of earnings and build the foundation we needed for fast growth. I predicted that we would lose money for three years.

In fact, that's precisely what we did. In 1987, we lost $330,000. The next year losses more than doubled, to $764,000. The third year we lost $1.2 million. It wasn't until 1990 that we finally turned a profit.

That was a nerve-wracking period for all of us, filled with many white-knuckle days. Although we knew we were investing in the future and had accepted the fact that we wouldn't be profitable, I was often filled with doubts.

One night in 1988, Ron Lawrence, then Starbucks' controller, knocked at the door of my house at 11 P.M. Sheri and our son were already asleep upstairs, and when I led Ron into the kitchen, I saw that his face was ashen. He had just calculated our monthly numbers, and we had lost four times more than we had budgeted for. A board meeting was scheduled for the following week, and as we sat at the table with the figures spread before us, I was appalled.

"I can't go to the board with these numbers," I said. "This is unbelievable. How did this happen?"

Ron explained that it was an unusual circumstance, in which everything hit the P&L at once. It was unlikely to happen again. Still, I didn't sleep well that night, trying to plan how I would explain the huge shortfall to the directors.

The board meeting was as tense as I had expected it would be. "Things aren't working," one of the directors said after hearing my report. "We will have to change strategy." We had only about 20 stores at the time, and some directors thought my plans were far too ambitious. I began to imagine conversations among board members, before and after those meetings, in which directors complained: *We've got to get this guy out of here. Howard doesn't know what he's doing. How much of our money are we going to let him lose before we pull the plug?*

The pressure was on, and I had to justify those losses. I had to prove that they were necessary for my investment strategy and not just money poured down the drain. Although I was quaking inside, I had to summon every ounce of my conviction to convince them.

"Look," I told the board, keeping my voice as steady as possible, "we're going to keep losing money until we can do three things. We have to attract a management team well beyond our expansion needs. We have to build a world-class roasting facility. And we need a computer information system sophisticated enough to keep track of sales in hundreds and hundreds of stores."

Although it took various forms in the years to come, that message became like a mantra, repeated every quarter: "We have to invest ahead of the growth curve."

Fortunately, the board and investor group showed remarkable patience in supporting me and my plans. If Starbucks hadn't turned a profit in 1990, they would have had good reason to kick me out.

Looking back now, I realize how sound our strategy proved to be. In those early years, 1987–1989, we laid a solid base for rapid national expansion by hiring key managers and by investing early in facilities we would soon need—far sooner than we realized. It was expensive, but without it, we would never have been able to accelerate our growth, year after year, without stopping to catch our breath.

When you're starting a business, whatever the size, it's critically important to recognize that things are going to take longer and cost more money than you expect. If your plan is ambitious, you have to count on temporarily investing more than you earn, even if sales are increasing rapidly. If you recruit experienced executives, build manufacturing facilities far beyond your current needs, and formulate a clear strategy for managing through the lean years, you'll be ready as the company shifts into ever higher gears.

What we did was try to figure out how big we wanted to be in two years and hire experienced executives who had already built and managed companies of that size. Their background enabled them to anticipate the pitfalls of growth and plan and react accordingly. Hiring ahead of the growth curve may seem costly at the time, but it's a lot wiser to bring in experts before you need them than to stumble ahead with green, untested people who are prone to making avoidable mistakes.

Of course, building an infrastructure takes money. Ideally, capital should be in place even before you need it, not only to fund the expansion itself but to respond quickly to problems and opportunities as they arise. Convincing shareholders to increase their investment is probably the hardest part of an entrepreneur's work. It's a humbling experience to stand before these financially savvy individuals, who are already full of doubts, and tell them, "We're losing money. Can you invest more?"

In our case, just a year after we raised $3.8 million to acquire Starbucks, we had to raise an additional $3.9 million to finance our growth plans. By 1990, we needed even more money, and we brought in $13.5 million from venture capital funds. The following year, we completed a second round of venture capital, for $15 million. That added up to four rounds of private placements before Starbucks went public in 1992. If Starbucks had failed to perform, if investors had lost faith in us, obtaining those levels of funding would never have been possible.

Luckily, Starbucks' revenues were rising at more than 80 percent a year, and we were nearly doubling the number of stores annually. We pushed into markets outside our home base, including Chicago, to prove the idea could work in other cities. We were able to show attractive "unit economics" at each store, and investors could see that the overall specialty coffee business, both in supermarkets and in stand-alone stores, was catching on all over the country.

To supply our accelerating number of stores, we needed a much larger roasting facility than we had acquired with the purchase of Starbucks. With the help of Jack Benaroya, we built a new office and plant in Seattle in 1989, large enough, we thought, to last ten years. We installed a high-speed roaster and packaging equipment and moved across Airport Way to a building that seemed huge at the time. Now it houses only our mail-order business.

Securing good sites for new stores also became increasingly expensive as we expanded. For the first five years after 1987, I approved every site personally—for more than a hundred stores. We aimed for highly visible locations, either in downtown office buildings or in densely populated urban or suburban neighborhoods, near supermarkets. We worked with outside brokers in each region, and in 1989, we hired one of our best brokers, Yves Mizrahi, to be our vice president for real estate. Working closely with me, he pre-screened each site and closed each deal. Our process of site selection was enormously time-consuming, but we couldn't afford a single mistake. One real-estate error in judgment would mean a $350,000 write-down for leasehold improvements, plus the cost of getting out of the lease. That represented a minimum of a half million dollars at stake, not counting the opportunity cost of money we could have been using elsewhere.

Eventually I came to the conclusion that store development was too big a task to run out of the CEO's office, so I did something controversial: I hired an old friend from New York to be senior vice president for real estate. Arthur Rubinfeld, whom I had gotten to know during my single days in Greenwich Village, was a practicing architect and developer who had moved to San Francisco around the same time I moved to Seattle. Arthur started a firm that specialized in retail real estate brokerage in northern California, and we turned to him to represent us in our entry strategy into the San Francisco market. I realized I needed not only his expertise and professional judgment but also someone I could trust. Choosing the right sites is such a critical part of success for a retailer that it should be done by someone with a passionate commitment to the future of the company.

But Arthur didn't want to do just site selection. He convinced me that we needed real estate, design, and construction to speak with one voice, under the direction of one person, to avoid the conflicts that sometimes arise between those disciplines. He coordinated the departments and built a complete store-development organization that ultimately enabled Starbucks to plan for and open one store every business day. Of the first 1,000 stores we opened, we opted to close only two locations because of site misjudgments. Few other retailers could boast such a record.

Although we leased rather than owned our sites, we bore the entire cost of design and construction. Why? Because every store was company-owned. We refused to franchise. Although it would have been tempting to share costs with franchisees, I didn't want to risk losing control of the all-important link to the customer.

Behind the scenes, we also kept investing in new systems and processes for a far larger operation than we had at the time. In late 1991, when we had just over 100 stores, we hired Carol Eastin, a computer expert from McDonald's, gave her a blank slate, and asked her to design a point-of-sale system that would link all our outlets and would be able to accommodate the 300 stores we planned to have within three years.

When companies fail, or fail to grow, it's almost always because they don't invest in the people, the systems, and the processes they need. Most people underestimate how much money it will take to do that. They also tend to underestimate how they are going to feel about reporting large losses. Unfortunately, that's a given in the early stages of retail development, unless you raise money by franchising. Huge investments upfront mean not only potential annual losses but also a dilution of the founder's shareholding.

If you want to know what Starbucks did right, you have to look at our competition and find out what they did wrong. Clearly, Starbucks isn't perfect. But among our competitors in the specialty coffee business, you'll see examples of all the mistakes we didn't make: companies that didn't raise enough money to finance growth; companies that franchised too early and too widely; companies that lost control of quality; companies that didn't invest in systems and processes; companies that hired inexperienced people, or the wrong people; companies that were so eager to grow that they picked the wrong real estate locations; companies that didn't have the discipline to walk away from a site if they couldn't make the economics work. All of them lost money, too; some are still doing so. But they didn't use their years of losses to build a strong foundation for growth.

You can't create a world-class enterprise without investing in it. In a growth company, you can't play catch-up. But you also can't just excuse losses in the early stage of the business without examining each expenditure. Growth covers up a lot of mistakes, and you have to be honest about what's right and what's wrong about your operations.

Fortunately, we realized this in the early years. And our investors had strong stomachs.

IF NO MENTOR FINDS YOU, SEEK ONE OUT

Sometimes, in life as in business, you know exactly what you need to accomplish your goals and you have to go out to look for it.

During those tense years when we were losing money, I realized I was badly in need of a mentor. I had a faithful board of wealthy investors who believed in me and trusted me (for the most part!) to make the right decisions. They questioned me diligently, but because most of them had no experience building a retail company into a national brand, they could offer only limited guidance for future planning.

I had also never anticipated how isolating running a company would be. You can never let your guard down and admit what you don't know. Few people can share your frustrations and anxieties when you're losing money, when you have to deal with investors who have high expectations, when you suddenly find yourself responsible for hundreds of employees, when you face difficult hiring decisions. Trying to balance the intricacies of rallying people and forging complex strategies can feel like running a political campaign—with the same sense of accountability to many different constituencies.

Although they can hire executives with many talents and skills, many CEOs discover that what they lack most is a reliable sounding board. They don't want to show vulnerability to those who report to them. If they feel uncertain or fearful, or if they just want to think out loud, they need to have friends they can call up and complain: "Oh, shit! You wouldn't believe what happened today!"

In the Il Giornale years, the only person with whom I could talk openly was Sheri. I'd come home so tired, so beaten down, so out of sorts that I'm sure I wasn't easy to live with. But she listened, and she gave me much-needed support. She anticipated what I was going to need and made sure she off-loaded the pressure I would have on other things so I could concentrate on my work. So much of that period is a testimonial to Sheri's forbearance and wisdom, but still I felt acutely the lack of a professional confidant.

Not long after taking over Starbucks, I strengthened a friendship with one of my investors, Steve Ritt, a relaxed and genial guy who runs a leather-cleaning company in Seattle. For almost two years, until my daughter was born, we ran together, three mornings a week, starting at 5:30 A.M. During these runs, I was able to get Steve's reading on any number of problems I was facing. It was great therapy for me. Steve proved a valued adviser because he had no vested interest other than to be supportive of me. I could share my doubts with him as comfortably as I could my triumphs. He had great confidence in me and became a close friend. But even he didn't have experience in building a retail company.

I knew that what I needed was advice from a person who had been there before, someone who understood what I was trying to accomplish. I wanted someone who had built a fast-growing company, who lived and breathed the retail business, who could guide me and direct me whenever I reached an unfamiliar fork in the road.

I did a mental audit of the Seattle business community, thinking about the many individuals who had built successful retail companies. One in particular had both the experience I lacked and a willingness to help: Jeff Brotman.

Jeff is a seasoned veteran of retailing, eleven years older than I. As the son of a retailer, he understands the operations instinctively. He ran a family-owned chain of twenty clothing stores and founded several other companies. In 1983, he made his biggest, boldest move when he founded Costco Wholesale, a company of membership-only wholesale club stores. In ten years, he and Jim Sinegal built Costco into a national operator of more than a hundred outlets with annual sales of $6.5 billion. In 1993, they merged with Price Club, and now Jeff is chairman of the combined company, which has $19 billion in revenues and more than 250 warehouse stores. Starbucks is a dwarf by comparison.

I first met Jeff Brotman when I was trying to raise money for Il Giornale. Later, after I bought Starbucks, I called on him several times, asking his advice. He offered his time and counsel unselfishly, well before he had any connection to Starbucks. He had a sixth sense for good opportunities and an understanding for the range of issues entrepreneurs face. I confided in him, and I realized I could trust him. Listening to his counsel, I appreciated how talented he was. He became, de facto, my mentor.

After several meetings, I asked him to join Starbucks' board of directors. It took a while to court him. Jeff is careful about his investments, of both time and money, but once he makes a commitment, he takes it seriously.

Jeff eventually joined the board in 1989, a rough time in Starbucks' history. We were losing money for the third year in a row, and it was by no means clear we would make it in Chicago. Although I had assured the board that we would turn profitable in fiscal 1990, it took Jeff Brotman to give my arguments credibility in the face of escalating losses. His was the voice of authority and experience, and much easier to believe than my promises based on sheer faith.

Jeff also understood what a fast-growing retail company just emerging on the national scene would need to do to raise capital. By late 1989, it was clear that Starbucks had to reach outside Seattle for institutional investors, which meant approaching the venture capital community. As the chairman of a company that had recently gone public, Jeff had the connections and the credibility to make contacts for us.

At first, I was wary of taking this step, for I had heard that some venture capitalists intrude on entrepreneurial ventures and ultimately ruin them with short-term thinking. At best, venture capital can energize a company with both dollars and expertise and help it grow and mature. But the wrong partners can pursue their short-term self-interest at the expense of the long-term future of the company.

Once we decided to go ahead, though, we had more difficulty than we expected. In the early 1980s, retail start-ups had become highly popular with institutional investors. Then, the market collapsed, and several venture-backed retailers collapsed. The funds that had invested in them performed so poorly that some were unable to continue to raise money. Many venture funds refused to invest in retail after that, sticking to companies in technology and health care. Many turned us down.

Craig Foley, who then headed Citibank's Chancellor Capital Management Inc., was one investor who decided to take a chance on us. Unlike other fund managers, who quickly dismissed us as a coffee-shop chain, Craig was a coffee lover who missed the quality of coffee he had tasted in Europe. He did have a long-term commitment to retail investments and had heard of Starbucks through a colleague. But after visiting a poor-performing store in Chicago, he had decided not to invest. He had, though, supported Costco, so when Jeff Brotman asked him to take another look at Starbucks, he did.

Craig's biggest concern was that our idea was not "portable," that it wouldn't appeal to customers outside the cool, rainy Northwest. I rose to the challenge and went to great lengths to convince him he was wrong. He closely examined all our Chicago stores and decided that not only was gourmet coffee potentially a big growth opportunity but it could also be a "lifestyle phenomenon." To compensate for the weakness he saw in Chicago, he negotiated a somewhat lower valuation in the company, $3.75 a share, only slightly above the $3 share price of the previous round, in 1988. Still, because of Chancellor's high profile, his decision to invest $4.5 million, a rather risky leap of faith in Starbucks, attracted several other institutional investors. In all, we were able to raise $13.5 million in March 1990, by far our biggest financing at that time.

Our Chicago stores proved critical, too, in attracting another investor in that round, Jamie Shennan, a general partner of Trinity Ventures. He first saw Starbucks by happenstance, while walking down a street, and he later heard from a colleague that we were looking for venture capital. An experienced marketer, he was attracted by the power of the Starbucks brand and the buzz he heard from our customers. So was Ken Purcell, of T. Rowe Price.

My initial fears about venture capitalists proved unfounded; what I found, in fact, was the opposite. Instead of interference, I gained another set of trusted advisers with long-term horizons. We were fortunate that our venture capital partners genuinely understood and appreciated the culture of Starbucks.

Craig Foley and Jamie Shennan joined the Starbucks board when their funds invested, in March 1990. They pushed me to conduct market research and to begin strategic planning, and also gave invaluable guidance on how to make the transition from an entrepreneurial, private company to a professionally managed public one. Jamie, who spent many years as a brand manager at Procter & Gamble and later as a consumer marketing consultant, provided astute insights into the building of the brand, establishing joint ventures, improving the catalogue, and introducing new products.

Craig contributed financial know-how, guided us in our strategic planning, and helped evaluate new business opportunities. It speaks volumes about their contributions and their commitment to Starbucks that Jamie and Craig both remained on the board long after their funds sold their Starbucks stock, as planned. (Venture capital funds, by nature, usually distribute profits to their investors after a company goes public.)

Craig and Jamie's joining the board meant that several of my earliest, staunchest supporters had to step down. Of the original Il Giornale board and investor group, only Arnie Prentice remains a director. Just as every business has a memory, every board should have one, too, and it's been critical for me to have the presence of someone who understands me and where Starbucks came from, to have someone from the past who is linked to the future.

My relationship with the board took an unusual turn when I came to view them more as trusted advisers rather than as supervisors. Unlike many CEOs, I was direct with them, confiding in them my problems in running the business. They always challenged me to defend my ideas, and we had open and frank discussions at board meetings. They continually pushed me to sharpen my focus and set clear priorities, fearing that my entrepreneurial zeal would send the company in too many directions. The board also strongly encouraged me to strengthen my management team ahead of the curve, hiring people with bigger company experience. Debates were at times intense and sometimes difficult but also healthy and constructive. We never needed to take a vote. When one person disagreed strongly, we took the time to work it out and come up with an acceptable solution.

With time, the board's culture and values evolved into a mirror image of those of Starbucks. The outside directors gradually developed more trust in me than they had in the early period, when they thought perhaps I was just another raw young entrepreneur who would have to be replaced, at some point, by a professional manager and CEO. They, too, have poured their hearts into the company.

Starbucks' board remained stable for six years, adding only two inside directors. Then, in 1996, as we faced the reality of becoming a $1 billion company, we once again looked for someone who had the expertise that comes with experience. That person was Barbara Bass, who had risen at Macy's and Bloomingdale's before becoming CEO of I. Magnin and later of Carter Hawley Hales' Emporium Weinstock, which had annual sales of nearly $1 billion. Barbara brought not only a rich store of knowledge and insights about national retailing but also a fresh perspective to what had too long been an all-male board.

To any entrepreneur, I would offer this advice: Once you've figured out what you want to do, find someone who has done it before. Find not just talented executives but even more experienced entrepreneurs and businesspeople who can guide you. They know where to look for the mines in the minefield. If they have thought and acted boldly in their own careers, and proven successful, they can help you do the same. If they share your values and aspirations, and if they freely share their counsel, they can help you through rough patches and celebrate your victories as their own.

That's the kind of mentor I never had as a kid or as a young adult. If one doesn't find you, beat the bushes till you find one who will take you on. And with the right mentor, don't be afraid to expose your vulnerabilities. Admit you don't know what you don't know. When you acknowledge your weaknesses and ask for advice, you'll be surprised how much others will help.

11

Don't Be Threatened by People Smarter Than You

*The best executive is the one who
has sense enough to pick good men [and
women] to do what he wants done, and self-
restraint enough to keep from meddling
with them while they do it.*

—*Theodore Roosevelt*

There's a common mistake a lot of entrepreneurs make. They own the idea, and they have the passion to pursue it. But they can't possibly possess all the skills needed to make the idea actually happen. Reluctant to delegate, they surround themselves with faithful aides. They're afraid to bring in truly smart, successful individuals as high-level managers.

But an intelligent executive team is vital for a company to prosper. Strong, creative people are a lot more stimulating to be around than yes-men. What can you learn from those who know less than you? They may massage your ego for a while and take orders easily, but they won't help you grow.

From the beginning, I knew I had to go out and hire executives with greater experience than I had, people who would not be afraid to debate with me, who were strong-willed, self-reliant, and confident, and make them part of the management team and the decision-making process.

When I began Il Giornale, a start-up with no stores at first, I was fortunate to work with Dave Olsen, who not only had a passion for coffee but also had run a successful café for years. In November 1987, I brought in Lawrence Maltz, a seasoned executive who had managed a beverage company.

For a small enterprise, that team was appropriate. But as Starbucks expanded into more markets, we needed someone familiar with the process of opening and running many retail stores at once. In 1989, we hired Howard Behar for that job, a man who had twenty-five years of retail background in the furniture business and at Thousand Trails, an outdoor resort developer. I found out about Howard through Jeff Brotman and Jack Rodgers.

In 1990, as we prepared for more sophisticated financing, we began scouting for a chief financial officer with broad experience. We hired a sophisticated headhunter to do the search for us but were frustrated because he kept talking only about professional qualifications and didn't get our point about character and culture. We found Orin Smith instead through a personal recommendation of one of our partners who had worked for him before. With an MBA from Harvard, Orin had managed far larger and more complex organizations than Starbucks was then. He had worked as budget director for the State of Washington for five years and before that for Deloitte and Touche for thirteen years, including three years as partner-in-charge of their consulting practice in Seattle.

Howard and Orin were both older than I was, by about ten years. Both took pay cuts to come to Starbucks but joined because they understood the passion and the potential and they believed their stock options would one day be valuable. To a lot of entrepreneurs, hiring more seasoned executives can be threatening, and actually delegating power to them is even more so. In my own case, I have to admit, it wasn't easy. My identity had quickly become so closely tied up with that of Starbucks that any suggestion for change made me feel as if I had failed in some aspect of my job. Inside my head, it was a constant battle, and I had to keep reminding myself: *These people bring something I don't have. They will make Starbucks far better than I could alone.*

Both Howard and Orin brought not only skills and experience but also attitudes and values that were different from mine. What I found, as we worked together year after year, was that Starbucks was enriched and broadened by their leadership. If I had let my ego or my fears prevent them from doing their jobs, we could never have matured into a sustainable company with strong, people-oriented values.

Then as now, I was conscious of having to show the people around me that my self-esteem and confidence were strong enough to absorb the arrival of new talent, managers who were more qualified than I to handle certain segments of the business. At the same time, I also had to make sure that I clearly handed them the authority to do what they needed to do, for their departments would be reporting to them, not to me. I tried to make the message I sent to them—and by extension, to the entire company—as unequivocal as possible: "I hired you because you're smarter than I am. Now go and prove it."

I can't pretend I never made any hiring mistakes. A few management choices I later regretted, and, valuing loyalty as I do, I also let some managers stay on longer than I should have. Some people could not keep up with the company's fast pace of growth; though they gave a lot in the early days, they did not stay to face the challenges of the steep learning curve that came with growth. Overall, Starbucks has had remarkably little turnover at the top, especially considering the stresses we were subjected to as a result of such rapid expansion.

By 1990, I had assembled a management team that worked together so tightly and synergistically that people called us "H2O," for Howard, Howard, and Orin. We stood for the vision, the soul, and the fiscal responsibility. In many respects, Howard and Orin are polar opposites, but each of us has provided an essential ingredient to Starbucks' success.

DON'T BE THREATENED BY CANDOR

In August 1989 Howard Behar hit Starbucks like a tornado.

A compact man with round glasses and a neatly cut salt-and-pepper beard, Howard Behar arrived at Starbucks at a point when we sorely needed him. We then had about 28 stores and were planning to nearly double that number annually. With his retail expertise, he was able to put in place the systems and processes we needed to run our current operation at the same time as we were opening new stores.

But he had an even deeper impact on the corporate culture. In meetings, he would often raise his voice. One minute his eyes would sparkle with excitement; the next, he'd be pounding the table in anger. Sometimes tears would well in his eyes. He thinks deeply, not only about business but about poetry, philosophy, and meditation. Self-effacing and humorous, he cares passionately and worries incessantly. He wears his vulnerabilities on his sleeve and embarrasses people with his candor. You never have to wonder what is on his mind.

By his very nature, he was many things that Starbucks was not. Like many Seattlites, Starbucks people tended to be reserved and polite, equating respect with a disinclination to openly disagree. The downside of this characteristic was that we would sometimes beat around the bush to avoid offending one another. We couldn't talk straight to underperforming employees.

Howard Behar made us question that attitude. From his first day, he began openly disagreeing with me, and with anyone else, in meetings, on the roasting plant floor, in the hallways, wherever he happened to be.

"Why do you have to go to page three of the Starbucks hand-book before you find the word 'people'?" he asked. "Shouldn't 'people' be first, with respect to both customers and employees?"

"Why don't we give customers whatever they ask for?"

"Why are store managers timid about speaking up?"

Whatever the subject, if Howard had an opinion, he'd voice it.

His confrontational approach was tough on me, at first. We had started with such a small, close-knit team and worked hard to build trust and confidence. While I like passion and enthusiasm and initiative, by nature I tend to avoid confrontation.

Gradually, I came to learn that when Howard disagreed with me, it wasn't out of lack of respect. He simply disagreed with the point of view I was expressing on a particular subject. His anger, his beliefs, his emotions are all honest and all immediate, but once they were aired, he was open to listening to others' viewpoints.

One of the first, and most valuable, critiques Howard made was his opinion that Starbucks was too product-oriented. It's *people* who make the coffee, he kept insisting. People directly affect the quality of products and services our customers receive. People will determine the ultimate success of Starbucks. Products are inert. You have to hire great people, he urged us, celebrate their passions and their skills, and give them the freedom to do their jobs right. "We're not filling bellies," he likes to say. "We're filling souls."

That advice resonated with me. It reflected my own values, but I had never articulated them so clearly.

Howard taught us how to be more strongly customer oriented. In the course of building the business, we had been so focused on the quality of the coffee that we had sometimes overlooked customer preferences. To address this problem, he initiated a "snapshot" program, which involved unannounced visits to each store to monitor customer service. He trained our employees to go out of their way and to take heroic measures, if necessary, to meet customer demand. In an era when Nancy Reagan popularized "Just say no" to drugs, he encouraged our people to "Just say yes" to customer requests. He urged us to make ourselves more accessible to a wide range of consumers. Even if someone brought in coffee beans from another store, we should be willing to grind them for him. We began to give a "Starbuck," or free-drink certificate, to each customer who was dissatisfied. We gave stickers to kids. "As long as it is moral, legal, and ethical," Howard likes to say, "we should do whatever it takes to please the customer."

Howard's priorities went against the grain of longstanding Starbucks traditions, for it had always been our goal to educate customers to appreciate coffee the way we liked it. The two sets of values clashed often and loudly—sometimes even within my own head. But what we learned, ultimately, is that it's equally important to value our coffee, our partners, and our customers. Neglect any one, and we would have a weak link.

Howard also taught Starbucks people to speak their minds. He believed as a matter of principle that anyone should be able to say anything at anytime without worrying about how others would react. One day he met with all our store managers and told them his number-one expectation was that they should be straight with him. "If someone has something to say, say it," he declared. "What's on your mind? What's going right? What's not going right?" He looked around the room expectantly, but nobody uttered a word.

As the group began to disperse, though, one of the store managers came hesitantly up to him. "If I'd have known that you really meant that," she told him, "I would have had a lot to say." Howard asked her to write a list of everything she didn't like about Starbucks, including all her suggestions for change. A few days later, they arrived, and he immediately began responding to them, one by one.

To encourage people to speak their minds, Howard came up with the idea of holding Open Forums each quarter. At these gatherings, senior managers meet with all interested employees to update them on the company's performance, answer questions, and allow them to air grievances. They are now held quarterly in every region where we do business. Sometimes the comments are painful, but once we are aware of widespread concerns, we can fix them. Whenever we begin to move away from our center line, our partners are the first to warn us. And the majority of them feel proud of the company they work for.

At times Howard would create conflict in an Open Forum, just to force us to think outside the box. He once recommended that, as a way of exceeding expectations, every store should open ten minutes earlier than the posted time and stay open ten minutes later. The store managers, predictably, went nuts, flooding him with complaints.

For Howard, the point was not whether his proposal was good or bad, but that our partners felt comfortable enough in an Open Forum to challenge him. If people in a company are upset about some issue but are not talking about it openly, the most productive approach for management is to bring up the subject directly. Getting them to talk openly, however awkward and uncomfortable, will ultimately help dissipate the anger and solve the problem.

"Walls talk" is a favorite Howard Behar expression, and anyone who steps into his office immediately sees why. His walls talk more than most, for they are covered with more than twenty sayings, poems, and quotations that express his philosophy of life:

> *Thou shalt not stand idly by.*

> *When you're in a hole, quit digging!*

> *Think like a person of action; act like a person of thought.*

> *The best minute I spend is the one I invest in people.*

Another tradition Howard established was to send hand-signed birthday cards and starting-date anniversary cards to every Starbucks partner. At first, he himself signed all of them, but now that the company has grown so large, the duties are shared.

Some have dismissed those little touches as hokey and not sincere, but Howard is undaunted. "Gestures like that add up and make Starbucks feel human," he says. Even when there are 25,000 employees, managers have to recognize that each is an individual. Howard also started several recognition programs, encouraging partners to nominate their colleagues as *trendsetters* or *store managers of the quarter.*

After several years of spearheading our retail operations and expansion, Howard did something many executives talk about but few do: He hired and trained his successor. He found Deidra Wager at Taco Bell in southern California and eventually trained her to take over his job. Deidra proved to be a skilled manager who knew what information and systems we needed and could systematize our retail operations.

If Dave Olsen personifies our impossibly passionate attitude toward coffee, Howard Behar embodies our impossibly passionate attitude toward our partners. If I had let myself feel threatened by him, if I had reined him in or pushed him out, Starbucks would never have developed the strong values it has today.

Candor can hurt. It can feel intimidating. But, as I learned from Howard Behar, it's the kind of environment Starbucks needs if we're going to continue relying on the enthusiasm and commitment of our people.

DON'T BE THREATENED BY PROCESS

"It's hard to execute entrepreneurially." Orin Smith has to keep reminding me of that.

Without romance and vision, a business has no soul, no spirit to motivate its people to achieve something great. But a successful company can't sustain itself on exhilarating ideas alone. Many business visionaries have failed as leaders because they could not execute. Processes and systems, discipline and efficiency are needed to create a foundation before creative ideas can be implemented and entrepreneurial vision can be realized.

That's been a hard lesson for an entrepreneur of my temperament to swallow. I'm always afraid that, as we grow larger, Starbucks will become too bureaucratic, too process-oriented, too narrowly focused on specific functions at the expense of the passion and the need to achieve big dreams. It's an ongoing tension within the company.

To be successful, every business needs to achieve a balance between the two forces. And that requires leaders who both understand the vision and know how to put in place the infrastructure needed to realize it.

Building processes is not a skill I have. It's beyond my interests and abilities. What I did to compensate, what every visionary entrepreneur needs to do, is find an executive who can build the infrastructure the company needs without sacrificing the need for innovation. But it has to be someone who also understands the value of unconventional thinking. At Starbucks, that executive is Orin Smith.

Orin's approach couldn't be more different than mine. Orin is quiet and reserved and almost always in his shell, like a tortoise, and he works steadily and faithfully at problems until they get solved. He always carries a pen and notebook in his pocket, and when he wears his big-framed glasses, he looks as wise as he is. When a dilemma arises, I tend to make a snap judgment and want to take action immediately, while Orin listens calmly, gathers all the information he needs, and ponders carefully until he comes up with a logical, reasoned response.

When Orin came to us in 1990, Starbucks was not a professionally managed business. We were totally entrepreneurial, with an approach Eric Flamholtz, one of our consultants, characterizes as "Ready, Fire, Aim." To his credit, Orin didn't make a big show of turning Starbucks into a professionally managed company. If he had, it probably would have spooked me and many others inside the company. Instead, he led by example. Thanks to his equanimity and his leadership skills, the organization began to gravitate naturally toward a more balanced approach—just as we got big enough to need it.

Very subtly, he created an environment in which there was for the first time a strong appreciation of the disciplines necessary to run a large and profitable business. He built an organization by recruiting seasoned professionals in the key areas that had to be strengthened in the company: management information systems, finance, accounting, planning, legal affairs, and supply-chain operations.

However warily, I began to recognize that in building discipline into a company, it's possible to not only honor the creative process but also make it stronger and more dynamic. By strengthening the foundation and structure of the company, we can stop wasting time reacting to small problems and instead devote our attention and resources to new products and new ideas. With a clearer strategic direction, we can focus our creativity on issues that matter for Starbucks in the long term.

When Starbucks went public, Orin and I went together to do the "road show," a presentation in which we explained the Starbucks story to potential investors. What Wall Street saw in us was an energetic, passionate young guy, thirty-eight years old, inspired and visionary, but perhaps a little too inexperienced, a little too idealistic. But sitting next to him was a fifty-year-old, gray-haired, stable, conservative, prudent executive, explaining all the projections and numbers in calm, measured tones. We were a well-matched team: entrepreneurial zest and managerial control, which together inspired confidence that Starbucks could achieve its high goals but also remain fiscally responsible.

Many young companies can't make the leap to maturity because they either don't support the creative spirit with structure and process, or they go too far and stifle that spirit with an overdeveloped bureaucracy. The most successful examples have been led by both a visionary, like Walt Disney, and a business-like implementer, like

Roy Disney. That kind of joint leadership works even better if the two partners have the strong bond of trust and confidence like the one Orin and I developed.

Orin took care of the back room, while I was able to focus on what the customer saw. I realize now, with hindsight, that the back room is really the arena where points are scored. In football, it's often said that "Offense scores points; defense wins games." In business, the front room is what the world sees: in our case, the coffee, the stores, the style, the brand. But the back room is where we win. The efficiency of the back room is really what's made Starbucks a financial success. That's been Orin's crucial contribution to the company. He's made me look much better than I am.

12

THE VALUE OF DOGMATISM AND FLEXIBILITY

*The only sacred cow in an organization
should be its basic philosophy of doing business.*

—THOMAS J. WATSON, JR., "A BUSINESS AND
ITS BELIEFS" AS QUOTED IN BUILT TO LAST,
BY JAMES C. COLLINS AND JERRY I. PORRAS

If you want a half pound of hazelnut-flavored coffee beans, you can't buy it at Starbucks. But if you would like hazelnut syrup to flavor your caffè latte, no problem.

That distinction may seem like splitting hairs to some people. Why be so purist about refusing to sell artificially flavored coffee beans when we'll add flavorings to espresso drinks?

Deciding when to make compromises to please its customers is one of the trickiest questions any business faces. At Starbucks, we have two articles of faith that on the surface may seem contradictory:

We believe that every business must stand for something. At its core must be an authentic product, one that's better than most customers realized they wanted.

We also believe we should "just say yes" to customer requests. Good retailers go out of their way to please their customers.

In our early years at Starbucks, we found ourselves always debating how far we ought to go toward reconciling these principles. On some issues, I refused to budge. One was franchising: We would not trust our quality to franchisees. Another was artificially flavored coffee beans: We would not pollute our high-quality beans with chemicals. Another was supermarket sales: We would not pour our beans into clear plastic bins, where they could get stale. And finally, we would never, never stop pursuing the perfect cup of coffee by buying the best beans and roasting them to perfection.

Those were key decisions, ones where our values and desire to create a clear brand image sometimes left us at a competitive disadvantage. By the late 1980s, the specialty coffee business had begun growing quickly, and the majority of it was in the form of whole-bean coffee sold in supermarkets. Brands like Millstone and Sarks took off, and their volume far surpassed that of Starbucks. We could have doubled or tripled volume easily by selling in supermarkets. But it was important to us that Starbucks maintain a clear distinction from grocery-store coffee. So we chose at the time not to sell our beans in supermarkets.

In that same period, about 40 percent of the increase in specialty coffee sales was the result of the new fashion for coffee beans with such flavors as vanilla, Irish cream, and mint mocha. We saw little point in buying the best beans in the world only to mask their flavor. Initially, we also refused to add flavored syrups to lattes, for the same reason.

A third choice faced us when several competitors began using franchising to expand nationwide, threatening to leave Starbucks as an also-ran. In 1991, one even surpassed us in number of stores, though not for long. Still, I insisted on company-owned stores, so we could keep our fate in our own hands.

Although I started out with a long list of these and other things Starbucks would "never" do, I gradually learned the need for compromise. What I won't do, though, is compromise our core values.

Each time a difficult decision came up, we debated long and hard, and we adopted new ways only when we were confident that we were not diluting the integrity of what we stand for.

WHEN IT'S OKAY TO GIVE THE CUSTOMERS WHAT THEY WANT

It was Howard Behar who forced us to shed some of our most dogmatic views. Until he arrived, most of us had an almost reverent attitude toward the coffee. But he came from a different tradition, from companies where, if you weren't customer-driven, you went out of business.

When Howard joined Starbucks in 1989, he was already familiar with Starbucks as a consumer, but he immediately began frequenting our stores and talking to baristas and customers. By listening carefully, he heard things to which we had closed our ears, and he forced us to examine our values in light of our customer preferences.

One message he heard loud and clear: Many customers wanted us to offer nonfat (or skim) milk.

Howard had been at Starbucks less than a month when he came to me one day and asked: "Have you been reading the customer comment cards?"

"Sure," I said, "I read them. I read them all."

"Well," he replied, "how come you're not responding?"

"Responding to what?"

"Look at all the people who want nonfat milk."

"Well," I explained, "I did a formal tasting a number of times this year of lattes and cappuccinos made with nonfat milk and they just didn't taste good."

"To whom?" Howard was clearly growing impatient with my answers.

"To me, to Dave."

"Well, read the customer comment cards. Our customers want nonfat milk! We should give it to them."

I answered—and Howard never lets me forget it—"We will *never* offer nonfat milk. It's not who we are."

At that point in Starbucks' history, even *mentioning* nonfat milk was tantamount to treason. Our goal, then as always, was to bring the authentic Italian espresso bar experience to the United States. But in fact, lattes and cappuccinos—espresso with steamed milk and foam—had quickly become our most popular drinks. Some coffee purists scoffed at them, saying that in offering warm milky drinks we were catering to people who weren't hard-core coffee lovers. But these beverages enabled us to introduce great coffee to people who normally didn't even drink coffee.

By 1989 several of our smaller competitors, especially in Seattle, were offering lattes with nonfat or 2 percent milk. For reasons of health and weight, more and more Americans were avoiding whole milk. But we still thought skim milk tasted thin and sharp, and altered the taste of Starbucks coffee.

Still, Howard had found a crusade, and he started figuring out ways we could give our customers what they wanted—however unpopular the idea was with coffee purists. One day one of our most dogmatic coffee defenders confronted Howard in the narrow hallway outside his office. Standing nose-to-nose, he told him, "That's not in keeping with the quality of our coffee. That is bastardizing it. It's getting to the point that we'll do anything the customers want us to."

"Are you nuts?" Howard Behar remembers responding. "Of *course* we'll do what they want us to!"

Believe it or not, the issue of nonfat milk led to one of the biggest debates in Starbucks' history. I fought it. Dave Olsen fought it. The store managers were scandalized. What kind of person is this Howard Behar, they wanted to know, and does he really want us to introduce nonfat milk?

Some store managers went to Howard and argued: "We will

never be able do it operationally. It's impossible to handle more than one kind of milk. If we offer two kinds of milk, it will ruin the business."

But Howard was adamant, and he insisted that we at least test the idea.

The controversy forced me to do some soul-searching. It might seem inconsequential, but it struck at the very heart of our fundamental commitment to quality. If we stuck to our conviction that "everything matters," how could we serve espresso drinks that didn't taste right to us?

One morning I woke up early, still wrestling with the idea after a restless night. I got dressed and drove to one of our Starbucks stores in a residential neighborhood of Seattle. I paid for a double espresso and took a seat at a table. Even though it was early, there was already a long line. I was reading the newspaper but also keeping my ears alert to hear what people ordered. The atmosphere felt good, with a smooth, steady coordination between the two baristas, one taking orders, the other making drinks. I noticed one customer, a young woman in her late twenties, dressed in sweats and sneakers and slowly nodding her head to the music on her Walkman. It looked as if she had just finished her morning run. When she got to the counter, I could hear her say the words I'd been waiting for:

"I'll have a double tall latte, with nonfat milk."

"Sorry, we don't have nonfat," the barista replied politely but firmly. "We only have whole milk."

I could hear her sigh in frustration and then ask, "Why not? I always get it at the place down the street."

The barista apologized, but she strode out of the store, apparently headed for a competitor.

A lost customer is the most powerful argument you can make to a retailer.

I went in to the office that morning and told Howard Behar to go ahead with his test, and to make sure to include that store.

We had only about thirty stores then, and Howard convinced half a dozen store managers to volunteer to try nonfat milk. Despite all the concern beforehand, they managed to work out the operational issues pretty quickly. They even figured a way to offer 2 percent milk by blending whole and nonfat. Seeing how pleased their customers were with the option, those first store managers became advocates and eventually won over the others. Within six months, all our stores offered it. Today, almost half of the lattes and cappuccinos we sell are made with nonfat milk.

In hindsight, that decision looks like a no-brainer. But at the time, we weren't sure what impact it would have on our brand and our identity. When a caffè latte is made with nonfat milk, is it still an authentic Italian drink? Most Italians wouldn't recognize it. But an Italian can still come to a Starbucks store and order a cappuccino that *is* truly authentic, just as another customer can request a nonfat vanilla mocha.

How did we deal with our consciences? We had to recognize that the customer was right. It was our responsibility to give people a choice.

Howard Behar had made the right call. The way we resolved the nonfat milk controversy also is a great example of the autonomy of decision-making we encourage within Starbucks. Although he had been with the company only a few months, his retail acumen and experience gave him the credibility and authority to persuade us to do the right thing.

In subsequent years, we have moved farther and farther from our initial dogmatic stance. In addition to nonfat milk, customers can have vanilla or raspberry syrup mixed into their espresso drink if they request it. We have used our coffee to flavor ice cream and beer and icy blended drinks. But we deliberated long hours before taking each of these steps. And when we did move forward, we did so very tactically, clear about what we hoped to accomplish.

Does that mean we've sold out? Does "never" ever really mean "never"?

Here's how I see it:

Our customers have the right to enjoy their cup of coffee how-ever they prefer it. Milk and sugar are always available at our condi-ments counters, and baristas will mix in certain flavored syrups if customers ask for it.

What we won't do, however, is mess with the real stuff in a way that violates its integrity. The real stuff is the coffee, roasted dark, fresh and full-flavored. It is our touchstone, part of our lifeblood, our legacy. Our customers have to be able to count on Starbucks to provide it. Whatever else we do, we won't buy cheaper coffees. We won't stop roasting dark. We won't pollute our coffee beans with artificial flavors and chemicals.

We want Starbucks people to go out of their way to please cus-tomers, but we won't allow them to pass flavored beans through our grinders. Some portion of the chemicals used to treat them would remain behind and alter the flavor of beans ground in that machine afterward. Artificially flavored beans also have a chemical smell that would pollute the air of our store and be absorbed by other coffee beans.

Dave Olsen and his coffee-department colleagues represent the purists at Starbucks, our collective conscience. Dave has a great analogy:

> Think of coffee as a music CD. You can listen to it in a special listening room that you designed especially for the purpose in the basement of your home, where there are no distractions, where you can put the headphones on and really listen for the string section or the oboes or try to hear every little click of every fingernail on Eric Clapton's guitar. Or you could put it in the stereo of a car, roll all the windows down, and scream and shout. The music is the same; the application is different.

As long as we remain respectful of our core product, as long as our customers can come into any Starbucks and buy the greatest coffee in the world, as long as we bring the same pursuit of quality to our new products, then we can feel comfortable offering customers different ways of enjoying our coffee. Options like these help introduce a far wider range of people to Starbucks coffee. And that, after all, is our abiding mission.

WHEN IT'S OKAY TO BE FANATICAL ABOUT CONTROL

Imagine if a company like Nike not only designed and marketed shoes but also owned all its factories and all the retail stores that sold its shoes.

Or try to picture a national book publishing company that employed its own authors, manufactured its own paper, operated its own printing presses, and sold only through its own bookstores.

What if you had to go into a Pepsi shop every time you wanted a can of Pepsi? Or a Kellogg's shop whenever you wanted Corn Flakes?

Starbucks has an unusual approach to business, one that is perhaps unique among brand-name consumer-products companies. We're so fanatical about quality control that we keep the coffee in our hands every step of the way from the raw green beans to the steaming cup. We buy and roast all our own coffee, and we sell it in company-owned stores. That's vertical integration to the extreme.

Why? The answer can be found in the last cup of lousy coffee you drank. Unlike shoes, or books, or soft drinks, coffee can be ruined at any point from its production to its consumption. To begin with, the beans themselves could be poor. They can be roasted wrong. If the beans aren't fresh, if they're ground wrong, if they're brewed with too much or too little water, if the water tastes bad to begin with, the coffee can taste wrong. The worst, most common sin in coffee preparation is leaving the pot on the burner for too long, which results in a foul, burned taste.

Coffee is a product so perishable that building a business on it is fraught with peril. The minute we hand our coffee over to someone else, we're extremely vulnerable to its quality being compromised.

Many people assume Starbucks is a franchise operation because we are growing so quickly and are present in so many markets. We receive hundreds of calls a month from people who want to open a Starbucks franchise. What about Alaska? they've asked. What about Sun Valley, or Jackson Hole, or any number of smaller markets the company won't get to for years? We turn them all down. Our approach is to rely instead on company-owned stores.

In the early days, Jack Rodgers, our senior vice president for new business development, was a particularly strong advocate of franchising. Jack was one of the early McDonald's franchisees, starting in St. Charles, Illinois, in 1959, and knew Ray Kroc as a close family friend. Over time, he became a multi-franchisee, owning several McDonald's, Red Robin, Benihana, and Casa Lupita restaurants, as well as the Athlete's Foot stores.

Franchising is the logical route to national expansion, Jack argued. It's a quick, reliable way to raise capital. It allows you to preempt the competition and enter new markets in a hurry, to get ahead of the pack. And franchise owners are committed to the financial success of their store.

But I refused to franchise. In the 1980s, we didn't need an extra source of capital, for investors were willing to fund all of Starbucks' growth. In the early days, too, we had little competition, and the competitors who did grow by franchising never developed a strong brand. And by offering stock options, we were able to generate in-house even more of enthusiasm and sense of ownership that franchise owners bring to their businesses.

In fact, "franchising" is almost a forbidden word at Starbucks. To me, franchisees are middlemen who would stand between us and our customers. We prefer to train all our own people and operate all our own stores, so that each cup of coffee you buy from Starbucks is the real thing.

If we had franchised, Starbucks would have lost the common culture that made us strong. We teach baristas not only how to handle the coffee properly but also how to impart to customers our passion for our products. They understand the vision and value system of the company, which is seldom the case when someone else's employees are serving Starbucks coffee.

At first, we were immovable in our position: Our customers could buy Starbucks coffee only in a Starbucks store. I was just as opposed to wholesaling as I was to franchising, and I wouldn't let our coffee be sold at any other type of store.

But gradually, we began to give up that control. The opportunities to attract new customers were too appealing to pass up, and the window would not be open indefinitely. Each new venture, though, is part of an ongoing struggle. We keep asking ourselves: At what point do we give up so much that we lose our soul?

The first big concession was airports. We knew they would be a great location for us. At airports like O'Hare in Chicago, travelers from all over the world can encounter Starbucks coffee for the first time. These sites give us a chance to raise awareness among new customers.

But because airport stores everywhere are run by concession-aires, in 1991, we decided to make an exception: We signed a licensing agreement with Host Marriott for airport locations. We started in Seattle and gradually expanded to airports across the United States.

As it happened, we went through some rocky times in that relationship. Starbucks had no experience managing a licensing arrangement, and Host Marriott had probably never dealt with a company as hands-on as Starbucks. We had to learn to maintain our standards by influence rather than direct control. We knew next to nothing about airports, which are tough environments in which to operate. Customers are often stressed out, in a hurry, and suspicious that they'll be faced with higher prices. They're not willing or able to spend time to be educated about different coffees or espresso drinks.

I travel a lot, and in the early period of our partnership with Host, I occasionally was dissatisfied with what I saw at airport stores. Lines were too long, the employees lacked knowledge of our coffee, and service was slow and sometimes unfriendly.

Host Marriott responded positively to our concerns, and Starbucks people worked with them to come up with solutions. We improved the training of Host Marriott employees, giving them the full twenty-four hours we provide for new hires at Starbucks. Host added cash registers to busy stores, beefed up staffing during hours of heaviest traffic, and increased its management support for the venture. As Host Marriott's employees became better versed about coffee and grew more comfortable in Starbucks stores, they were better able to provide friendly service. Today, both sides are satisfied that the partnership is successful.

As the relationship with Host Marriott improved, so did my opinion of licensing. It's like a marriage: Whether it works is a matter of whom you choose as a partner, the amount of due diligence you do beforehand, and how things go during the courtship. If you jump in with little preparation, you risk setting yourself up for failure.

Today, less than 10 percent of Starbucks stores are licensed—only 75 out of our first 1,000. But the number of airport locations is growing rapidly; in O'Hare alone we have 12 outlets. And we are considering other license arrangements in locations where we cannot operate company-owned stores. We've recently licensed Aramark to open Starbucks stores on a few college campuses.

Keeping true to our ideals while expanding the brand requires great discipline and a delicate sense of balance. We want everybody to experience our coffee, yet letting someone else serve it means giving up the reins. Over the years, we have done that very carefully, turning down hundreds of companies that wouldn't add value. We reject more business proposals than we accept and have walked away from deals that would have earned us millions of dollars.

If we weren't so obsessed with control, our business would be a lot easier. But the coffee wouldn't be as good.

As you're growing a business, you never know the long-term implications of decisions you make. In the early years after 1987, we seldom thought in terms of brand-building, yet everything we did to protect the quality of the coffee and the atmosphere of our stores was strengthening and expanding the reputation Starbucks had created in Seattle. The executives we hired, the plants we built, the decisions we made on how to raise money all laid a foundation that made possible a smooth and rapid national rollout of the vision I had had back in Milan. I was learning on the fly, creating the kind of work environment that appealed to me. What I only half realized is that I was also creating a different kind of company, one that works because its people care deeply about what they're doing.

Today, when I look back on the years before we went public, 1987 to 1992, I call them "the imprinting years." Like parents struggling to raise a child, Dave and I, Howard Behar, and Orin Smith brought our values to the workplace and tried to figure out how to apply them even as the company was moving and changing by the day. What I tried to do was honor the individuals around me, let them paint colors and make mistakes without telling them they were wrong. We struggled during that early part of the journey, as we do today, and we made mistakes. But we also forged a team and a mission and built the confidence that we could, indeed, reinvent the coffee experience in America and build a worldwide brand.

PART
THREE

Renewing the

Entrepreneurial Spirit

The Public Years,
1992-1997

13

WALL STREET MEASURES
A COMPANY'S PRICE,
NOT ITS VALUE

There are only two guidelines. One, what's
in the long-term best interests of the
enterprise and its stakeholders, supplemented
by the dominant concern of doing what's right.

—ROBERT D. HAAS, PRESIDENT,
LEVI STRAUSS & CO.,
AS QUOTED IN THE CORPORATE CONSCIENCE

More than most managers, I rely heavily on my instincts about people. Whether I'm hiring a key executive, selecting an investment banker, or assessing a partner in a joint venture, I look for the same kind of qualities most look for in choosing a spouse: integrity and passion. To me, that's just as important as experience and abilities. I want to work with people who don't leave their values at home but bring them to work, people whose principles match my own. If I see a mismatch, or a vacuum where values should be, I prefer to keep looking.

• • •

THE VALUE OF VALUES

When Starbucks finally decided to go public, we could have hired any investment bank in the country. Many of the biggest national investment banks, as well as a number of smaller, local ones, sought us out in our roasting plant/offices on Airport Way South in Seattle.

At the time, in 1991, we were still a relatively modest-sized, regional company. We ended fiscal 1991 with just over a hundred stores, all of them in the Northwest and Chicago, and $57 million in sales. But the major investment banks were looking for just the sort of promising, high-growth profile we had. They liked our financial projections and our plans for aggressive national expansion. When they examined our books, they were impressed with our *unit economics*—sales per store, average cost, return on investment.

It was flattering to be the object of so much attention, and I met with more than twenty suitors over the course of six months or so. But to my dismay, I found that most of the investment bankers I talked to viewed Starbucks as simply one of many options on a long list of potential IPOs—companies planning their first stock market listing, or Initial Public Offering. I began to get the feeling they were playing the odds: doing their due diligence to make sure there were no obvious errors of judgment and then backing a certain number of candidates, fully aware that some would fail and some would succeed.

Almost all of them seemed to tune out when I started discussing our company's Mission Statement. If they were taking notes, their pens stopped moving when I brought up values, as if I were indulging in rhetoric unrelated to Starbucks' financial performance. Experience has taught me that it's easy to talk about values, hard to implement them, and even harder for an outsider to determine which values are heartfelt and which are window-dressing. Wall Street cannot place a value on values.

I began to get discouraged. I knew Starbucks could carry off a successful IPO, but I wanted to work with investment bankers who got it, professionals who understood that Starbucks was more than another retail/restaurant play, more than a chain of cafés, more than just the latest transaction. These people were from a different world, where everything was weighted by its financial value; if you couldn't put a number on it, it didn't show up in the equation. They wanted to know what we could deliver to shareholders, not how we treated our employees.

One day in August of 1991, another investment banker showed up for an appointment. Dan Levitan was from Wertheim Schroder, a firm more experienced working with large, well-established companies than with small ones like ours. He had flown from Los Angeles to Seattle and joined up with a colleague from New York. They were probably about the tenth set of investment bankers to approach us. Neither had ever been in a Starbucks store, so they stopped by one that morning before coming to my office.

At that time, my office had a huge glass window, covering an entire wall, through which I could see the plant and the roasters. I pointed out to them our three big Probat roasting machines, with a combined capacity of 7 million pounds per year per shift. As we took our places at a small conference table I once again tried to explain. Starbucks is fast-growing and profitable, I told them. Overall, the U.S. gourmet coffee market had risen by 18 percent a year, from $270 million in 1984 to $750 million in 1991, and it was expected to reach $1 billion by 1994.

But, I told them, Starbucks was attempting to accomplish something more ambitious than just grow a profitable enterprise. We had a mission, to educate consumers everywhere about fine coffee. We had a vision, to create an atmosphere in our stores that drew people in and gave them a sense of wonder and romance in the midst of their harried lives. We had an idealistic dream, that our company could be far more than the paradigm defined by corporate America in the past. I told them about Bean Stock, our revolutionary new program of granting stock options to all employees. Our first priority was to take care of our people, because they were the ones responsible for communicating our passion to our customers. If we did that well, we'd accomplish our second priority, taking care of our customers. And only if we achieved both of those goals would we be able to provide long-term value for our shareholders.

I waited for their eyes to glaze over.

But this time, they didn't. These guys seemed to get it—at least more so than many of the others—and they immediately started asking some good questions.

After the meeting ended, I walked them out. As we headed down a long hall toward the front stairs, I said something to Dan Levitan that took him aback.

"Do you know what the problem with your business is?" I asked.

Dan braced himself for a major indictment of the investment banking industry. "No, what?" he said warily.

"There are not enough *mensches*."

I assumed Dan would know the word *mensch*, a Yiddish way of describing someone who is basically decent, honest, and full of integrity.

Dan jerked his head up and looked me directly in the eye. I could see that he took my point, instantly. My guess had been right: Dan was a *mensch*.

He later told me that he got on the plane that day, completely hyperactive, and used the in-flight telephone to call his colleagues in New York, telling them he had just discovered an amazing company.

He found it to be a hard sell. Starbucks didn't have any stores in New York then, and most New Yorkers thought of coffee shops as bland, purely functional places, not as fast-growing enterprises. In an era when biotechnology and fiber optics were the hottest investments, coffee didn't strike Dan's colleagues as an obvious moneymaker. Even when they came to understand and appreciate the business, they figured that Starbucks couldn't maintain such rapid growth, that it would spin out of control, or self-destruct, or quickly saturate the market. Ironically, Dan got to experience first-hand what I had been going through in Seattle, learning how tough it was to communicate intangibles like passion and values to hard-bitten skeptics. He got a lot of grief from his colleagues before he convinced them Starbucks was worth the risk.

Dan kept in touch with me by phone, and we had dinner together the next time I went to Los Angeles.

In early April of 1992, we had our "Beauty Contest"—a parade of seven investment banks, the finalists we invited to formally pitch for the business of handling our IPO. The contenders included some of the biggest names in the business, and the process took two intense days. We were rigorous and demanding, asking each group to fill out and submit a five-page questionnaire before its two-hour session. We wanted to see who cared enough to devote the most care and thought to the presentation. Laura Moix, who had advanced from being my trusted assistant to a marketing position, gave them all a tour of the roasting plant and reported back to us how much interest each of them showed. Professional and personable, a true believer in the company and its dream, Laura was the perfect person to take the pulse of those investment bankers.

One of our key goals was to find out who was genuinely passionate about both our product and our company. Some of the bankers all too clearly had the attitude that we at tiny Starbucks were lucky such a huge, successful investment firm had taken the trouble to pitch for our business. One such crew showed up in a big limousine but had never bothered to visit our stores.

Dan Levitan poured his heart into his presentation, and the effort showed. He brought along his chairman, Jim Harmon, and they lingered longer than anyone in our roasting plant, showing a sincere interest in the coffee. Laura reported back that they understood our passion. That put them a point ahead.

After the bankers left, Orin Smith and I had long discussions with Craig Foley and Jamie Shennan of the board, who had guided our IPO process from the beginning. Our plan was to pick two of the seven. We already had close ties with several of the investment banks, including some top-rated ones, so it would be hard to break ranks with them. But I had a gut instinct about Dan and his company, and the others agreed.

We selected two firms: Alex. Brown & Sons, which had many years of experience in taking companies like ours public, and Dan's firm, Wertheim Schroder & Co. (now Schroder Wertheim).

Dan called me that Sunday from Minnesota, where he was watching his alma mater Duke play in the Final Four basketball games. I couldn't tell him of our decision yet, because I hadn't yet informed the unsuccessful candidates. I tried to reassure him to be patient.

Finally, I phoned him on Monday morning. "Congratulations. You got the business." He was overjoyed.

Our choice of Alex. Brown as lead underwriter was not a surprise, since they specialized in working with smaller companies like ours. Alex. Brown had three great people, who, not unlike Dan, understood our mission and viewed our IPO as far more than just another transaction: Mayo Shattuck, the president, Peter Breck and David DiPeitro, in capital markets. But some people didn't expect us to pick Wertheim Schroder since it was not on the A list of pedigree firms for our type of business. Time has proven that we made the right choice, and we still work closely with both firms. As time went on, I developed close working relationships with all of them, as well as with Robert Fisher, another managing director at Schroder Wertheim.

In my experience, relationships and loyalty have become undervalued commodities at many American companies. So many of us have lost sight of the vital importance of dealing with people we can trust. Adversarial or distant relationships are not inevitable—nor are they the best way of doing business. There is much to be gained by enlisting partners and colleagues who are committed to the same goals.

Any of the seven finalist investment banks could have done the job we needed. They were all first rate. For me personally, what made the difference in the winners was their obvious commitment and passion. They both brought an intangible something extra that I knew would take us over the top.

DON'T GET DIZZY ON WALL STREET'S EMOTIONAL ROLLER COASTER

If I had to pick the happiest day of my business career, it would have to be June 26, 1992. That was the date we went public, when Starbucks stock was listed on NASDAQ.

Our target range was $14 to $16 per share, a figure considered high at more than sixty times the previous year's earnings. Some worried about whether we could sustain that high a price, since the market for IPOs, hot in March, suddenly went soft, and most new issues started selling at prices below projections. Our advisers recommended the low end of that range. Local newspaper articles warned small investors to be wary of buying our stock since prices of most new issues drop after the initial offering. Once again, we defied conventional wisdom. We priced Starbucks stock at $17 a share, just above the initial range.

On the big day, several of us in the senior management team went to a brokerage office in downtown Seattle and huddled around a terminal, watching as the name SBUX came up on the screen, open for trading. At the opening bell, the stock price immediately jumped to $21. We cheered.

Starbucks was the second most active stock traded on NASDAQ that day. The IPO raised $29 million for the company, $5 million more than we had expected. By the closing bell, Starbucks' market capitalization stood at $273 million—just five years after I bought it for slightly under $4 million.

The IPO was one of the most successful of the year—one that

made Wall Street brokers search eagerly for "the next Starbucks." Our share price maintained its strength far longer than Wall Street pundits had predicted. It never fell significantly below the opening price, and within three months, it reached as high as $33 a share, making Starbucks worth nearly $420 million.

Being a public company has lent Starbucks a certain patina, taking it to the big leagues. Our stock market listing provided the liquidity that has allowed many people at Starbucks, including me, to cash in stock options and buy things we need or have long wished for. It has likewise served as a great incentive to attract talented people, who join us not only because of the excitement of building a fast-growing company but also because of the value we are creating.

Our success on Wall Street also added dimension to the brand. It allowed us to go back to the market almost every year and ask investors for more money to underwrite our growth. We've raised close to $500 million since going public, by issuing new stock or selling bonds that convert into stock if the price goes above a certain level. I personally enjoy the intellectual stimulation of interacting with the bright people I've met on Wall Street, people who have done their homework and understand the company. I also like the challenge of formulating a strategy for Starbucks to finance its growth.

But becoming a public company has its downside, too. It exposes your business to a high degree of scrutiny and your personal life to a sudden lack of privacy. Most importantly, it increases the weight of responsibility to shareholders and imposes a burden of meeting Wall Street's expectations.

Around the time we went public, one newspaper report appeared that really irked me. A Wall Street pundit who often forecasts disaster and sells stock short predicted that Starbucks would stumble. He believed we were way overvalued and said the stock would fall to $8 by the end of the year. The piece cast a shadow over the glory of the moment. I cut it out and stuck it in a drawer in my office. Every morning for the next six months, I pulled out that clipping and re-read its gloomy prediction. Fortunately, the pundit was wrong: We didn't stumble, and our stock price continued to rise, albeit with some dramatic ups and downs along the way. His forecast reminded me, every day, of the cost of even a minor trip-up.

Alongside the exhilaration of being a public company is the humbling realization, every quarter, every month, and every day, that you're a servant to the stock market. That perception changes the way you live, and you can never go back to being a simple business again. We began to report our sales monthly, including *comps*—"comparable" growth of sales at stores that have been open at least a year, also called same-store sales growth. When there are surprises, the stock reacts instantly. I think comps are not the best measure to analyze and judge the success of Starbucks. For example, when lines get too long at one store, we'll occasionally open a second store nearby. Our customers appreciate the convenience and the shorter lines. But if, as often happens, the new store cannibalizes sales from the older store, it shows up as lower comps, and Wall Street punishes us for it.

Over the past few years, we've faced many a skeptic in the financial community. Starbucks' stock has always traded at a high multiple to earnings, which has made it a favorite for short-sellers, who bet against it because they are convinced that our company is overvalued. Since 1992, we've had the dubious honor of consistently being one of the top names on the short-sellers' list. But so far, most of our steadfast believers have been rewarded, and the skeptics have been proven wrong. Investors in every new Starbucks stock issue have seen the price go up. But when your stock is trading high, you become familiar with the business version of vertigo: It's a long way down.

While Wall Street has taught me a lot, its most enduring lesson is an understanding of just how artificial a stock price is. It's all too easy to regard it as the true value of your company, and even the value of yourself.

In early December 1995, Starbucks' stock price reached a record high—the sort of news that normally lifts moods around the office. But in fact, we had just learned that our Christmas merchandise was not selling as well as we had predicted, and tension ran high as we waited for the final results of the critical holiday selling season.

In early January, when we announced December comps of only 1 percent, the stock fell dramatically, from $21 to $16. In just a few days, we lost $300 million in market value, even though we had announced only a $5 million shortfall in sales. Concerned investors called me up, asking: "Why is the company performing so poorly?" *The Wall Street Journal* declared that we were a "shining light" that "may now be fading." Analysts seemed sure that our growth days were over, that the bloom was off the rose.

In fact, Starbucks hadn't changed in that month. Although our sales were lower than expected, our overall annual sales growth was nearly 50 percent. We were still buying and roasting coffee. We were opening a store a day. We continued with our plans to enter new cities and introduce new products.

Three months later, the stock rose to another all-time high. Comps were healthy again for the first three months of the year. Goldman Sachs, one of the pedigree bankers on the Street, with no vested interest in Starbucks, predicted even higher profit margins and a higher stock price.

Investors were now phoning to congratulate me—some of them the same people who had called with serious concerns during the Christmas season.

What had changed? Again, nothing substantial. Starbucks was the same company in April that it was in January. The difference was that Wall Street suddenly decided the company was worth a lot more.

Running a public company is an emotional roller coaster. In the beginning, you accept the congratulations as if you really deserve them. Then, when the stock price falls, you feel you have failed. When it bounces back, it leaves you dizzy.

At some point, you have to divorce yourself from the stock price and just focus on running the business. You need to maintain a controlled calm throughout both the heady highs and the sickening lows. That sort of composure comes hard for me, because normally I respond very emotionally. But I've discovered how critical it is to exert strong, consistent leadership through both good and bad times, to be able to temper the morale swings of those around you. Most importantly, I've tried to make decisions based on what's right for the company, not what's right for the stock price. That's one of the achievements I'm proudest of at Starbucks.

Every entrepreneur dreams of building a public company. But how many of us really know what we're getting into? Not every company leads as charmed a public life as Starbucks has. If it's been a wild ride for us, what must it be like for those whose companies do stumble?

Another old saying rings true here: Be careful what you wish for. You might get it.

14

AS LONG AS YOU'RE REINVENTING, HOW ABOUT REINVENTING YOURSELF?

*The difference between great and
average or lousy in any job is, mostly, having
the imagination and zeal to re-create yourself daily.*

—*TOM PETERS*, THE PURSUIT OF WOW!

WHY ARE WE GROWING SO FAST?

After Starbucks went public in 1992, I basked in the glow of our success. Our expansion plan sprinted ahead of schedule, with more than 50 new store openings in fiscal 1992 and 100 in fiscal 1993. Each year we exceeded our internal targets for both sales and earnings, and Wall Street analysts cheered as our same-store sales growth remained in double digits. In 1992 we expanded to San Diego, San Francisco, and Denver. Everywhere we went, the enthusiastic response bowled us over.

In April 1993, we made our initial jump to the East Coast, deciding to open first in Washington, D.C., which had the highest concentration of mail-order customers in the East. Washington also had the benefit of being home to a large number of both Europeans and transplanted West Coasters. We sent invitations to all our area catalogue customers for the opening of our first D.C. store, in Friendship Heights on Wisconsin Avenue, and attracted a sizable crowd. We later had an even bigger turnout when Kenny G played at the Grand Opening of our highly visible Dupont Circle store, which quickly became one of our highest volume outlets.

We began to rely more and more on information from our mail-order group to decide which markets to enter. Catalogue customers tend to be the most loyal, since they go out of their way to ensure that they will have a steady supply of Starbucks coffee. The average Starbucks mail-order customer, we've found, is a connoisseur, highly educated, relatively affluent, well-traveled, and technologically savvy, with a significant interest in the arts and other cultural events. These were just the right kind of ambassadors we wanted to get the word out about Starbucks.

In July, the month of my fortieth birthday, my picture appeared on the cover of *Fortune* magazine, illustrating a story on America's fastest-growing companies. "Howard Schultz's Starbucks grinds coffee into gold," it said. *Fortune* by forty! I was proud but, frankly, a little embarrassed at all the attention. It's always been hard for me to celebrate success, because I'm always thinking: *What next?*

On the surface, everything was going flawlessly. But in my own mind, I found myself growing apprehensive. Much of the company's zeal was motivated by swimming against the tide, by scaling impossible mountains. We had proved our idea would work—far better than even we had imagined. Could we maintain our edge?

Now that specialty coffee was catching on all over the country, national expansion looked like an easy goal to attain. It wasn't that simple, of course, for the competition was heating up. In cities across North America, coffee stores were adapting the Starbucks model, serving lattes and cappuccinos, stocking shelves with mugs and coffee grinders, sometimes selling whole-bean coffee, too. The Specialty Coffee Association of America predicted that the number of coffee cafés, including espresso bars and carts, would rise from 500 in 1992 to 10,000 by 1999. The espresso business was attracting thousands of small entrepreneurs, some with little overhead. Many middle managers in downsizing companies dreamed of opening a little coffee place, and some actually did. It seemed there was no barrier to entry, since anybody could buy an espresso machine and steam milk for a latte.

Starbucks has never felt threatened by the mom-and-pop coffee stores. In Seattle there's one on just about every street corner, and we've all benefited from the growing market. But other coffee companies, seeing our success, started to undertake ambitious expansion plans. One of our competitors, SBC in Seattle, announced that it would franchise 500 stores in five years; another, Brother's Gourmet Coffee, bought out mall-based Gloria Jean's and declared plans to open at least 80 more Starbucks-type stores.

Because of the growing competition, some observers predicted we had already "missed the train" to the East Coast. So we accelerated our plans: Instead of opening 125 stores in fiscal 1994, we quietly upped the goal to 150. After our success in Washington, D.C., we decided to enter New York and Boston in 1994. New York held special symbolism for me, since it's my hometown as well as the nation's biggest city. But with its high rents and tough labor market, it also concerned us. Arthur Rubinfeld and Yves Mizrahi devised a real estate strategy of first opening stores in nearby Fairfield and Westchester counties, home to many opinion-makers who work in Manhattan. By the time we made our first foray into the city, at 87th Street and Broadway in March 1994, we were already rated the best coffee in New York.

In Boston, we made a move we had never tried before—or since. After opening a handful of our own stores, we bought out the leading local competitor. Founded in 1975 by George Howell, The Coffee Connection was different from competitors we faced elsewhere. Like the founders of Starbucks, George had discovered fine coffee at Peet's in Berkeley, where he was a graduate student. When he returned to Boston and opened his own stores, however, he quickly realized that New Englanders preferred a lighter roast. After much trial and error, he switched loyalties and began to strongly advocate light-roasted gourmet coffees.

By 1992, The Coffee Connection had 10 stores, including prime sites in Harvard Square and Faneuil Hall, and an intensely loyal customer base, built largely by word of mouth. Realizing Starbucks would soon be coming to town, George hired a former hotel executive, Curt Bean, to help him tap into venture capital funding to speed up growth. They added 15 more stores by mid-1994 and started to expand outside Boston, with plans to open another 60 stores by 1997.

Rather than starting a local coffee war, we offered to buy The Coffee Connection, and George Howell agreed. In June 1994, in a stock swap worth $23 million, Starbucks completed the acquisition, moving overnight into a leading position in Boston, a hub for the Northeast. George Howell became a consultant, and Curt Bean stayed on to oversee the transition. The move gave Starbucks a jump start on our brand-building and retail strategy, as well as immediate access to a core of well-informed coffee drinkers.

By the end of calendar 1994, we had also entered Minneapolis and Atlanta, as well as Dallas, Fort Worth, and Houston. The lightning-fast, multi-pronged move into Texas was partly based on the availability of great sites, with rents priced at the bottom of the cycle. In 1995, we opened stores in Philadelphia, Las Vegas, Austin, San Antonio, Baltimore, Cincinnati, and Pittsburgh. The pace was dizzying. Opening up in so many regions at once was risky, but we were building the kind of sophisticated, mature management team we needed in each region to oversee the process.

To an outside observer, our growth may have seemed effortless, and in fact, there weren't many hitches along the way. Once we had set up a smooth-running engine for growth, opening stores became as routine as pulling shots of espresso.

What really made it work so well was the people we were able to employ. In only a few years, the Starbucks name had acquired a mystique that attracted skilled managers, many of whom had left far larger operations to join us at the regional level. Howard Behar and Deidra Wager recruited zone vice presidents to direct the development of each region, and gave them the responsibility of duplicating the Starbucks culture throughout North America. In Canada, Roly Morris came to us with extensive operations and marketing experience in the retail industry. Stuart Fields, heading the Midwest zone, had been vice president for operations of the Custom Shirt retail chain. Bruce Craig had overseen the growth of 1,600 Burger Kings before building up Starbucks' Southwest region. Marcia Adams, now head of our Gulf Atlantic zone, had executive experience with 7-Eleven in operations, merchandising, and new concept development. Each of them took ownership of their region and outperformed even our expectations.

To accommodate fast growth, we developed a system to recruit and train baristas, ensuring high-energy, knowledgeable people, helping them develop their palate for coffee, and replicating our standards and values in city after city. Under Deidra Wager, our retail operations had not only to install systems that could handle large numbers of stores but simultaneously to oversee the opening of hundreds of stores in new markets every year.

At our Seattle offices, our real estate, design, store planning, and construction people developed a sophisticated store-development process based on a six-month opening schedule, so well-oiled that eventually we were able to open a store every business day. There got to be so many that I couldn't visit them all.

In 1992 and 1993, we refined our real estate strategy, creating a three-year expansion plan based on a matrix of regional demographic profiles and an analysis of how best to leverage our operations infrastructure. For each region, we targeted a large city to serve as a "hub," where we located teams of professionals to support new stores. We entered large markets quickly, with the goal of rapidly opening 20 or more stores in the first two years. Then from that core we branched out, entering nearby "spoke" markets,

including smaller cities and suburban locations with demographics similar to our typical customer mix.

To supply so many new stores, we also had to build a new roasting plant. Just after Christmas 1992, we realized we couldn't get
through another holiday season with our existing plant, although it
had been planned to last ten years. In February 1993, we asked
Howard Wollner, our vice president for administration, to do the
impossible: find a new site, assemble a team to build a far larger
roasting plant, and start operations in only seven months. In
September of 1993, roasting began in a new 305,000-square-foot
plant in Kent, Washington, just south of Seattle.

The old plant eventually became dedicated to roasting for our
mail-order group, headed by Buck Hendrix since mid-1993. Buck
grew that business from $6 million to more than $20 million by
1997, which, though representing a small percentage of our overall
sales, served as a visible showcase for our products and an important link to customers all over the United States.

In October 1993, we outgrew our old offices as well. Howard
Wollner found us space in a building a few blocks away, still in the
light industrial area south of Seattle, an area called SODO because
it is SOuth of the KingDOme, the stadium where the Mariners and
Seahawks play. We rented several floors in a building that once
served as the Northwest warehouse for Sears' catalogue division.
It's nothing like the high-rise buildings or sprawling corporate campuses other companies inhabit. Each one of its nine floors has the
equivalent square footage of six stories in a typical office high-rise.
The old warehouse used to be so large that people moved around
it on bicycles and roller skates to fulfill orders. We created a space
centered around a "commons area" with food service, espresso
kitchens, and rest rooms, to encourage people to interact.
Industrial lighting and exposed pipes and ducts create a mood that's
far from the stylish image some might expect of us.

I hated the idea of moving away from the roasting plant, so I
insisted on elements that would remind us of our roots. Just inside

the main door is a mock store, showcasing our latest products. Posters on the walls throughout the office display our newest marketing materials. Coffee plants grow in pots. And once we expanded into the top floor, we installed a small antique coffee roaster, retrofitted with modern technology, to use for demonstrations and sample batches and, most importantly, to tie us all the more closely to coffee.

From the window of my office, a modest one by CEO standards, I look out over the cranes of Seattle's port, where our coffee beans arrive, and the towers of the city where the company was born. Yet I still miss the days when my office overlooked the roasting plant.

By 1994, we could see that our aim of becoming the leading retailer and brand of specialty coffee in North America was within reach. So we framed a bigger goal: to become the most recognized and respected brand of coffee in the world. There were still many American and Canadian cities we hadn't entered, but since the Starbucks model and logo were already being copied—sometimes blatantly—around the world, we knew we needed to act quickly to lay plans to go global.

But it wasn't enough simply to speed up and spread ever farther afield. Just as I had changed the paradigm for Starbucks once, selling coffee beverages as well as coffee beans, I wanted to shift it again. I wanted to jump to a new level, with a move that would be truly innovative and daring. The Starbucks brand was gaining favor so quickly that I figured we could leverage it for new coffee products that could be sold far beyond our stores. I began to imagine a Starbucks that was more than coffee and larger than the four walls of our stores.

In 1994, Starbucks exploded into a whirlwind of activity. We invented Frappuccino. We signed a far-reaching joint venture with Pepsi. Orin Smith became president of the company. We formed Starbucks International, and Howard Behar became president of that. We moved to our new offices. We upgraded our mail-order computer system. We chose a site in York, Pennsylvania, for a huge $11 million roasting facility that could ultimately grow to 1 million square feet, to supply our East Coast stores. And we faced our first major crisis: a 300 percent rise in coffee prices.

They were all major moves, many taking place simultaneously, and I've devoted entire chapters of this book to some of them. And the pace of change hasn't slowed more recently: 1995 and 1996 found us facing challenges of growth and ubiquity, conflicts over ethics and style, and fantastic new opportunities with risky downsides that made the debates of the late 1980s seem minor by comparison.

FAST GROWTH TAKES ITS TOLL

What kept us balanced during this storm of activity was our values and our commitment to each other. Yet as we ran ever faster, those values came under more and more strain. Within the company, people who had helped me grow Starbucks in the early years became fearful and threatened, as professional managers came in over their heads. I no longer knew everyone's name, even though we worked in the same building. The same pace and passion that made us great also at times burned people out. And while we were winning thousands of new customers a week, I heard reports of some who defected.

Nowhere were these conflicts more intense than inside my own head. Whenever someone came to my office upset about some new change, I felt personally responsible. I had thought my job would get easier as the company expanded, but it grew more difficult instead.

The issues became far more complex. Can a company double and even triple in size but stay true to its values? How far can you extend a brand before you dilute it? How do you innovate without compromising your legacy? How do you create widespread trial and awareness without losing control? How do you stay entrepreneurial even as you develop professional management? How do you keep pushing through on long-term initiatives when short-term problems demand immediate attention? How do you continue to provide customers with a sense of discovery when you're growing at the speed of light? How do you maintain your company's soul when you also need systems and processes?

Most of these questions, I discovered, do not have answers you can find in books. The best guidance comes from observing how other admired enterprises act. Only a few, unfortunately, have openly grappled with the difficulties of sustaining high standards and values during rapid growth.

With no easy answers, I explored every avenue I could. I've always been a voracious reader, but now I began to read even more widely. I consulted experts. I got to know other CEOs and entrepreneurs. I hired managers who had done it before. I picked the brains of everyone I met: reporters, analysts, investors, store managers, baristas, customers.

With growth, the daily pace of my life intensified as well. On any given day, I might have up to a dozen meetings, dealing with an extremely wide range of subjects. Sometimes, I'd have very little time to mentally prepare and would have to quickly shift gears between discussion of the company's strategic vision, the following month's sales promotion, a new blend of coffee, profit margins, an employee's personal worries, a major investment opportunity, a policy change, and a board member's objection. Sometimes my brain would almost literally ache.

In the middle of that, I'd sometimes get a call from Sheri or one of my kids. I always try to make time for family and friends; I couldn't stand the pressure if I didn't. But keeping up those personal relationships is stressful, too. Sheri has been able to gauge the pressures on me as the business matured, and during times I was distracted she somehow managed to keep the family on an even keel. I can't imagine that I could have built Starbucks, that I could have managed the tensions and conflicts involved and still feel as good about it as I do, without having a strong, secure wife like Sheri.

Still, it's always a struggle for me to pursue my dreams at the office without impinging on family time. I try never to travel on weekends. We always make an effort to have dinner at home together, whenever I'm not on the road. For us, that time is sacrosanct, and though we may eat a little later than most families, my kids look forward to it. I coached my son's Little League team for two years, planning my travel schedule around his games. I take the kids to see the Sonics and Mariners, and they always attend the Starbucks annual picnic.

The balancing act has never been an easy one. I've struggled to harmonize the needs of the family, the needs of the business, the needs of my marriage, and my individual needs, too. I sometimes wonder: *When is there time for me? What do I get out of this?* It's a relief to get out on the basketball court every Sunday morning and play a fast, running, sweaty game. For two and a half hours, I concentrate on that ball, and all of the work world melts away.

THE ENTREPRENEUR'S BIGGEST CHALLENGE: REINVENTING YOURSELF

Nobody has a greater need to reinvent himself than the successful entrepreneur. Think of it: How many entrepreneurs have founded a company and then managed to grow successfully along with it, even as it reaches and surpasses $1 billion in sales?

Bill Gates of Microsoft has done so, as has Phil Knight of Nike. But far more entrepreneurs can't adjust to the transition into professional management. Most are better at creating start-ups than at guiding mature businesses. As the companies beneath them balloon ever larger, the odds diminish that their skills will grow fast enough to maintain control.

Sometimes I feel like one of those cartoon characters who somehow winds up straddling two jet planes. I've got one foot on one jet and one foot on the other, and both are racing faster and faster ahead. I have to decide: *How long can I hang on? Should I jump off? Am I going to break my legs?*

I figure I've had to reinvent myself at least three times, each time at top speed.

I started off as a dreamer. That was the thirty-two-year-old who knocked on every investor's door in Seattle looking for money to realize his business plan.

Then I moved to entrepreneur, first founding Il Giornale and then taking over Starbucks and re-creating it as a fast-growth company. Then I had to become a professional manager, as the company grew larger and I needed to delegate more and more decisions. Today, my role is to be Starbucks' leader, its visionary, cheerleader, and keeper of the flame.

For me, dreamer is the most natural role, and one I still enjoy. Growing up in the 1950s and 1960s has a lot to do with that. It was the era of the Kennedys and the Peace Corps, when capitalism meant opportunity, not oppression. The prevailing mood was optimism, and I absorbed it deep in my bones.

But being a dreamer isn't enough. If you want to achieve something in life, you need a different set of skills to set those dreams in motion.

Once you cross the divide where your dream begins to take shape, you graduate from being a dreamer to being an entrepreneur. The entrepreneurial stage of a young business is probably the most exciting one.

I didn't realize it at the time, but I'm now convinced that one of the greatest responsibilities of an entrepreneur is to imprint his or her values on the organization. It's like raising children. You start with love and empathy, and if you've imprinted the right values on them, you can trust them to make reasonable decisions when they become teenagers and young adults. Sometimes they will disappoint you, and sometimes they will make mistakes. But if they have absorbed good values, they will have a center line to return to.

In building a business, you'll often come to forks in the road. Intel CEO Andy Grove calls them "inflection points." You may not even be aware of it at the time, but the decisions you make at these junctures have repercussions for years to come. You may realize, for example, that you've discovered an opportunity to create a much larger, more meaningful business. But in order to take advantage of that chance, you will have to make a dramatic change in the way the business is managed.

It is precisely at points like this when a lot of entrepreneurs cut and run. Some are intimidated by the new opportunity and reject it. Others who do accept the challenge often can't develop the skills to handle it.

At a certain stage in a company's development, an entrepreneur has to develop into a professional manager. That often goes against the grain. Early on, I realized that I had to hire people smarter and more qualified than I was in a number of different fields, and I had to let go of a lot of decision-making. I can't tell you how hard that is. But if you've imprinted your values on the people around you, you can dare to trust them to make the right moves. You have to build a foundation strong enough to support the pressures, the anxieties, and the fears of growing to the next level.

If you're a creative person, an entrepreneur at heart, introducing systems and bureaucracies can be painful, for they seem like the antithesis of what attracted you to business in the first place. But if you don't institute the right processes, if you don't coordinate and plan, if you don't hire people with MBA skills, the whole edifice could crumble. So many companies do.

In the early 1990s, we worked hard to make the transition from an entrepreneurial to a professionally managed company. But even as we did so, we tried to retain as much as we could of our entrepreneurial spirit, our esprit de corps, our ability to innovate and renew ourselves. We invited Eric Flamholtz, business professor at UCLA, to advise us on making that passage. He had written a book called *Growing Pains*, and recognized the symptoms all too well when he arrived at Starbucks. Fast-growing companies, he believes, go through predictable stages; no one is immune to them. He has developed management strategies to help company founders at each stage deal with the personal and professional challenges they confront as their enterprises mature into professionally managed firms. At Starbucks, Eric Flamholtz worked with us to develop strategic planning and management systems. Slowly, painfully, we're learning how to set priorities and better manage rapid growth.

At first, I battled against these changes. I'm not process-oriented. I hated the very notion of strategic planning and systems, which always struck me as limiting. I'm used to tossing the gauntlet on the table, saying, "I challenge you to do this," and it's done. Eric Flamholtz calls that the "John Wayne school of management: a shoot-from-the-hip mentality." Gradually, though, I gained respect for processes and plans as I came to realize that the better Starbucks can handle routine business and growth, the more well-equipped it is to move boldly into new arenas.

But I knew I would ultimately have to grow beyond even the role of manager to become a leader. I was lucky in that respect to become acquainted with the man who wrote the book on leaders, USC professor Warren Bennis. After he did some consulting at Starbucks, our friendship developed to the point where I could call him up late at night or early in the morning, whenever I reached a turning point and was at a loss for what to do. He took a personal interest in the company and in me, and helped me over some hurdles in my evolution to leadership.

RECOGNIZING YOUR LIMITATIONS

In mid-1994, I realized that my role needed to change again. Managing the day-to-day operations of a big company was not what I wished to do. It was beyond the scope of my skills and also fell outside my interests. I wanted, rather, to continue to create the vision, to anticipate the future, to experiment with creative ideas. That's the value I can add, and it's the work I love.

So in June 1994, the board and I promoted Orin Smith to take over some of my day-to-day responsibilities. He took on the titles of president and chief operating officer, while I remained chairman and CEO. Over the years, Orin had grown into a world-class executive with a thorough understanding of the logistics of managing administrative systems, someone who was much more qualified to manage our daily operations than I was. The move freed me up to spend time on such projects as the Pepsi joint venture, brand-building, the design of the Store of the Future, and new product development.

If you've raised a company as if it were your child, it's difficult to let go of the instinct to care about every detail. For years, I used to monitor sales and profits numbers daily, for every store, watching them come off the printer. I'd compare their actual performance against budget, looking for numbers that were off the charts, whether good or bad. If a store had a phenomenal day, I'd call up its manager and congratulate him or her. If I noticed a weak performance, I'd call, too, to find out what could be done to help improve sales.

By the time the company had 400 or 500 hundred stores, I realized I could no longer keep watch over it so closely. I had to trust Orin and the rest of our operations people to do so. Still, it was frustrating not to be included in meetings about new products, new merchandise, new marketing campaigns. To this day, I'll often pass a room where an interesting discussion is in progress, and I'm sorely tempted to drop in. But I know my presence will change its tenor, and it's no longer appropriate.

For me, picking Orin was an obvious move. I had so much confidence in him that I couldn't have entertained the idea of bringing in someone from the outside. Although Orin and Howard

Behar had long been equals, each overseeing about half the functions in the company, by mid-1994 Howard Behar wanted a different sort of challenge. We were just ready to begin planning overseas expansion, and he wanted to build up that side of the business from scratch. So we created Starbucks International, appointed Howard as its president, and gave him the leeway to develop an enterprise that had the long-term potential of doubling the size of the company.

When Orin became president, I moved into a new role, which I call leader. As chairman I play the role of pathfinder, trying to look far into the future to see what's coming at us. I try to anticipate competition and envision the strategic changes our company may need to make to face it. When a regional manager or plant manager needs someone to come and speak to his or her people, to reinforce the values of the company, to fire them up around the cause, I take on the charge. I spend a lot of time visiting stores, touring new markets, building excitement.

Here's the irony: I've remade myself into a professional manager and a corporate leader. But in my soul, I'm still a dreamer and an entrepreneur. I have to retain that outlook even as I develop new skills.

So does Starbucks. We've got to develop systems and processes, but not at the cost of stifling our creative people. If we bog down innovative ideas in bureaucratic nonsense, we will have made the same mistake hundreds of American corporations have made before us.

To stay vigorous, a company needs to provide a stimulating and challenging environment for all these types: the dreamer, the entrepreneur, the professional manager, and the leader. If it doesn't, it risks becoming yet another mediocre corporation.

I'm determined that won't happen at Starbucks.

15

Don't Let the Entrepreneur Get in the Way of the Enterprising Spirit

*No organizational regeneration, no
national industrial renaissance can take
place without individual acts of courage.*

—*Harvey A. Hornstein,* Managerial Courage

Frappuccino: The Best Mistake I Didn't Make

It's not difficult for me to retain my entrepreneurial spirit; it's part of my nature. But encouraging others at Starbucks to feel and act like entrepreneurs within the company takes effort. Sometimes what's hardest—for me and strong-minded leaders like me—is restraining myself, allowing other people's ideas to germinate and blossom before passing judgment.

Many entrepreneurs fall into a trap: They are so captivated by their own vision that when an employee comes up with an idea, especially one that doesn't seem to fit the original vision, they are tempted to quash it. I almost did the same for one of Starbucks' most successful products, the icy blend of dark-roasted coffee and milk that we call Frappuccino.

Here's how it happened.

Dina Campion managed a district of about ten Starbucks stores in and around Santa Monica, California. She and her store managers were becoming increasingly frustrated because nearby coffee bars were doing great business with their granitas—sugary, blended, cold coffee drinks that were very popular during hot weather, especially in the afternoon and evenings. Starbucks did offer iced lattes and iced mochas, both of which were served with ice cubes, but more and more customers came in asking for a blended drink. When informed that Starbucks didn't sell any, they went to a local competitor instead.

People working in our southern California stores had asked us many times to create such a blended beverage, but because we didn't regard it as a true coffee drink, we declined. I, especially, resisted the idea. It seemed to dilute the integrity of what we stood for and sounded more like a fast-food shake than something a true coffee lover would enjoy.

In September of 1993, Dina saw an opportunity to make her case more strongly. Dan Moore, a former Los Angeles–area store manager, had moved to Seattle to work in retail operations. He understood the needs of the southern California market, and he could champion the cause in Seattle.

After Dina approached him with her idea, Dan arranged to purchase a blender for her. As her test case, Dina picked a store in the dry San Fernando Valley, where requests for blended drinks ran as high as the summer temperatures. The partners installed the blender and began experimenting. They didn't ask for permission; they just went ahead, wondering if they'd get in trouble. Their first attempt was far from perfect; it wasn't sweet enough and the consistency was uneven. Dina and Dan presented their initial results to our food and beverage department, which then agreed to develop a proprietary blended drink for further testing.

Early in 1994, a prototype of the new beverage was brought to my office for me to taste. That version used a powder base and had a chalky, pasty taste. I thought it was awful, which only confirmed my opposition to the notion.

Still, remembering the nonfat milk experience, I agreed to let them test it with customers, beginning in May 1994. Dina handed the project over to Anne Ewing, who at the time managed our Third Street Promenade store in Santa Monica, in an outdoor mall where tourists and a wide variety of shoppers congregate in the afternoon and evening. In a warm climate, hot coffee doesn't appeal much at those hours.

Anne and her assistant manager, Greg Rogers, quickly discovered that neither of them liked the drink. Instead of complaining about it, they took ownership and improved upon it.

Greg, who is a comedian on the side, had worked with Anne at an entrepreneurial California company that invented variations of fruit shakes, smoothies, and yogurt drinks, so they knew how to innovate. They dumped the powder and used freshly brewed coffee for the base instead. They varied the ingredients. They lengthened the blending time from ten to twenty-five seconds. They changed the ratio of ice to liquid. They tasted all the competing products. They got feedback from customers.

That summer, Howard Behar visited Los Angeles. Dina took him to the Third Street Promenade store and presented him with two versions of the drink—the food and beverage version and Anne and Greg's revision. Hands down, he preferred Anne and Greg's drink, and he brought it back to Seattle for me to taste.

"We've got to pursue this," he insisted. "Customers are asking for it."

Our beverage director took the recipe to a team of food consultants, who applied their professional knowledge of food chemistry and product development to refine it. They came up with a great-tasting product that used low-fat milk, so its texture was more icy than creamy. In October, we began testing the beverage at 12 southern California stores, half using blenders and half using soft-serve machines. We then conducted formal research in three cities to get broad consumer perspective.

The results revealed that the blended product was fantastically popular and had wider appeal than the soft-serve variation. When I tasted it, I could see why. It was delicious.

We wanted to use a distinctive name for the drink, one that would be proprietary to Starbucks. In June 1994, when we had acquired The Coffee Connection in Boston, we inherited one of their products called a *Frappuccino*, a cold, slushy drink made from a soft-serve machine. We didn't like the drink but the name was perfect, evocative of both the cold of a *frappe* and the coffee in a cappuccino. So we decided to extend the name *Frappuccino* to the new blended beverage.

I still had reservations. We were already working with Pepsi to develop a lightly carbonated cold coffee drink in a bottle, which I thought had much greater promise. Although I agreed that *Frappuccino* was an appealing name, I still thought it was a mistake to sell it in our stores. It seemed more like a milk product than a coffee product. And blenders whirring away next to our espresso machines? How could we?

In the end, though, I gave in. Once again, our customers had voted, and our partners, who are closest to them, had understood their needs best. We put the blender in a metal shroud to dampen the noise, and nobody seemed to mind.

By the end of 1994, we decided to roll Frappuccino out, nationwide, to all Starbucks stores. Our goal was to formally introduce the drink on April 1, before the weather got hot. That may sound easy, but to our retail operations people, it seemed nearly impossible. We had less than five months to retrofit more than 550 individual stores, to install blenders, and to train our baristas to make the new drinks. We asked Dan Moore to coordinate the effort.

We made it, and Frappuccino was an instant hit—a runaway home run. Word of mouth about the new product spread quickly, and our regular customers introduced it to their friends. A lot of women, in particular, appreciated the fact that it is low-fat, and stopped in for a Frappuccino after a run or a workout. Frappuccino accounted for 11 percent of our summer sales that year. It pushed up our profit numbers, and our stock hit a record high.

In fiscal 1996, the first full year on the national market, we sold $52 million worth of Frappuccinos, which represented 7 percent of our total annual revenues. That's $52 million we would not have registered had we not listened to our partners in California.

I was wrong, and I was delighted about it. Turning down Frappuccino was the best mistake I never made. In late 1996, *Business Week* named it one of the best products of the year.

And did it dilute the integrity of Starbucks? A coffee purist might think so, but, most importantly, our customers didn't. Frappuccinos not only gave us a welcome alternative for warm-weather months but also provided a way to introduce non–coffee drinkers to Starbucks coffee. Besides, the more I drank Frappuccinos, the more I liked them.

Perhaps the most remarkable thing about this story is that we didn't do any heavy-duty financial analysis on Frappuccino before-hand. We didn't hire a blue-chip Establishment consultant who could provide 10,000 pages of support material. We didn't even con-duct what major companies would consider a thorough test. No cor-porate bureaucracy stood in the way of Frappuccino. It was a totally entrepreneurial project, and it flourished with a Starbucks that was no longer a small company. Even when I doubted it, it went ahead.

If we had been a typical leaden corporation, Frappuccino would never have emerged as it did. Its story epitomizes the enterprising spirit we still have at Starbucks, an innovative edge that keeps our customers coming back and our competitors grous-ing. It's experimental. It's adventurous. It fires people up and engages their imagination.

In October 1995, Dina, Anne, and Greg received the Starbucks President's Award. Dan was named nonretail Manager of the Year. They would laugh if someone asked if Starbucks is corporate and bureaucratic.

• • •

How Does a Coffee Company
Get into the Music Business?

During 1994, another idea percolated up from the store level. It pushed Starbucks into a new direction that I never could have imagined: the music business.

The idea began brewing in University Village, one of the original Starbucks locations, an urban shopping center with an eclectic clientele that included college students, professors, and wealthy homeowners. Timothy Jones, the store's manager, had worked for twenty years in the record industry and loved music as much as he loved coffee.

At that time, we had long been working with AEI Music Network, which provided a "tape of the month" for us, primarily jazz and classical instrumentals. Starting in 1988, Timothy asked if he could be the one to select the tape from AEI's monthly programs. We were happy to oblige. He began reviewing the monthly selections and experimenting with various types of music in his own store, gauging customers' reactions during different times of day. Gradually, he added jazz vocals, such as Ella Fitzgerald and Billie Holiday, and varied the classical offerings. Because of his personal interest and initiative, Timothy became Starbucks' music conscience.

Again and again, customers complimented him on the music that was playing, and asked where they could buy it. He had to tell them it was a special compilation for Starbucks, not for sale.

In late 1994 Timothy approached us with an unusual idea. "Why not compile our own CD or tape?" he asked. "Customers would snap it up."

At about that time, AEI had made a few tapes for us called "Blue Note Years," using jazz cuts from the 1950s and 1960s, most of them recorded by the acclaimed Blue Note label. They included such great instrumentalists as John Coltrane, Art Blakey, Bud Powell, and Thelonius Monk. Customers loved them.

One day, by coincidence, Jennifer Tisdel, our director of retail marketing, was having Sunday brunch with a friend visiting from Los Angeles, Dave Goldberg. Dave worked in new business development for Capitol Records, which owns Blue Note, and he told her about an idea he had for marketing Capitol's music through a retail company.

"Well, how about Starbucks?" she suggested. "We play a lot of jazz in our stores."

The idea clicked. Dave had heard the Blue Note tunes played in our stores, and they saw many possibilities for synergy. Both Blue Note and Starbucks had a "coolness factor" in their image and we could benefit from association with each other. Capitol had been looking for ways to get a wider audience for its music, especially jazz, and would benefit from having it played in our stores more regularly.

Jennifer put him in touch with Timothy Jones at University Village. Together, they explored an idea: What if Starbucks compiled great recordings from Blue Note in a CD and sold it exclusively in our stores?

They revised the idea and brought it to Howard Behar. He found it intriguing enough to turn it over to Harry Roberts, one of the most creative executives we've had at Starbucks. As vice president for merchandising, Harry was always looking for fresh and imaginative new products to sell. The idea set Harry on fire, too, and he became the executive who championed our entry into the music business.

We had to do some research first. Timothy looked through two years' worth of customer comment cards, from all the Starbucks locations, and found hundreds that asked us to sell the music we played in our stores. It was an overwhelming demand we had neither anticipated nor noticed. Many of our customers are middle-aged with young kids and don't have time to hang out in record shops and flip through albums or listen to new tunes. But if they hear something good playing at Starbucks, they want to buy it on the spot.

In December of 1994, we had a trial run. Kenny G had recorded an album of holiday music, *Miracles*, which we decided would be a good test case in our stores. Would people buy music with their coffee? In fact, as soon as they went on sale, Kenny's CDs flew off the counters. Jazz and java, it seemed, were a natural fit.

Anyone who's ever been to Hollywood would probably recognize the Capitol Records building, a tall white cylinder shaped like a stack of records, with a spire on top. I remember seeing it years ago and wishing I could go inside.

On January 31, 1995, I found myself walking into that landmark building with Harry and Timothy to meet with Gary Gersh, the president and CEO of Capitol Records. Photos of famous singers and musicians lined the corridors. We passed studios where Frank Sinatra, Nat King Cole, and numerous other greats had recorded their famous hits.

We took an elevator to the top floor and were greeted by Gary, Bruce Lundvall, president of Blue Note, and a dozen other executives.

Blue Note Records loved the idea of allowing Starbucks to compile a selection of its jazz greats and offer them on an exclusive compact disk. For them a Starbucks CD was a way of reviving interest in some old Blue Note titles. The entire record industry was looking for alternative venues to showcase music, since the old sales formula, radio stations and record stores, was failing to reach a lot of listeners.

We agreed that it was in our mutual interest to work together. We decided to produce as many as five CDs in the coming year, using not just Blue Note titles but also other music from the Capitol catalogue.

Timothy left his store and began working on music full time. He got to spend hours in Blue Note's archives and listen to its incomparable recordings of jazz greats. He discovered a seldom heard piano-only version of "I Get a Kick Out of You," played by Nat King Cole. The album was ready in just a few weeks.

We kept the whole project as secret as possible so we could take the world by surprise. A $1 million promotion was designed to highlight the release of the album, called *Blue Note Blend*. Our coffee specialists, Mary Williams, Tim Kern, and Scott McMartin, even developed a Blue Note blend of coffee, "smooth and spirited," our first new coffee blend in four years, to complement the soulful sounds. Our creative people designed jazzy blue packaging for it. Jennifer and Timothy arranged for local school jazz bands to play in our stores in thirty-eight different cities that month. We also developed in-store campaign materials drawing from the coffee and CD packaging, wrapping the store in blue. Some store managers, caught up in the enthusiasm, even hung blue notes made of paper from the ceiling.

The introduction of *Blue Note Blend*, on March 30, 1995, coincided with the grand opening of our largest store yet, at Astor Place in New York City's Greenwich Village. It is a huge 4,000-square-foot site in a prime location, with high ceilings and windows on three sides. Thelonius Monk, Jr., came to the celebration, and we had a special performance by Blue Note recording artist Benny Green. Dave Olsen and I were there to soak up the mood, as were Gary Gersh and Bruce Lundvall. We were all—dare I say it?—jazzed.

Despite our enthusiasm, we still didn't know how customers would react. Retail stores like ours normally didn't sell CDs, and it was certainly conceivable that we might sell only 10,000 copies.

As it happened, *Blue Note Blend* sold 75,000 copies before going out of print, and we still get calls for it, from San Diego to Atlanta. Ralph Simon, then vice president of Capitol Records, told us, just a few weeks after the disc was released, that it would have hit the Top Ten on the Billboard jazz charts if its sales had been tracked like those of a traditional album.

Later that year, we produced three additional CD compilations, followed by six others in 1996, branching out from jazz to classical and blues. In April 1996, when we introduced the *Blue Note II* album, we created an event in Seattle called "Hot Java/Cool Jazz," inviting high school jazz bands to perform downtown, with a panel of prominent local musicians to judge them. In many instances, we were able to raise funds for these schools' music programs, as a way of giving back to the community. Our second biggest hit came in the summer of 1996, with *Blending the Blues*, a historical look at Chicago blues, including vocals by Howlin' Wolf, Etta James, and Muddy Waters.

Did this foray into the music business make sense for a company like Starbucks? I would answer an unqualified yes. On the one hand, it gave a boost to sales, especially in April 1995, the month of the Blue Note introduction. But more important, it sent a message to our customers that we would continue to surprise and delight with unique products they never expected to find in a coffee store.

Selling music CDs wasn't just a marketing ploy imposed from on high. The idea was generated right there in our retail stores. It was a perfect demonstration of the character of Starbucks, one that was maturing in harmony with its customers. It added to the warmth and atmosphere that people were seeking when they came to our stores. And it showed our people, again, that we were willing to take a chance on a ground-breaking idea if it appealed to our sense of esthetics.

I realize it's easy for one person among our 25,000 partners to feel like a single digit in a rapidly growing company. But Dina and Dan, Anne and Greg, Timothy and Jennifer, at all different levels of Starbucks, proved that we're sincere when we say we believe in encouraging initiative. Rather than stifle the entrepreneurial spirit in our people and then try to resurrect it, as so many companies are trying to do, I'm convinced we should nurture it from the beginning in each new hire. It's demoralizing, I know from experience, to get fired up about a great new idea only to have it dismissed by higher-ups.

Quite possibly, the most promising inspiration for Starbucks' future is unfolding now in the mind of someone who joined the company as a barista yesterday. I hope so.

16

SEEK TO RENEW YOURSELF EVEN WHEN YOU'RE HITTING HOME RUNS

To stay ahead, always have your
next idea waiting in the wings.

—*ROSABETH MOSS KANTER*

When you're failing, it's easy to understand the need for self-renewal. The status quo is not working, and only radical change can fix it.

But we're seldom motivated to seek self-renewal when we're successful. When things are going well, when the fans are cheering, why change a winning formula?

The simple answer is this: Because the world is changing. Every year, customers' needs and tastes change. The competition heats up. Employees change. Managers change. Shareholders change. Nothing can stay the same forever, in business or in life, and counting on the status quo can only lead to grief.

At Starbucks, we had always aimed to build a company healthy enough to sustain itself for many years to come. We discovered along the way that sustainability is directly linked to self-renewal. Even when life seems perfect, you have to take risks and jump to the next level, or you'll start spiraling downhill into complacency without even realizing it.

In 1994, Starbucks undertook the second paradigm shift in its history. The first was adding the beverage to the bean sales, beginning in 1984. After that we weren't selling just coffee but also the coffee experience. The second shift came when we moved outside the four walls of our stores and invented new ways to enjoy the flavor of coffee, in bottled beverages, ice cream, and other innovative products.

This wasn't a natural or obvious move, and it wasn't one that was forced upon us. It was a deliberate attempt to spring ahead of the curve, to create a future no one would have imagined, while retaining our core values.

IT TAKES A FRESH OUTLOOK TO REINVENT AN AGE-OLD PRODUCT

Coffee has been around for a thousand years. Could it possibly be reinvented? This wasn't a question we at Starbucks spent much time thinking about in the early years. We figured we already had the best coffee around.

Yet any product-oriented company has to keep reinventing its core product if it expects to prosper, let alone survive. Ask Andy Grove of Intel, who obsoletes a whole generation of personal computers every eighteen months when he develops a new microprocessor chip.

We had devoted a lot of time to thinking about how to refresh and invigorate various elements of the Starbucks experience, whether store design, merchandise, espresso drinks, coffee blends, even new products like our jazz CDs. That's a conventional retailing approach, however creative a twist we put on it.

We consciously reinvented the coffee experience in America, but it never occurred to us to reinvent coffee itself. It took an immunologist to convince us to try it.

In 1988, Don Valencia began experimenting with coffee. Why he picked coffee, I'll never know. But we're lucky he did.

Trained in cell biology at University of California at Davis, Don had founded and run a biomedical business in Sacramento called Immuno Concepts, to develop tests to diagnose autoimmune diseases, such as lupus and rheumatoid arthritis. In his biomedical research, Don had explored the delicate task of isolating molecules within human cells without destroying them.

One day, on a whim, literally at his kitchen table, he applied some of the same techniques to coffee. He discovered that he was able to capture its flavor and aroma in a concentrated extract.

Although Don himself wasn't even a coffee drinker, his neighbors were. Every morning at 7:30, he would wake them up and put two wine glasses of coffee on their fence. One contained freshly brewed coffee; the other was made from his scientifically prepared coffee extract.

"Which is the control?" Don would ask them. He kept refining the technique until they couldn't distinguish the two.

When Christmas came, Don's wife suggested he bring along some of his coffee extract as a gift for her parents, who live in Seattle. During their visit, Don's wife took him to the Starbucks store in Pike Place Market. It was his first exposure to Starbucks.

Half-embarrassed, Don pulled out a sample of the extract and asked the barista to mix it with hot water and have a taste. The baristas were pretty skeptical, but they agreed to try it. They made his coffee, smelled it, and took a careful sip.

"It's okay," they said. "But it's nothing like Starbucks."

Don remembers walking out to the street, feeling foolish and deflated. His wife wanted to know what had happened to her latte, which he had forgotten to order. When he returned to the store, several of the baristas were still examining his cup of coffee.

"You said it wasn't very good," Don said.

"Well," they admitted, "it's actually pretty good, considering what it is. What kind of coffee did you make it from?"

Don had been using beans from a different company. So they sold him a pound of one of our best-selling coffees, Sumatra. He promised to try to prepare an extract from it and send it back to them.

Excited, he returned to Sacramento and worked on the Starbucks Sumatra. When he got it right, he sent a sample to the Pike Place store by overnight express.

Two days later, Don got a call from one of our coffee specialists. "I tasted this," he said, "and it's revolutionary. I don't know if you realize what you've got here."

The next day, he got a call from Dave Olsen. "This is surprisingly good," Dave told him. "If you're ever in Seattle, I'd love to sit down and talk to you."

The next day he got a call from me. I told him I had to meet him as soon as possible.

The day before, Dave had come into my office with a cup of coffee that he told me was Sumatra. When he insisted I try it, I figured he had discovered some new estate.

"How do you like it?" Dave asked

"It's great," I said. "Is it a new arrival?"

"Nope," he said. "It's from the same lot we're selling in the stores, but it's made from an extract!"

He had fooled me. The coffee in my cup tasted 100 percent as good as fresh-brewed Sumatra. He led me into his tasting room and showed me how it was made.

A few days later, I flew to Sacramento to meet Don Valencia. He has intense brown eyes and an infectious boyish excitement. We fed off each other's energy, like two kids getting ready to build the world's biggest fort. This scientist had the key to Starbucks' future, right there in his kitchen. I proposed that he form a joint venture with Starbucks.

Getting him to join forces with us wasn't easy, for he had made a career in the medical field and didn't want to leave it. Also, the timing was wrong for Starbucks. In 1990, we were just beginning to make money. We were in the midst of preparing for another round of private financing and still trying to fix problems in Chicago. The

Starbucks board wanted me to concentrate on retail expansion, which was critical to the success of the company.

The board hasn't often turned down my proposals, but they rejected the idea of a joint venture with Don Valencia. I was terribly disappointed, for I could envision a raft of future products this technology would make possible. But they thought his idea would drain a lot of time and money from Starbucks' top priority, which was to expand rapidly before other companies started copying us.

Don was more philosophical when he heard the news; his company was growing and taking all of his time. But in the years that followed, we kept in touch with each other. We sent him lots of coffee and a commercial espresso machine from one of our stores, and Don came to visit us in Seattle every Christmas. Dave and I got to know him well.

Then in spring of 1993, we made a formal overture. By then, Starbucks had grown to nearly $150 million in sales, with 250 stores in 10 regions. The company had gone public and was on much sounder financial footing. We could finally afford to set up our own in-house research and development facility.

Even then, Don wasn't a shoo-in. If you're going to hire an R & D guy, people advised me, hire a world-class R & D expert. But an immunologist? It was hard to justify how someone from the field of immunology could add value in a coffee company's pursuit of new products.

But I knew instinctively that Don's lack of experience in coffee was one of the factors that made him such an ideal candidate. We didn't need someone whose gaze was turned toward the past. Nontraditional results are more likely to arise from someone who can think out of the box. You're not likely to find such a person by looking inside the box.

Don had recently turned forty and was, in fact, contemplating a change of career. But he did not want to join us to work on just one product. He said he would accept Starbucks' offer only if he could develop a long-term strategic vision for technology and support it with a lab and researchers within a new department. After a lot of discussion, Don finally arrived in 1993 as vice president for research and development.

The extract that Don first developed in his Sacramento kitchen has opened new worlds for Starbucks. It enabled us to capture the unmistakable taste of fresh-brewed coffee as the key ingredient in a wide range of new products, including coffee-flavored beer, coffee ice cream, and ready-to-drink bottled beverages.

In 1996 we invested several million dollars to build a Technology Resource Application Center for Don. In a locked-off section on the seventh floor of our building, he's equipped seven labs and hired thirty scientists and technicians who work with such sophisticated technologies as gas chromatography, high-pressure liquid chromatography, and capillary electrophoresis. Ask Don what all that means! Some of the equipment is found only rarely in the top labs in the world.

At the same time, we devoted more than $4 million to a state-of-the-art pilot plant, set up in our parking garage, to produce the extract and test other new technology. At first we planned it only for small test batches, but as new products caught on quickly, we had to ramp up to commercial production levels.

It was wild: a coffee company, hiring scientists and investing millions in R & D.

It's a long way from espresso.

It's a long way from immunology.

What it wasn't far from was the market.

WHAT IT TAKES TO SHIFT TO A NEW PARADIGM

For all his scientific brilliance, Don Valencia did not have the background to develop a commercial product on his own. That step required another major move by the company—a partnership that few could fathom at first.

In 1992, I attended a top-secret meeting in Purchase, New York, in the imposing, mahogany-paneled boardroom of PepsiCo. Accompanying me was George Reynolds, then Starbucks' senior vice president for marketing, who had worked for Frito Lay and Taco Bell for thirteen years and knew Pepsi well.

I approached Pepsi the same way I've approached every one of Starbucks' partnerships: looking, first and foremost, for the right people. We had arranged to meet the then-president of Pepsi-Cola North America, Craig Weatherup. I had half-expected a top executive of a $33 billion company to be formal, detached, impersonal, and bureaucratic, so I was pleasantly surprised when Craig proved to be the very opposite: a hands-on, warm, personable man who genuinely valued the entrepreneurial spirit. Craig and I quickly developed a mutual trust and respect, which later proved vital in cementing the relationship between our companies.

Initially, neither of us had a clue how Pepsi and Starbucks might work together. But I figured there had to be a way to leverage Pepsi's tremendous distribution power to help move Starbucks out of our retail stores and into a more visible position in the mainstream market. Craig suggested we have a discussion with Pepsi's new beverage group, which had developed and marketed successful bottled beverages for Lipton and Ocean Spray.

I had discovered, during a trip to Tokyo in 1991, how popular cold, ready-to-drink, coffee-based beverages were in Japan, in both bottles and cans. The Japanese consume $8 billion worth of these drinks a year, about one-third of their coffee consumption. By contrast, this market is only $50 million a year in the United States—so far. Coke had found a ready market in Japan for its Georgia Coffee, and I was certain that if Starbucks could create a better product, it could be a huge success in North America and ultimately the world. I knew we would need a partner with strong national distribution to help us break into this category; who better than Pepsi?

In July 1993, on Don Valencia's first day at Starbucks, we held our first meeting with Pepsi's new-beverage group. Don didn't even have a lab yet, let alone support staff. But when the possibility of a bottled coffee product was proposed, he and our coffee specialist Tim Kern began experimenting immediately.

A few months later, working with the Pepsi R &D group, they had developed a wonderful coffee drink, made from Don's extract. Its taste was far superior to that of Georgia Coffee or any other cold coffee beverage on the market. We hoped it would be the first of many products with the potential to redefine the experience of coffee drinking in America.

Pepsi was excited, and so were we. We set up a task force, studied the market, and discussed the alternatives. Tiny Starbucks, with annual sales barely over $200 million, sat down with Pepsi and negotiated a fifty-fifty joint venture with a company more than a hundred times its size. Pepsi had huge marketing muscle and one million points of distribution, yet they agreed to cede us a high degree of ownership and control over our brand equity and product formulas.

In August 1994, Pepsi and Starbucks publicly announced the formation of the North American Coffee Partnership, with the goal of creating new coffee-related products for mass distribution, including cold coffee drinks in a bottle or can.

From the outside, the venture may have seemed an odd sideline, with little relevance to Starbucks' core business, or to Pepsi's, an unusual experiment unlikely to substantially affect the bottom line of either company. But I viewed it as an earth-jolting paradigm shift, a sign that our business might evolve in unimaginable directions. Our core business was now about to expand to a far wider concentric circle: coffee-based products. That meant leaving the comfortable confines of our stores, where we firmly controlled the quality and the environment, and entering intimidating new channels of distribution, where we were a bit player. It meant creating products that would carry the Starbucks brand name but would not be sold by Starbucks directly. It meant working with joint-venture partners who had a different agenda. It also meant reaching out to far more potential customers than those who came into our stores.

While we all perceived the risks involved, almost no one appreciated the ambiguities and complexities such a relationship would force us to grapple with.

For example, there was considerable debate about the appeal of cold coffee. In Japan, people are accustomed to it, and they even buy it from vending machines. But in America, cold coffee was always regarded as something brackish that deserved to be tossed down the drain.

Others viewed Pepsi and Starbucks as strange bedfellows. Starbucks appeals to sophisticated customers with discriminating tastes, while Pepsi aims to appeal to the broadest consumer base possible. Purists in the coffee business accused us of selling our soul.

In fact, it was straight uphill in the early stages of our relationship, with a clash of cultures that shook people in both companies. The tensions between Pepsi and Starbucks were predictable, if only because we came to the venture for such different reasons. Starbucks was looking to leverage Pepsi's distribution, while Pepsi wanted to leverage the quality and integrity of Starbucks' trademark. Because of their company's huge size, Pepsi people tend to be process-driven and focused on one project at a time, where Starbucks people tend to work on multiple projects simultaneously. Pepsi is so big that one division can be involved in a project that another knows nothing about, as we discovered when Pepsi International announced a joint venture in China with Maxwell House.

But differences can be complementary, as long as each side values what the other can bring to the table. Rather than slug it out until one party or the other won, we resolved our disagreements the hard way, assuming positive intent and aiming for win-win solutions. We learned to celebrate our differences rather than getting frustrated by them, and with time began to get along surprisingly well. I give great credit to Craig Weatherup, now chairman of Pepsi-Cola Company worldwide, Brenda Barnes, president of Pepsi-Cola, Mark Mangelsdorf, general manager of the joint venture, and Brian Sweete, head of marketing, for making the partnership work, because they recognized the long-term value of the joint venture and the Starbucks brand.

As it happens, the joint venture's first attempt was a failure. Mazagran was a cold, lightly carbonated coffee drink with a name borrowed from the French Foreign Legion posted in Algeria in the nineteenth century. When we test-marketed it in southern California in 1994, it polarized people. Some loved it; others hated it. A lot of customers were willing to try it because of the Starbucks brand name, but Mazagran didn't get the repeat business we had hoped for. We finally realized, with disappointment, that we had created a niche product, one that would catch on, if at all, only after a slow build.

Pepsi was remarkably patient. If Craig Weatherup and I had not established so forthright a relationship from the start, that episode might have ended it. But we both believed in each other and, obviously, in the capabilities of the partnership.

So we kept pushing until, in 1995, we found a better approach. Frappuccino had been a surprise hit that summer, drawing in tens of thousands of customers who were not normally coffee drinkers, filling our stores in afternoons and in hot months when the coffee business is usually slow. One day, in the midst of an agonizing discussion about the future of Mazagran, I said: "Why not develop a bottled version of Frappuccino?" The Pepsi executives were immediately enthusiastic.

But coming up with the idea was the easy part. Actually getting Frappuccino into a bottle in the supermarket was a challenge. In our stores, Frappuccinos are made in a blender, with crushed ice. They also contain milk, which has a limited shelf life. The first few efforts at a bottled version tasted wrong. It took months of experimentation before our joint venture R & D teams came up with a shelf-stable Frappuccino that tasted as delicious as the blended ones in our stores. When they did, I knew it would be a winner.

We were so confident of our product that we didn't even test-market it. Pepsi ramped up production as quickly as possible, but even then we could supply only West Coast supermarkets for the summer of 1996.

The response overwhelmed us. Within the first few weeks of introducing bottled Frappuccino, we were selling ten times the quantities we had projected. We couldn't make it fast enough. Supermarkets kept running out of it, and customers grew frustrated. We had to cancel all marketing support.

Pepsi, too, was blown away. Frappuccino was getting twice the level of trial they had predicted—and more than 70 percent repeat business, well above that of other New Age beverages. Sales of bottled Frappuccino were matching or exceeding early returns on Lipton and Ocean Spray. Finally, we had to withdraw it from the shelves until we could increase our manufacturing capacity.

Bottled Frappuccino was the runaway hit we had been hoping for. It ushered our way into the supermarket and into the ready-to-drink beverage business.

Throughout the summer, we met frequently with the Pepsi people to assess the unexpected surge of demand and the shortage of supply. In September, we jointly decided to invest millions of dollars to simultaneously build three bottling facilities for Frappuccino. It was the largest single investment Starbucks has ever made. With supermarkets continuing to clamor for the product, we planned a summer 1997 date for a nationwide launch. Once again, we set our sights on what seemed like a stretch goal. But we were confident we could make it.

• • •

How Can You Be Authentic Yet Also Innovative?

The equity of the Starbucks brand is a priceless asset. Every decision we make has to contribute to its sustainability and differentiation. Yet each time we create a new Starbucks product, we're weighing a risk against a potentially great reward. If we capture the public imagination with innovative products, Starbucks could become larger than life. But we have to make sure that nothing we do dilutes the integrity of the Starbucks brand.

Creating new products through joint ventures has now become a central part of how we do business. In 1995, we worked with Seattle's Redhook Ale Brewery to create Double Black Stout, a stout beer with a shot of Starbucks coffee extract in it. It amazed and delighted many of Redhook's customers. We then moved into another line Starbucks' founders could never have imagined: coffee ice cream.

In October of 1995, Starbucks ice cream wasn't even in our business plan. By July of 1996, it was in supermarkets around the country, number one in its category.

Although Howard Behar had been pushing for ice cream for years, it had never seemed to me to be a serious business proposition. But Don Valencia's extract opened my eyes to the possibility that we could bring authentic Starbucks flavor to a variety of products we had long dismissed as unlikely. So when Harry Roberts, our vice president for merchandising, came to me with an ice cream proposal in August 1995, I agreed to let him invite a few manufacturers to discuss it with us. After a few intriguing meetings, we picked Dreyer's Grand Ice Cream as a partner because they had nationwide distribution and experience making super-premium ice cream. Dreyer's was also willing to produce and distribute Starbucks ice cream without co-branding, or putting their name on the ice cream along with ours.

Don Valencia took his coffee extract to Dreyer's, and their ice cream experts began working with our coffee experts to come up with some flavor profiles.

In September, Dreyer's president Rick Cronk brought a high-level team to Seattle to meet with us and taste several samples. Like us, the Dreyer's people were dressed in plaid or striped shirts, and were genial and informal, open and excited. I asked them, "How do you guys stay so thin?"

They laughed and responded, "How do you guys stay calm?"

In a slide presentation they outlined the size of the market opportunity (potentially a $100 million market) and proposed five to six coffee-related flavors of premium ice cream in quarts, as well as two or three novelty items, on a stick. Then they broke out the ice cream: three prototypes they had prepared. It was wonderful, rich and creamy, with the distinct taste of Starbucks dark-roasted coffee.

I flashed a look across the table at Behar and said, "You're going to get your wish after all."

It seemed like a big opportunity, good timing, and the right partners. I knew that this product would enhance our brand equity and burnish our image. So I set a goal.

"July Fourth, 1996, nationwide, that's the target," I announced. "Super-premium ice cream, better than Ben and Jerry's, better than Häagen-Dazs. Best of class. Go for it."

Developing a new product at such high speed with a new partner is fraught with potential difficulties, but our legal department helped us work them out. The final products were of a quality that made both sides proud.

When it hit the supermarkets in April, Starbucks ice cream sales blew off the charts. We introduced five gourmet flavors: Italian Roast Coffee, Dark Roast Espresso Swirl, Javachip, Caffè Almond Fudge, and Vanilla Mocha Swirl, adding Low Fat Latte the following year. During the month of July, before we even completed our national rollout to 10,000 grocery stores, we passed Häagen Dazs as the number-one premium coffee ice cream brand in the United States—with very little promotional expense.

The customers voted yes on both ice cream and bottled Frappuccino. People who had never entered a Starbucks store were trying our products.

We were leveraging the equity of the brand, but in a way that was very risky, one that could either reward us handsomely or do great harm. The compressed timetable added to the potential dangers. Other companies might have declined that gamble.

Did we make the right decisions?

Conventional marketing wisdom says that every brand has its limitations. If you slap it on just anything, it will be cheapened beyond recognition. We put the Starbucks brand only on best-of-class products that take advantage of our recognized expertise in coffee.

Ice cream and Frappuccino are almost certain to become profitable and fast-growing businesses for Starbucks, but that's only part of the point. We want to attract new customers to Starbucks, and we want it to be known that this company is not sitting on its haunches. New products show that Starbucks the company is dedicated to innovation and self-renewal.

These opportunities were open to us only because we had already validated the brand at retail, through word-of-mouth reputation with consistently high-quality coffee. Once people came to trust the Starbucks brand, we were free to experiment, within a carefully drawn set of parameters. In fact, we've recently begun testing whole-bean coffee in supermarkets, an outlet we avoided in the early years because grocery-store coffee was generally, and correctly, regarded as inferior. If we had done this before the Starbucks brand was firmly established, it could have hurt us. But now, we are bringing premium whole-bean coffee to markets too scattered or small to merit a dedicated store. Although no barista is present to explain the different blends, many grocery shoppers already know that Starbucks stands for the highest quality of coffee.

All the goodwill and trust we've built up over twenty-five years could evaporate if customers thought these supermarket products were shoddy or mediocre. It's a delicate balance. We have to bring our consciences to the table every day. If we succeed, new products will refresh the brand, not dilute it. The market will always let us know how we're doing.

Living in the same city as Microsoft, I'm only too aware that, even in low-technology businesses like coffee, the Next Big Thing could knock the dominant player into second place tomorrow. I keep pushing to make sure that Starbucks thinks of the Next Big Thing before it has even crossed anybody else's mind. In fact, Don Valencia is working on it even as I'm writing this book.

17
CRISIS OF PRICES, CRISIS OF VALUES

It is by presence of mind in untried emergencies
that the native metal of a man is tested.

—JAMES RUSSELL LOWELL, "ABRAHAM LINCOLN,"
PRINTED IN NORTH AMERICAN REVIEW, JANUARY 1864

THE DAY THE FROST HIT

In June 1994, I awoke one morning to face the worst crisis in Starbucks' history. It came without warning. It was no one's fault, nothing we could have predicted, nothing we knew how to handle.

I had just set off on what I had intended to be my longest vacation in ten years. Sheri had suffered through a series of delayed or canceled vacations as I had become more and more preoccupied with growing the business. But I was finally convinced that Starbucks was in good hands and I could afford to take off a full two weeks. After four years as chief financial officer, Orin Smith had just assumed the responsibilities of president. Neither of us realized that he was about to be tested by fire.

I had rented a cottage on the beach in the Hamptons, not far from where Sheri and I had met, not far from where we were married. The kids would have a chance to spend some time with my mother, my sister Ronnie, my brother Michael and his family, and my other relatives in New York. Our cottage would be like a little island, a refuge in a place where no one knew us, where family and friends could come to visit without the daily demands of work and school. Sheri and the kids planned to stay for a month. I would spend the first two weeks with them, return to Seattle for two weeks, and then fly back to New York to pick them up.

The cottage was everything we had hoped for: a modest white shingle house with a big deck, only a hundred yards from the beach. The sun was shining brightly when we arrived, and the kids jumped into their swimsuits immediately. Sheri was smiling and humming as she got us settled in, the happiest I'd seen her in years. We passed the first two days setting the house up and exploring the town and the beach with the kids.

On our third morning there, Monday, June 27, I called the office to check in—a daily habit that, unfortunately, I've not yet been able to break. I had waited till 11 A.M. so that I could reach Seattle at the start of the West Coast business day. I was standing in the kitchen when I punched in the number, wearing shorts and a loose shirt, looking out over a small backyard where the kids liked to play. I had just come in from shooting baskets with my son and still heard the sound of his dribbling outside.

I heard the note of alarm the instant that Georgette Essad, my assistant, recognized my voice.

"You need to talk to Orin and Dave immediately."

"What's wrong?" I asked.

"You just need to" was all she would tell me.

My stomach clenched as a fast montage of ugly possibilities raced through my imagination. I could tell something serious had happened.

My phone call was patched into a conference room, where Dave Olsen and Orin Smith were waiting for me.

"Howard," Orin said, his normally calm voice pinched, "there's been a severe frost in Brazil. Coffee prices are going crazy."

Brazil? Starbucks didn't even buy any coffee from Brazil. Most Brazilian coffee ends up in cans.

But I understood the significance of that frost immediately. Brazil produces more than a quarter of the world's coffee, and a serious shortfall there would send up prices for coffee everywhere. Because Starbucks buys only top-quality coffee, we normally pay a premium above the commodity price of coffee on the Coffee, Sugar & Cocoa Exchange in New York. The standard bellwether price for green coffee is the widely quoted C contract on that exchange, a composite price for green coffee, and when it goes up, our prices do, too.

That morning, Orin told me, the C contract was shooting straight up; it had just surged from $1.26 to $1.80 a pound, the highest price since 1986, and far above the 80-cent price we had counted on for the first four months of the year. In effect, one of our basic costs of business had doubled, and green coffee prices were still rising. Starbucks' stock price began to drop.

The last time Brazil had had a serious frost, in 1975, coffee prices had soared as high as $3.40 a pound and stayed high for years. That legendary "black frost" had decimated much of Brazil's crop. Back then, Starbucks had only three stores. Now, with 350 stores to supply, we had a huge exposure. What if the price doubled again?

Within five minutes I knew my vacation was over. I would have to take the next available flight to Seattle. Though they didn't ask me to return, we all knew we had to be together to deal with the problem. It wasn't right that Orin, in the first month of his new job, should have to resolve this on his own.

With that call, my whole life changed—not only for the summer but for the year that followed. In fact, it took two full years to finally work through the problems that hit us that day.

I hung up the phone and stood still for a second as the magnitude of the emergency hit me. I called for Sheri, who was in the next room, and she could hear the edge to my voice. When she came into the kitchen I could see, with a pang, that she was both filled with concern and bracing for disappointment.

"You're not going to believe this," I said to her. "I've got to go back to Seattle."

SHOULD WE RAISE OUR PRICES?

I got a flight early the next morning and was in my office at 12:30 P.M. Orin had set up a meeting, so when I walked in I was immediately surrounded by the worried faces of Starbucks' leadership. Our task was to respond to the worst crisis that had confronted us as a team. The fear and uncertainty of everyone in the room were almost tangible. I wanted to reassure them that we could handle this problem, but I was filled with doubts myself.

Seated around the conference table were the managers who represented every major area of responsibility: coffee buying, inventories, roasting, finance, planning, retail operations, mail order, and wholesale. First we needed to understand the breadth of the issues we were facing and the risks involved. The size and scale of Starbucks demanded unusual discipline and sensitivity to things that were not in our control.

Each person gave a status report—a term that in this case was really an oxymoron, since the situation was literally changing, from minute to minute, as coffee prices jumped.

Dave Olsen put the frost in a historical context for us. Ironically, for the past two years, he had been worrying that coffee prices were too low. In the late 1980s, coffee-producing countries in the International Coffee Organization had tried to prop up prices using an export quota system. But in July 1989, that agreement fell apart, and coffee prices dropped to historic lows. The world was awash in coffee as global production reached an all-time high, rising well above the level of consumption. By 1992, the C contract had drifted down to around 50 cents a pound, far below the cost of production.

You'd think that Dave and other coffee buyers would have been pleased with such low prices, but in fact, he was concerned about their negative consequences. Coffee growers around the world couldn't afford to buy fertilizer and didn't bother to prune, so in many regions coffee crops were weakening. Some farmers uprooted their coffee bushes and planted other crops, such as sugar cane. Although that cut world production back sharply, to well below the level of global consumption, the oversupply from earlier years kept prices relatively low for a time. By early 1994, the C contract had risen to only 80 cents, still low by historical standards.

Dave was actually relieved when prices began to rise in April 1994. He had traveled widely and worked for years to forge relationships with coffee growers and exporters, so he had seen firsthand the punishing effect low prices had had on them. More normal prices, he knew, were needed to ensure a continuous supply of quality coffee. In May, the market recovered, to a level above a dollar a pound.

During the time prices were low, Dave had, fortunately, locked in about a ten months' supply of green coffee, through long-term contracts at fixed prices—more for some origin countries, less for others. Buying ahead was our normal strategy of protecting ourselves, the theory being that it was both necessary to ensure our inventories and a good investment for Starbucks' capital. Long-term contracts also allowed us to lock in the more limited supplies of top-quality coffee. Overall, we were in a better position than many specialty coffee companies because we are vertically integrated: We buy and roast all the coffee we sell, rather than purchasing pre-roasted beans from independent roasters.

After the frost hit, I was relieved to hear we had so much inventory on hand. But what if green coffee prices kept rising? Should we buy more coffee now before they rose even further? Those weren't decisions we could make that first day.

Over the next few days, the phones lit up as big shareholders, stock analysts, traders, and reporters called to find out how we were reacting. We had to make some decisions. Would we raise prices? If so, by how much and when? What impact might that have on sales?

The big three roasters, Nestlé, Kraft General Foods, and Procter & Gamble, increased prices immediately on their canned coffee. Between them, they control about 70 percent of the U.S. coffee market. With fewer months' supply on hand and thinner profit margins, they had little choice. The price of Folgers jumped twice that week alone.

We decided not to raise retail prices right away. It wasn't fair to our customers. We remembered how outraged everyone had felt when gasoline companies jacked up prices the minute oil prices rose, to reflect replacement costs, even though they had months of inventory on hand. We decided to wait and see what happened to green coffee prices.

Exactly two weeks after the first shock, we got a second. On July 11, another Monday, I woke up and heard the worst. Brazil had suffered another frost, this one even more bitter. Early estimates had suggested that the first frost had damaged 30 percent of Brazil's crop; this one appeared to have destroyed another 10 percent, at least. Starbucks stock responded by dropping to a three-month low that day.

Within days, the green coffee price jumped to $2.74 a pound — more than 330 percent of the level just three months earlier. To me, it felt like it happened overnight. It was a body blow.

We held daily conferences, hushed and hurried. I don't think most Starbucks people really understood the gravity of the situation and how fearful we were. Earnings had been growing more than 50 percent a year for four years, and Wall Street investors were counting on a continuing stream of profits in coming years. If we failed to meet their expectations, our stock price might drop so low we would have trouble raising funds for future expansion. Traders were now predicting coffee prices might reach $4. All the information we had at hand—about the 1975 frost, about depleted world coffee supplies, about lower production every-where—led us to believe those estimates could well be true.

The big three once again quickly raised their prices.

Inside the company, we debated intensely about whether and when to raise retail prices. Some board members urged caution, saying price hikes tended to be easy, short-term fixes that discouraged the hard work of lowering costs and improving efficiency. They thought it would put us at a competitive disadvantage. But with our main raw-material cost skyrocketing, we had to respond.

On July 13 we announced that we would increase prices by just under 10 percent on July 22. Although coffee drinks went up only 5 cents or 10 cents a cup, our whole-bean coffee prices rose by around $1.25 a pound, on an average price of about $8.50. How would our customers react? Our prices were already higher than supermarket coffees. Would our whole-bean coffee sales volume drop?

We consciously chose a different path than the oil companies and the big packaged goods companies. We did not raise our prices to cover current replacement costs, passing raw material price rises immediately on to the consumer. If we had, our prices would have gone up far more dramatically, as the canned supermarket coffees did. Instead, we tried to offset only our actual cost increases for fiscal year 1995.

During those days, my role was to provide the company with the leadership to instill confidence that we were going to get through this crisis intact. I also took the lead in communicating with the outside world about the problem. We had a lot of constituencies to deal with, not the least of which was Wall Street, where investors worried about the extent to which Starbucks was exposed. They were making bets on the short and long side. With Dave Olsen, I explained the situation to our partners, and then Orin and I discussed it with investors. We made frequent conference calls and left voice-mail updates nationwide, as well as posting signs in our stores, trying to keep people abreast of the situation.

What we tried to do with our customers was to honestly and directly explain that our costs had risen and we had no choice but to pass on a certain amount to them in order to continue to do business. We were fortunate in that the relationship we had built with our customers and most importantly with our partners gave us license to do what we needed to do. For the most part, they responded by being willing to pay higher prices for coffee they knew was best of class.

THE LONG-TERM COST OF SHORT-TERM DECISIONS

Behind the scenes, we had other tough decisions to make. Should we buy more coffee at current prices, lest they surge even higher? Or would $2.74 be the peak, and would it be better to wait and buy at lower levels? When the market was at 80 cents, we had dreamed of 70 cents and worried about $1. Now that the market was around $2.50, we dreamed of $2 and worried about $4.

The issue came to a head on one tense day in July, when we had to decide whether to commit to buying a substantial quantity— thousands of bags—of Colombian coffee. At these high levels, it was a multimillion-dollar decision, three times the amount of money we would have paid for the same coffee a few months earlier. The purchase could be either a wise hedge against even higher prices or a disastrous obligation incurred at the top of the market.

While we all agonized, Orin's calm manner and training in financial markets helped maintain our equilibrium. "It's futile to try to outguess the market," he advised. "Let's look at it this way. Assume there are two equally likely risks: On the one hand, the coffee price might go higher; on the other, it might go lower. Which is a more acceptable risk?" We debated and finally agreed that it would be better to go long, buying extra inventory at current prices. If the price were to fall, Orin reasoned, we'd be stuck with high-priced contracts, but we could manage through it. If it were to rise to $4, we would definitely fail to meet our financial expectations. So we insured ourselves against a further increase. We also examined the option of hedging our long position against a price decrease, but the cost was prohibitive.

As it happened, we purchased that batch of Colombian coffee at what turned out to be nearly the peak. That summer we also had to buy other types of coffee, in smaller quantities, to fill in specific inventories that were low. It took two years to work through all the high-priced coffee in our warehouse.

After July, green coffee prices came down. What we hadn't understood at the time was the degree to which speculative trading had driven up prices. When the speculators dropped out of the market, the price retracted quickly relative to how it had behaved in earlier years. Within a few months, we saw a price more reflective of supply and demand, close to $1.10 by year's end.

Because we bought coffee in July 1995, we were left with a high-priced inventory that lasted so long that we had to raise prices slightly again the following year. That decision was hard to explain to our customers, who didn't realize we had protected them against the full impact of the increase after the frosts. But given what we knew, we made our decision the right way.

Despite the burden we had taken on, there was never any finger-pointing or attempts to place the blame for the ill-timed purchase. Given the tremendous fear and confusion and concerns that were affecting us all, it was important that we keep our balance through absolute harmony and trust in one another.

To me, what's even more remarkable about our decisions during those tense months of June and July is that we never once wavered in our dedication to providing the highest quality coffee. The easiest thing for us to have done, without question, would have been to tell Dave Olsen and Mary Williams, our coffee buyers, "Okay, the time has come. We want you to start buying lower-quality coffee. We have to keep costs under control and protect our profit margins." That conversation never took place; no one even considered it as an alternative. We could also have tried the tactic other companies seemed to be using: blending high-grade coffee with cheaper beans and raising the price anyway. Many customers would not have noticed the difference. We would have saved a ton of money, but we would have had a different kind of crisis on our hands.

. . . AND LONG-TERM BENEFITS

Once prices started to fall, the immediate crisis was over. But a messy aftermath now awaited us. We did not charge the customer for the full financial burden, so how could we meet our earnings targets?

Orin came up with a game plan, insisting we could find the answer in our backroom. We could make up for the increased green-coffee cost by becoming more efficient and taking advantage of economies of scale. He called it the "profit improvement plan."

I was skeptical at first. Starbucks had never before turned to the backroom for cost savings and efficiencies. When you're growing at 50 percent a year, you can't cut back on the support side. You need the flexibility of those systems. Many of our hardest-working, most committed partners were working in less visible jobs in accounting, legal, finance and planning, production, and management information systems. They were already feeling the strains of rapid growth; it seemed unfair to ask them to do more with less. But we had no alternative.

Putting his plan into action is where Orin really began to demonstrate his leadership skills. He hired an expert to direct the effort, formed committees, and began holding regular meetings with every department. He transformed the crisis into an opportunity to begin to manage the company in a more systematic, professional way. We discovered that there were a lot of synergies we weren't taking advantage of, chances to renegotiate contracts, to lower other costs, to plan better, to work smarter, to use our resources more wisely. We probably would have gotten around to making these improvements sooner or later, but this emergency forced us to recognize, earlier than we might have, the need for a tighter ship.

We knew that many of the savings would have to come from our warehouses and roasting plants. Ted Garcia, who joined us from Pillsbury to take over supply-chain operations in April 1995, had already begun to raise our roasting, packaging, and distribution operations to a world-class level. He led an effort to install state-of-the-art, computer-integrated manufacturing systems that improved our efficiency and lowered cost-per-pound by 8 to 10 percent a year for three years. At the same time, our manufacturing was becoming more complex, as we began to need many new package sizes as well as more ground coffee for United Airlines and other large customers. Ted's group also cut transportation costs and paper-cup costs significantly by renegotiating contracts. He set a five-year goal to continue lowering costs through the year 2000, without compromising quality.

Although not anywhere near as visible or dramatic as jumping into the ice cream or music business, what Orin and his team accomplished that year was firmly in Starbucks' tradition of defying the odds.

The high-priced coffee inventories didn't start hitting the bottom line until a year later, in the fall of 1995. Quarter after quarter, Wall Street analysts doubted that we'd make our numbers. Some quarters it was touch and go. But by the end of fiscal 1996, we had sold almost all of the high-priced coffee, and earnings for fiscal 1996 hit the mark. We signed on some large-volume customers during the year, but the main reason was the slow, methodical process of trimming costs, rooting out inefficiencies, and improving processes.

I've always been struck by the irony that a business is more likely to attract attention when it loses money, or lays people off, or fails spectacularly. Pundits can wisely analyze what went wrong and what should have been done. But pundits are not as proficient at analyzing success. What does it take to achieve 50 percent annual growth in both sales and profits for six years in a row? What enabled Starbucks to do that was a combination of discipline and innovation, process and creativity, caution and boldness that few companies have mastered.

When Starbucks made its numbers after two years of working through a crisis of such magnitude, I was elated. So was Orin. But no one asked us: How on earth did you accomplish that?

It may sound trite, but I believe that managing through the coffee-price crisis made Starbucks a better company. It made us aware of our vulnerabilities and it forced us to develop skills we hadn't possessed.

Starbucks reached maturity that summer. Before 1994, everything we touched turned to gold. Every time we tried something daring, it succeeded. When this crisis hit us, without warning, it forged our managers, a group that included many new senior executives recruited from other companies, into a well-bonded team. It demonstrated Orin's courage under fire and forced me to learn a new dimension of management.

Great companies need both a visionary leader and a skilled executive: one for the top line, the other for the bottom line. As *Fortune's* Ronald Henkoff wrote in November 1996, "The businesses that thrive over the long haul are likely to be those that understand that cost cutting and revenue growing aren't mutually exclusive. Eternal vigilance to both the top and bottom lines is the new ticket to prosperity."

It humbled me to realize how vulnerable we could be to outside forces that could instantly and dramatically change the course of the company. It taught me that we had to be in a constant state of preparation and vigilance. You can't manage just for the known; you have to manage for the unknown as well. Starbucks today is more prepared for the unknown crisis around the corner because it faced this one down.

When coffee prices again doubled in early 1997, we had a clearer idea of what it takes to weather such a storm. That time we knew how to calculate the costs, and we understood the need to take action while the news events were still fresh in the minds of our customers. Again, our increase covered only the incremental costs, not the replacement costs, of the higher-priced coffee.

The more profound lesson of the 1994 crisis hit me months after the event. What if we had opted for the easy solution and cut corners on our coffee?

We could save millions of dollars every year if we bought even slightly cheaper coffee. Starbucks spends more money per pound of coffee than almost any company in the world, even though probably fewer than 10 percent of our customers can tell the difference.

If you can raise profits by shaving costs on your main product and 90 percent of your customers wouldn't even notice, why not just do it?

Because *we* can tell the difference. Inside Starbucks, we know what great coffee tastes like. Authenticity is what we stand for. It's part of who we are. If we compromise who we are to achieve higher profits, what have we achieved? Eventually all our customers would figure out that we had sacrificed our quality, and they would no longer have a reason to walk that extra block for Starbucks.

But long before that happened, all of us inside Starbucks would have realized it, too. What, then, would keep us coming into work every day? Higher profits, at the cost of poorer quality? The best people would leave. Morale would fall. The mistake would eventually catch up with us. And the chase would be over.

Every business has a memory. The memory of sacrificing quality for profit would have been fixed in the minds of Starbucks people forever. It would have been an impossible price to pay.

18

THE BEST WAY TO BUILD A BRAND IS ONE PERSON AT A TIME

What comes from the heart, goes to the heart.

—SAMUEL TAYLOR COLERIDGE, TABLE TALK

In early 1988, during Starbucks' first winter in Chicago, I remember standing in an elevator and seeing customers carrying our cups, the distinctive green logo hidden behind their fingers. The brand name Starbucks meant nothing to them.

Six years later, when we opened our first store in Manhattan, a line formed immediately for espresso drinks; by 8:30 A.M., it snaked out the door. Why did so many New Yorkers choose to come to Starbucks that day?

Across North America, as we entered city after city, we attracted near-capacity crowds. In Atlanta, in Houston, in Toronto—each time we entered a new region, no matter how many miles from the nearest Starbucks location, people lined up on Day One. It wouldn't have made sense to advertise in our new markets; we couldn't have handled any more traffic than we got.

Our brand had achieved visibility and favor across the United States and Canada, but would it appeal in Japan? In August 1996, I flew halfway around the world to find out. Starbucks International was about to open its first store in Tokyo, on a visible corner location in the high-fashion Ginza District. Once again, we spent no money on advertising. What could the name *Starbucks* possibly mean to the Japanese? Tokyo has a coffee shop on almost every corner, not to mention a competitor with more than 500 stores. The odds against success were formidable.

On opening day, I was wilting in the 95-degree weather and almost 100 percent humidity. I had no idea Tokyo could be so hot. Yet from the minute the store opened until it closed, customers lined up forty to fifty people deep for a taste of Starbucks coffee. Men in dark business suits, women with elegant silk scarves, students with backpacks, all stood patiently in the unforgiving heat. Some of them ordered a blended Frappuccino, just a year after we invented the drink. We had been warned that, culturally, the Japanese refuse to carry to-go food or beverages on the street. Yet many customers were walking out the door proudly carrying their Starbucks cups—with the logo showing.

I stood there watching with Howard Behar, architect of our international expansion. He turned to me with tears in his eyes. The Starbucks brand had the same power in Tokyo that it had in New York and Seattle. It had taken on a life of its own.

STRONG BRANDS CREATE A POWERFUL PERSONAL CONNECTION

We never set out to build a brand. Our goal was to build a great company, one that stood for something, one that valued the authenticity of its product and the passion of its people. In the early days, we were so busy selling coffee, one cup at a time, opening stores and educating people about dark-roasted coffee that we never thought much about "brand strategy."

Then one day I started getting calls. "Can you come and tell us how you built a national brand in only five years?" It was unusual, people told me, for a brand to burst onto the national conscious-ness as quickly as Starbucks had. In some cities, it seemed to catch on overnight. When I looked back, I realized we had fashioned a brand in a way no business-school textbook could ever have pre-scribed.

We built the Starbucks brand first with our people, not with con-sumers—the opposite approach from that of the crackers-and-cereal companies. Because we believed the best way to meet and exceed the expectations of customers was to hire and train great people, we invested in employees who were zealous about good coffee. Their passion and commitment made our retail partners our best ambassadors for the coffee and for the brand. Their knowl-edge and fervor created a buzz among customers and inspired them to come back. That's the secret of the power of the Starbucks brand: the personal attachment our partners feel and the connec-tion they make with our customers.

I've learned a lot about great brands from Jamie Shennan, the Starbucks board member who has devised marketing strategies for Procter & Gamble, Anheuser-Busch, Pepsi, and General Foods. He invested in the company in 1990 because he believed Starbucks was already becoming a powerful brand. Great brands, he says, have a distinctive, memorable identity, a product that makes people look or feel better, and a strong but comfortable delivery channel, which in Starbucks' case was the store. To suc-ceed, you need to be in a category large enough to be robust and vibrant and to have a clear and original vision. All of these factors are essential, he says, but they fuse only if the management team can execute well. Jamie thinks Starbucks can eventually become as widely known as Coke around the world.

Most national brands in America are marketing-driven. Although my background is in marketing, that hasn't been the engine that drives Starbucks—at least not in the traditional sense. In the ten years after 1987, we spent less than $10 million on adver-tising, not because we didn't believe in it but because we couldn't afford it. Instead, we've been product-driven, people-driven, values-driven.

If you look for wisdom on brand marketing, most of what you'll find is based on the Procter & Gamble model. That is, you go after mass markets with mass distribution and mass advertising, and then focus on grabbing market share from your competitors. That's the basic way of life for mature products in established markets. If Pepsi gains a point or two, Coke loses. The same is true of cars and cigarette brands. The big packaged-goods companies spend many millions of dollars and design highly innovative ad campaigns with the goal of gaining a few percentage points of market share.

At Starbucks, we have a different approach. We're creating something new. We're expanding and defining the market. We didn't set out to steal customers away from Folgers or Maxwell House or Hills Brothers. We didn't go for the widest possible distribution. We set out, rather, to educate our customers about the romance of coffee drinking. We wanted to introduce them to fine coffees the way wine stewards bring forward fine wines. Just as they might discuss the characteristics of a wine grown in a specific region or district of France, we want our baristas to be able to intelligently explain the flavors of Kenya and Costa Rica and Sulawesi.

Starbucks built up brand loyalty one customer at a time, communicated through our people, in the setting of company-owned retail stores. Today, even managers of big consumer brands are starting to realize that if you can control your own distribution, you will not find yourself at the mercy of a retailer who may or may not understand your product. It's an enormously effective way to build an authentic brand, but it's certainly not the easiest way.

About 80 percent of the coffee sold in the United States is purchased on supermarket aisles. But from the beginning, we left these traditional channels to others and concentrated our efforts instead on our own retail stores in highly visible, high-traffic downtown sites and residential neighborhoods. We located in lobbies and on the going-to-work side of the street. We attracted people and got them to try our whole-bean coffee by first romancing them with espresso drinks.

Our competitive advantage over the big coffee brands turned out to be our people. Supermarket sales are nonverbal and impersonal, with no personal interaction. But in a Starbucks store, you encounter real people who are informed and excited about the coffee, and enthusiastic about the brand. Which brand name are you most likely to remember?

Today, there's a lot of marketing rhetoric about adding value to products. At Starbucks, the value was there from the beginning, in the coffee itself. When your average sale is only $3.50, you have to make sure customers come back. And ours do—on average eighteen times a month.

Starbucks certainly wasn't the first company to build a reputation through retail stores. Hundreds of local specialty retailers in cities everywhere do the same thing. Your local pizza shop may take pride in its unique spicy sauce. Or you may know a Chinese restaurant that has authentic *dim sum*, with a great chef from Hong Kong. Or you may frequent a local bookstore because the owner will special order obscure books for you. The point is, you know from experience, or from word of mouth, that they're the best in town.

Traditionally, local retailers have always thrived by differentiating themselves from the competition and by winning loyal customers with products or services or quality unobtainable nearby. What's extraordinary about Starbucks is that we used that model to become a national company and then leveraged our brand reputation beyond our stores, to wholesale and food-service channels as well as to new products sold through grocery stores and other outlets.

Starbucks' success proves that a multimillion-dollar advertising program isn't a prerequisite for building a national brand—nor are the deep pockets of a big corporation. You can do it one customer at a time, one store at a time, one market at a time. In fact, that may be the best way to inspire loyalty and trust in customers. By word of mouth, with patience and discipline, over a period of years, you can elevate a good local brand to a great national brand—one that remains relevant to individual customers and communities for years.

AUTHENTICITY MAKES BRANDS LAST

In this ever-changing society, the most powerful and enduring brands are built from the heart. They are real and sustainable. Their foundations are stronger because they are built with the strength of the human spirit, not an ad campaign. The companies that are lasting are those that are authentic.

Take Nike as an example. Few people remember that Phil Knight disdained advertising for years, preferring event promotions and athlete endorsements. He built Nike's reputation on the basis of authenticity, focusing on how its shoes improved athletic performance. Long after running shoes became a fashion statement and street wear, Nike continued to highlight technical superiority. Long after Nike became known for its megamillion-dollar award-winning TV ad campaigns, the company still embraced its legacy as the shoe of choice of the best athletes.

By contrast, take Gloria Jean's, a coffee company started near Chicago, which began franchising nationwide in 1986. By late 1991, it was ahead of Starbucks, with 120 stores, compared to our 110. But Gloria Jean's never developed the loyalty Starbucks did, and ownership ended up changing hands several times. One reason is that the company franchised the concept in more than 100 cities across the country, and each isolated franchise failed to create strong loyalty among customers. More fundamentally, though, the company never established a word-of-mouth reputation for authenticity and quality.

Mass advertising can help build brands, but authenticity is what makes them last. If people believe they share values with a company, they will stay loyal to a brand.

• • •

THE STARBUCKS BRAND
IS MORE THAN COFFEE

The number-one factor in creating a great, enduring brand is hav-ing an appealing product. There's no substitute.

In Starbucks' case, our product is a lot more than coffee. Customers choose to come to us for three reasons: our coffee, our people, and the experience in our stores.

Romancing the bean. Nothing matters more in our business than the taste of the coffee. We are fanatical about buying the high-est-quality arabica coffees in the world and roasting them to the desired flavor characteristics for each variety. It's become a bench-mark for us; everything else we do has to be as good as our coffee.

We make much of the romance of coffee buying, telling the story of how Dave Olsen and Mary Williams travel to origin coun-tries and talk to growers. But ultimately, the point is not the mys-tique but the performance in the cup.

Coffee is easily ruined. Even if you buy the right beans, they can go stale on the shelf, be under- or over-roasted, brewed improperly, or served lukewarm. We are fastidious about making sure nothing goes wrong any step of the way.

Behind the scenes, our retail partners go to great lengths to ensure our coffee stays fresh and flavorful. We keep the beans in vacuum-sealed bags or dark drawers to minimize the harmful effects of air, light, and moisture. We grind them to a precise level of coarseness or fineness depending on how they'll be brewed. Then we measure the proportions of coffee and water according to exacting standards. If a barista-in-training takes less than eighteen or more than twenty-three seconds to pull a shot of espresso, we ask him or her to keep trying until the timing is right.

Because 98 percent of coffee is water, bad water can ruin the taste of even the best coffee beans. So, behind the counter in every store, where most customers can't even see it, we even have a special water filtration system. Each of these careful steps adds to our cost of operation, but they make a difference customers can taste and guarantee a standard of flavor and quality that is consistent from store to store and region to region.

Romancing the customer. Dave Olsen has a saying: "Coffee without people is a theoretical construct. People without coffee are somewhat diminished as well."

And Howard Behar has another: "We're not in the coffee business serving people. We're in the people business serving coffee."

It's our partners who pass on to customers their knowledge and passion about Starbucks. If we greet customers, exchange a few extra words with them, and then custom-make a drink exactly to their taste, they will be eager to come back.

So much of the retailing experience in America is mediocre. At the dry cleaner or the supermarket or the bank, you're reduced to a number, or a credit card, or a personal identification code. You're just one transaction in a file of consumers that come before you and after you.

But when you meet with an experience at a higher level, where you are treated positively, where someone goes out of her way to make you feel special, where you're welcomed with a smile and assumed to be intelligent, the experience stands out.

Because we entrust the Starbucks brand to the hands of the baristas, it's vitally important that we hire great people and imbue them with our passion for coffee. We do that through a training program whose sophistication and depth are rare in retail.

For years, Starbucks spent more on training our people than on advertising our product. We've continually refined the twenty-four hours of training we offer to each hire. Every new barista has to take some basic courses in Coffee Knowledge (four hours), Brewing the Perfect Cup (four hours), and Customer Service (four hours), as well as classes in basic orientation and retail skills. From their first day, we try to immerse them in our values-centered culture, showing them the importance of treating customers and one another with respect and dignity. Our trainers are all store managers or district managers themselves, with on-site experience. We train baristas to make eye contact with customers, to anticipate their needs, to explain the different coffees simply and clearly, and to compensate dissatisfied customers with a *Starbuck* coupon that will get them a free drink.

Each time we open stores in a new market, we undertake a major recruitment effort. Eight to ten weeks before opening, we place ads to hire baristas and start their training. We send a Star Team of experienced managers and baristas from existing stores and use a buddy system for one-on-one training.

We also encourage a dialogue with customers by providing comment cards in each store. Typically, we receive about 150 responses a month. About half the comments are negative, 30 percent are positive, and the remainder are questions or requests. The number-one complaint is about long lines. Some customers identify with us so strongly that they write lengthy, eloquent letters, whose tones range from the sublime to the horrific. One man wrote a three-page, single-spaced epic about a tense drive to the hospital with his pregnant wife, and how a latte had eased the stress. To respond thoughtfully to such comments, we asked one of our longest-tenured employees, Barbara Reed, to set up a customer relations function in 1992. She had joined the company in 1982 as a barista, managed the Pike Place store for many years, and worked as a district manager in Canada, so she was familiar with the realities of customer service at the store level.

Romancing all the senses in the store experience. At Starbucks, our product is not just great coffee but also what we call the "Starbucks experience": an inviting, enriching environment in our stores that is comfortable and accessible yet also stylish and elegant.

More and more, I realize, customers are looking for a Third Place, an inviting, stimulating, sometimes even soulful respite from the pressures of work and home. People come to Starbucks for a refreshing time-out, a break in their busy days, a personal treat. Their visit has to be rewarding. If any detail is wrong, the brand suffers. That's why we love the saying, "Everything matters."

In effect, our stores are our billboards. Customers form an impression of the Starbucks brand the minute they walk in the door. The ambience we create there has as much to do with brand-building as the quality of the coffee.

Every Starbucks store is carefully designed to enhance the quality of everything the customers see, touch, hear, smell, or taste. All the sensory signals have to appeal to the same high standards. The artwork, the music, the aromas, the surfaces all have to send the same subliminal message as the flavor of the coffee: *Everything here is best-of-class*.

What's the first thing you notice when you approach a Starbucks store? Almost always, it's the aroma. Even non–coffee drinkers love the smell of brewing coffee. It's heady, rich, full-bodied, dark, suggestive. Aroma triggers memories more strongly than any of the other senses, and it obviously plays a major role in attracting people to our stores.

Keeping that coffee aroma pure is no easy task. Because coffee beans have a bad tendency to absorb odors, we banned smoking in our stores years before it became a national trend. We ask our partners to refrain from using perfume or cologne. We won't sell chemically flavored coffee beans. We won't sell soup, sliced pastrami, or cooked food. We want you to smell coffee only.

The sounds that fill our stores also contribute to the brand image. Until recently, our signature music has been classical or jazz instrumentals, but lately Timothy Jones has started to vary the musical mood with opera, blues, reggae, even Broadway show tunes. But music is only one element of what you hear. After you place your order, you'll usually hear the cashier call out the name of your drink, and then hear it echoed back by the barista. The hiss of the espresso machine, the clunk-clunk as the barista knocks the coffee grounds out of the filter, the bubbling of the milk steaming in a metal pitcher, and, at the bean counter, the swish of the metal scoop shoveling out a half-pound of beans, the clatter as they hit the scale—for our customers, these are all familiar, comforting sounds.

To match the warm feel of the cup in their hands, we have to pay attention to everything the customers touch: the style of the chairs, the edges of the countertops, the texture of the slate floors. Even cleanliness is part of the store experience, and it's one factor we monitor regularly, using "mystery shoppers" who pose as customers and rate each location on a series of criteria.

We build the romance of coffee into the visual design of every store. Many include displays of coffee beans at different stages of roasting, from the green raw beans to the cinnamon roast used for most canned coffee to the dark Starbucks roast—with an explanation of why we believe in roasting dark. Our latest store design brings the coffee beans out from their drawers and into large metal hoppers, a feature that piques people's curiosity and gets them asking questions.

We keep our look fresh by designing colorful banners and posters to evoke specific moods during different seasons, enriching the Starbucks brand with visual impact and interest. We receive hundreds of requests from customers for copies of their favorite posters, the most popular of which included an early one of Sumatra tigers and three original images of the siren we commissioned for our twenty-fifth anniversary from artists known in 1971 for their psychedelic imagery. We even use the cups themselves to carry messages, including three "chapters" of our history printed on cups during our twenty-fifth anniversary celebration.

The way merchandise is displayed also reflects on the brand. We pore over every detail and have great debates about whether or not to offer various products: Do bags of polenta reinforce or harm the brand image? Wristwatches? Jelly beans? We even work directly with Italian artisans to create original designs and hand-paint our mugs.

Authentic brands do not emerge from marketing cubicles or advertising agencies. They emanate from everything the company does, from store design and site selection to training, production, packaging, and merchandise buying. In companies with strong brands, every senior manager has to evaluate each decision by asking: "Will it strengthen or dilute the brand?"

CAN YOU REALLY BUILD A BRAND BY WORD OF MOUTH?

In Seattle, it took fifteen years for great whole-bean coffee to catch on. It took five years for espresso drinks. Yet, somehow, we underestimated how much time we would need to capture imaginations in other cities.

When we went into Chicago in 1987, we were so confident that we had developed a captivating formula that we took it for granted that customers would automatically come flocking. What we hadn't taken into account, however, was that our word-of-mouth reputation had not preceded us. Few people outside Seattle knew what Starbucks stood for.

From that experience, we learned that it wasn't enough to simply open our stores and assume customers would come. We had to create advance excitement in each city we prepared to enter. How could we get people to start talking about Starbucks the day we opened our first store in their neighborhood? With each market we entered, we learned new techniques, so that by 1994 and 1995, when we rapidly accelerated the number of new market openings, we had developed a multi-pronged approach.

Jennifer Tisdel, our vice president for retail marketing since 1992, organized a market entry strategy that began by hiring a local public relations firm to help us understand the heritage and concerns of a given city. Early in our store-opening sequence we always picked a flagship site, a very visible location in a busy part of the city, to build a high-profile store, such as those in Dupont Circle in Washington, D.C., and Astor Place in New York's Greenwich Village.

At the same time, our creative people designed artwork that celebrated each city's personality, whether it was Paul Revere and the name Beantown for Boston, twin coffee cups for the Twin Cities, a peach-shaped coffee cup for Atlanta, or New York's Statue of Liberty drinking coffee. We used the artwork on commuter mugs, T-shirts, and invitations for our partners and customers.

Unlike most other retail stores, coffeehouses are places where people naturally come together, so we try to integrate our stores into the fabric of their local communities. For each new market, we planned at least one big community event to celebrate our arrival, with the proceeds going to a local charity. In Boston and Atlanta, Kenny G gave benefit concerts, to which we invited local leaders.

Before each opening, we assembled a list of people who could serve as local "ambassadors" for Starbucks. We started by asking our partners if they had friends or family in that city, whom we then invited to pre-opening or Grand Opening events, along with local shareholders, mail-order customers, and sponsors of CARE or other causes we support. We sent them each two free-drink coupons with a note asking them to "Share Starbucks with a friend." We held tastings with local reporters, food critics, chefs, and owners of well-regarded restaurants. To give our baristas a chance to practice, we let them invite their friends and family to pre-opening parties, where the coffee and pastries were free, with a suggested $3 donation to a local nonprofit group. Finally, we'd throw a Grand Opening party, usually the Saturday after the store opened, sometimes with thousands attending.

Community events and sponsorships became an ongoing part of our marketing work, in part to build awareness but also because we believe it's the right thing to do. In addition to our support of CARE, we try to be sensitive to local issues, with our main emphasis on supporting AIDS programs; children's causes, especially children's hospitals; the environment, with a focus on clean water; and the arts, especially jazz and film festivals. For the past several years, 300 to 400 Starbucks partners and customers have marched in Seattle's annual AIDS walk. We have also developed a partnership with Doernbecher Children's Hospital in Portland that included selling specially designed commuter mugs; sponsored film festivals in Toronto, San Francisco, and Seattle; and raised money for Rhode Island's Save the Bay project. These activities, only a few of hundreds we've sponsored, grow directly out of our Mission Statement, which states our commitment to "contribute positively to our communities and our environment." Not only do these sponsorships create goodwill, but they also have a positive effect internally, making our partners proud to be associated with a company that gives back.

In the weeks after each opening, we often set up a reward system to thank our customers for their repeat business. Starting in 1993, we issued *passports* that entitled customers to a free half-pound of coffee once they had taken a *world tour* by trying coffee beans from different origin countries. In other cities, we invited them to try five different beverages, after which they were given a free local market tumbler.

We also offer company-wide printed in-store materials, which provide information for customers interested in learning more about coffee. Each store carries a display of brochures, including *The World of Coffee*, which details the different tastes of each type of whole-bean coffee we sell; *The Best Coffee at Home*, on how to grind and brew whole-bean coffee; and *A Quick Guide to Starbucks Specialty Beverages*, with diagrams explaining such drinks as cappuccino and caffè latte.

In addition, we publish and distribute *Coffee Matters*, a monthly newsletter focusing on the romance and culture of coffee through the ages. We use our annual reports to tell our story as well, from sections on "romancing the bean" and the "art of roasting" in 1992 through the innovative and unusual design of our twenty-fifth anniversary annual report in 1996. Another key contributor to brand-building has been our mail-order catalogue, which allows direct communication with customers. Our 800 number provides them with immediate access to coffee experts who can knowledgeably discuss the difference between Sumatra and Sulawesi, Gold Coast and Yukon blends.

With the rapid pace of expansion, our marketing people in Seattle can no longer monitor local needs and interests as well as people in the field. In response, we have decentralized our marketing efforts, with twelve partners in four zones scattered across the United States, handling store openings, events, and sponsorships for their regions and helping ensure our company-wide efforts are relevant on a local level.

Because Starbucks delivered a higher standard at a time when so many other retailers were lowering expectations, it has emerged as a beacon in the retail business. A typical customer might say, "Wow! I come in here and I'm treated so well. And when I come back the next day, they know my name and they know my drink! And there's a seat here, and I'm listening to jazz, and I can close my eyes and have five minutes of rest away from work and away from home. I can do it every day, and it's for me, and it's only a dollar fifty or two dollars. I can't afford a vacation to Hawaii, but this is something I can treat myself to! And I can afford it every day."

Enthusiastically satisfied customers like that are the power behind our word-of-mouth strategy. If every new store can evoke that kind of reaction, the Starbucks brand will stand for a meaningful, personal experience no matter how ubiquitous we become.

BRAND-BUILDING OUTSIDE OUR STORES

Today, the Starbucks brand is outgrowing the walls of our stores. Increasingly, people are encountering our coffee on airlines, on cruise ships, in bookstores, in supermarkets. That broader exposure has forced us to rethink our brand positioning.

Aside from restaurants and airports, we long refused to let anyone sell Starbucks brand coffee. To protect the brand, we especially refused to make it available at drugstores, convenience stores, or gas stations. In 1993, though, Nordstrom agreed to sell our coffee. With its reputation for top-quality clothing and superior service, Nordstrom was the kind of strategic partner who, we felt certain, would enhance, not dilute, our brand. Later, when we picked supermarkets to locate kiosks in, we aimed to find ones with the top reputation in their markets, such as Quality Food Centers in Seattle.

Now that we have such new products as ice cream and bottled Frappuccino, both of which are sold in supermarkets, an innovative approach to graphics is even more crucial. Our Frappuccino bottles evoke the milk bottles of yesteryear, but are decorated with a pattern of stars and swirls that promises an unexpected taste. When we reached bottling capacity constraints, we had to consider putting Frappuccino in an aluminum can. It was a tough call, since cans connote mainstream soft drinks. But once again, we created a great design in keeping with the brand equity of Starbucks and the sub-brand of Frappuccino.

Perhaps the most intense internal debate we have had regarding product design came over our ice cream packaging. One group argued that since Starbucks was entering unfamiliar territory, we should use the well-known brand graphics and sell the ice cream in white packages with the green logo, or in the familiar terracotta-and-charcoal colors of our coffee bags, with the steam pattern. Ice cream was enough of an innovation; we should pick something familiar and proven for packaging.

But another group argued that we ought to seize every opportunity to push the brand further with a new design that was bold and fresh and as playful and fun as eating ice cream. Using the existing design, they feared, would be admitting, "This is as good as we can get."

Ultimately, the innovative, playful approach won out. We adopted a bolder look developed by Terry Heckler, with a field of swirls and stars against a background of browns and oranges and yellows. I saw it as a chance to step out, instead of just stepping in place.

The Starbucks brand image has even affected the design of our offices. In 1997, when we redesigned our building and named it Starbucks Center, we wanted it to reflect a new sense of playfulness. When we took down the SODO sign on the clock tower of our building, we replaced it with the head of the Starbucks siren, peeking out over the top of the building. Now everyone visiting our offices, which were once unmarked and invisible from the street, will be treated to the sight of a tall tower topped by a pair of eyes and a starred crown.

Even though few of our customers ever visit our offices, our redesign reflects a new spirit that Starbucks is taking on as we move beyond our retail base. As fanatical as we remain about coffee and the store experience, we also want people to realize that Starbucks has a sense of humor and a playful side, a well-rounded personality with both exuberance and irreverence, one that can connect with people at many levels and in many moods.

ELEVATING THE BRAND TO A NEW LEVEL

By 1995, the Starbucks brand faced an identity crisis. Although we had built a reputation based on world-class coffee and a meaningful connection with people, the field was getting so crowded that some customers couldn't differentiate us from scores of competitors. Distracted by our size and ubiquity, they missed the point about our quality and commitment to community.

Clearly, word of mouth was no longer sufficient to get our message out. As long as we didn't clearly state what we stood for, we left room for confusion about our intentions.

We've always relied on our coffee to speak for itself. Gradually, though, we realized that we had to be more proactive in telling our story. Walking down the street you may pass two or three coffee places. How are you to know which one serves the best espresso drinks? How can you tell which one roasts its own coffee and sends its buyers all over the world, searching for the best beans? By the mid-1990s, we needed a better way to articulate our story and to weave it into a more comprehensive image, one that encompassed our soul and vision.

Great brands always stand for something far bigger than themselves. The Disney name connotes fun, family, and entertainment. Nike signifies superior athletic performance. Microsoft aims to bring a computer to every desktop. I wanted to raise Starbucks to the next level, to make it stand for something even more than a great cup of coffee and a warm, inviting atmosphere.

As we grew larger, it became clear that we needed a dedicated brand champion, someone whose responsibility it would be to clarify and elevate the Starbucks message. I had always taken a direct and active role myself in marketing and merchandising, because they are so closely integrated into the value of everything we do as a company. But by 1994, I was looking for a new senior marketing executive, and I wanted it to be someone who had already taken a brand to national, or even global, prominence. I left the top marketing position empty for eighteen months while we searched for the right person.

It proved to be a difficult job to fill. The right candidate had to be someone classically trained in marketing, who could both unveil the brand personality of Starbucks and bring it to life, working with the other departments of the company. It had to be someone who had both a creative mind and the ability to execute a strategy. In addition, I wanted someone I could learn from, someone who was considered to be the best and the brightest in brand development and marketing. The future of the Starbucks brand, I knew, would be in this person's hands.

In February 1995 I found Scott Bedbury in a cabin in snowy central Oregon, writing a book about unlocking the creative process in business. He had worked as Nike's director of advertising from 1987 to November 1994, the years when "Bo Knows" and "Just Do It" became part of America's vocabulary. Having just gone independent, he had written me a letter, offering to work as a marketing consultant. I had a different plan in mind.

"Yo!" he answered the phone, thinking it was his wife.

"Is that Scott Bedbury? This is Howard Schultz."

"Oh, hi!" he greeted me, and then laughed. "You won't believe this, but I just wrote a passage about Starbucks in my book."

He read me the piece, an entire page filled with good insights. He sounded young, bright, hip, energetic. He talked fast, the ideas spilling over one another. I invited him to Seattle so we could meet face to face.

Less than two weeks later, Scott was in my office, trying to sell himself as a consultant. He dressed in an impeccable casual style, as he always does, and his blue eyes flashed as he talked. He looked even younger than his thirty-seven years, like someone who would be in tune with the styles and needs of the twenty-something generation. He talked with excitement about his new consulting business and about the three other potential clients he had lined up.

Within five minutes, I turned the tables on him. "I really don't need a consultant," I told him. "What I need is someone to be our head of marketing."

He was taken aback. He had already planned his life out for the next twenty years. But he eventually accepted, and by June he had moved his family to Seattle and was beginning to think about a long-term marketing strategy for Starbucks.

Scott immediately found himself challenged by the fact that Starbucks is not only a brand but also an importer, a manufacturer, a retailer, a wholesaler, and a direct-mail business. No company that he knew of had done all five and survived. But he found some surprising similarities with Nike, too. Like Nike, Starbucks had entered a low-margin commodity industry and transformed its product into a cultural symbol. And I was surprised to hear that Nike, too, had started out by building its brand one customer at a time. Phil Knight initially hired running zealots to sell Nike shoes at track meets out of the trunks of their cars.

When Scott had joined Nike in 1987, it was in transition, just beginning its leap to national advertising. It had great athletic footwear but had never tried to appeal to anyone other than men and runners and basketball players. Scott helped Nike "widen the access point" to its brand to include women and "weekend warriors" looking not for a personal best but merely for the fun of physical exercise. Nike held tight to its core identity as a shoe for athletic performance but poked fun at itself and its loyalists, at basketball role models, amateur joggers, even dog-walkers. Its commercials and print ads hit an emotional chord that resonated far deeper than advertising normally does. Many are still remembered, five to ten years later.

When Scott arrived at Starbucks, he had more innovative ideas than any of us could keep track of. He was particularly intrigued by the idea that Starbucks needn't be confined within the four walls of our stores, and his imagination spun it even further than we had imagined. We should bring coffee to where people enjoy it most or want it most, he said, as long as we can ensure its quality. We had on staff thousands great baristas, many of them aspiring artists or musicians, who could get out onto the streets to proactively meet the needs of our customers.

Scott believes that Starbucks should be a "knowing" company: in on the latest jokes, the latest music, the latest personalities, up to date about politics, literature, sports, and cultural trends. He plans to shake up what some see as the predictability of Starbucks with ideas that are vibrant and innovative.

Until Scott joined, Starbucks had spent only a small percentage of our revenue on advertising. To someone used to Nike's $250 million worldwide marketing budget, our few million dollars seemed paltry. I wish I could have handed Scott a war chest of cash for advertising the day he walked in the door, but high coffee prices meant we had to temporarily put some costly projects on hold. In spite of that restriction, we went ahead and began the process of creating a voice to express our brand personality. The media dollars would come later.

Even before Scott had been hired, we had made the decision to find a new advertising agency. We selected four top-notch agencies and asked them each to prepare a presentation. That summer, a team of us first met with all four, and I explained my goals for Starbucks. They did market research with consumers and Starbucks partners before making their presentations, and they uncovered a disturbing theme: The key threat to the Starbucks brand was a growing belief among customers that the company was becoming corporate and predictable, inaccessible, or irrelevant.

The vehemence of those feelings shocked me. As CEO, I had deliberately kept a low profile, in order to keep the focus where I felt it belonged: on the coffee and our stores. But when I heard that some people viewed us as a faceless corporation, I knew I had to take a more visible role in explaining who I am and what my goals for Starbucks are.

Ironically, once a company is big enough to advertise heavily, it has to disarm people who are suspicious of size and ubiquity. Clearly, we had not told our story well enough. We needed to communicate who we are: a passionate, entrepreneurial company dedicated not only to providing great coffee but also to enriching everyday moments for millions of people.

Picking an agency was a tough choice, since all four had great creative ideas. I let Scott decide, and he went with Goodby, Silverstein & Partners, the award-winning San Francisco agency that created "Got Milk."

I told Scott and the Goodby people that I wanted Starbucks to become part of people's lives, to enrich them with a sense of discovery and hope. It should be human and real. Our advertising should tell people who we are and what we do.

Once we had signed with Goodby, Scott plunged into our own market research, hiring an expert from Nike, Jerome Conlon, to lead the effort. Jerome had been at Nike for fourteen years, including ten as the head of consumer insights. The two of them embarked on the Big Dig, a three-stage, nine-month research project, beginning with focus groups in three cities. They watched through one-way mirrors as customers and potential customers were asked about their perceptions of the coffee and the Starbucks experience. Why do people come to Starbucks? How do they envision an ideal coffeehouse? Scott was especially interested in hearing the opinions of young, college-aged people, tomorrow's coffee consumers, many of whom preferred offbeat local coffee places.

Again, we got blasted by some of the opinions we heard. Customers in their thirties and forties and whole-bean lovers are generally happy with the Starbucks experience. But twenty-somethings want more from a coffeehouse. They want a place that's funky and unique, not necessarily well-lighted and efficient. What matters to them is a place to hang out at night, not a quick to-go latte on the way to work.

The research helped us realize that customers have different need states, and that we have an opportunity to try to meet them in different ways in different stores. During the day, a college student may want somewhere to study with a cup of coffee. During the evening, that same student may prefer a place to meet with friends, free of the heavy influence of alcohol, that offers great music but also a chance to talk. On her way to work, a middle-aged attorney may want to buy a quick double latte at a drive-through, but at mid-morning she may need a table and relaxed atmosphere to discuss business with a client over coffee. The challenge we faced was to maintain, if not strengthen, the relevance of a brand that attracted such a diverse group of consumers.

The research forced us to rethink our marketing strategy. We see ourselves as the respectful inheritors of the European coffee-house tradition, with all its connotations of art, literature, and progressive ideals. We can strengthen and enrich the Starbucks experience by drawing from this legacy and finding parallels in contemporary America, as we did when we began offering high-quality books recommended by Oprah Winfrey in 1997. We need to continue satisfying our core customers at some locations but also "widen the access point" to appeal to those who want a stimulating Third Place in which to gather in the evenings.

National advertising poses a dilemma for a company like ours. With more than a thousand stores across the United States, we need to speak to people in many cities at once. But by its very nature, national advertising fuels fears about ubiquity. How do we reach a national audience while still being respected at the local level? We worked for months on a master plan, rejecting many concepts along the way.

However we approach our customers, we have to do so with respect, intelligence, humor, and energy. You can't hold the attention of people today unless you treat them as you would a respected friend of the family. In our case, these friends are our customers. The brand connects our partners, our customers, our products, and our core values the same way a family does.

Goodby has begun helping us craft an image that is simple, elegant, soulful, and uplifting, focusing on the emotional benefits we all look for in a coffee break, while embodying the playful and humorous spirit Goodby is known for. They are seeking to balance the successful corporate giant against the personal, human interaction our customers have every time they take time out to go get their favorite coffee.

A hint of Goodby's approach can be seen in these proposed advertising statements:

"We've got coffee down cold"—for our summer 1996 promotion of both ice cream and Frappuccino.

"Today, someone's writer's block will evaporate in the steam of a cup of Kona and the great American memo will be written."

"One sip of an icy Frappuccino creates a private personal cold front all around you."

We aim for the unexpected, the offbeat, the clever. Coming up with just the right message and tone has proved much harder than I imagined. My highest aim is to have not just our advertising but the entire Starbucks experience provide human connection and personal enrichment in cherished moments, around the world, one cup at a time.

19

TWENTY MILLION NEW CUSTOMERS ARE WORTH TAKING A RISK FOR

*Security is mostly superstition. It does not exist
in nature, nor do the children of men as a whole
experience it. Avoiding danger is no safer in the
long run than outright exposure. Life is either a
daring adventure or nothing.*

—HELEN KELLER, THE OPEN DOOR, *1957*

HOW NOT TO BET THE COMPANY ON A RISKY DECISION

In January 1996, almost overnight, Starbucks more than doubled the number of people it was reaching. United Airlines began serving our coffee.

Over the next few weeks, we received hundreds of phone calls from all over the country. "You've got to get out of this," people complained. "The coffee on United tastes weak and cold." "Nobody can believe it's really Starbucks." "You've got to fix it."

What was supposed to be a moment of glory was feeling instead like a disaster. We had taken a big gamble, and the early returns weren't looking good.

Every traveler knows that airlines can't serve a decent cup of coffee. Yet Starbucks lives or dies on the reputation of its coffee. So why did we risk the association? Because we had a chance to do something no one had ever done: redefine the image of airline coffee.

The gamble we took with United put to the test one of the foundations of our business: trust. If people can't trust the Starbucks name to mean quality coffee, the brand becomes meaningless.

The United Airlines partnership started in June 1995 with a phone call by Vincent Eades, who had joined Starbucks only three months earlier as senior vice president for specialty sales and marketing, the department that handles our wholesale and restaurant business. Vincent found out about a recently completed United Airlines study in which its passengers complained about the quality of its in-flight coffee. He proposed that Starbucks might be the answer to that problem.

Since United is based in Chicago, most of its employee/owners knew Starbucks and were excited about the potential of the idea, even though our coffee is typically more than twice as expensive as the competition. United pilots and flight attendants had to suffer daily with what the rest of us face only occasionally: bad airline coffee.

But inside Starbucks, the proposition provoked a strong debate. Did this move make sense for the company? What damage would we suffer if it didn't work? How many new customers could we gain from it? Ultimately, it came down to two key questions: Would it diminish the integrity of the brand? And, could we reliably deliver the quality our customers expected, on more than 500 planes all over the world?

It was a huge opportunity: Nearly 80 million people fly United annually, and between 25 percent and 40 percent of them request coffee. That's a potential market of at least 20 million people a year, many of whom would be tasting Starbucks coffee for the first time.

Vincent arranged with Ted Garcia, head of our supply-chain operations, to explore what it would take to supply coffee to United. Ted discovered that we would need to provide ground coffee in 2 1/2-ounce filter packs, yet guarantee the highest quality possible. That meant working with our supplier to create a one-of-a-kind packaging machine for our needs. Because the manufacturer needed a six-month lead time, Ted went ahead and ordered the equipment, not sure if the deal would be approved.

We were, in fact, already supplying coffee to Horizon Airlines, a high-quality regional carrier based in Seattle. Horizon was the first airline to recognize the added value that great coffee gives to its passengers. But Horizon brews our coffee on the ground, under controlled conditions, rather than on board, and then serves it quickly on short-hop flights.

United was far riskier. With its longer flights, it had no choice but to prepare its coffee in flight. That process is much more difficult than brewing coffee in a restaurant. Airlines pick up water from cities everywhere, and its quality and taste vary dramatically. On long-haul flights across continents and oceans, flight attendants are tempted to leave coffee sitting on a burner far longer than the twenty minutes maximum we recommend. Airplane brewing equipment varies in quality, and airlines are always looking for ways to lessen the weight of almost everything on board. United has more than 22,000 flight attendants worldwide, and training each of them to make a perfect cup of Starbucks coffee seemed almost impossible. The downside risk was tremendous: Twenty million potential customers whose first impression of Starbucks might be awful.

In September, we turned United down. Vincent Eades was devastated. So was Ted Garcia. But our marketing people, as well as some board members, feared that the brand could be irreversibly damaged if it were associated with a business that was perceived as big, mainstream, and too ordinary. They were afraid United would treat us like just another vendor. They didn't believe United was committed to serving our coffee the way we wanted it served. And finally, they weren't convinced that United would promote Starbucks as much as we had hoped.

But United wouldn't take no for an answer. The negotiations resumed until we finally worked out an arrangement that suited both companies.

We asked United to agree to a program far more comprehensive than any that they or we had ever signed before. We asked them to make a firm commitment to brew the best quality coffee. We wanted to train all their flight attendants, not only in the brewing of coffee and the fundamentals of what makes coffee fresh but also in the history and values of Starbucks, so flight attendants could answer questions asked by passengers.

We insisted on a comprehensive, grueling quality assurance program. We examined everything from the dosage and grind to the water filtration system. The brewing equipment on United was some of the best on any airline, but our research and development department found out they were planning to replace a stainless steel part with a less expensive plastic one. We tested the coffee made both ways, measuring the soluble solids, and asked them not to proceed with the substitution. They agreed.

To guarantee that there would be an immediate upside for us, United promised to promote the fact that it was now serving Starbucks coffee. In January 1996, it placed ads on the back covers of *Business Week, Time*, and *U.S. News & World Report*. It was not only our first national advertising but also a ringing third-party endorsement from the employee/owners of the nation's biggest airline—exposure we couldn't afford to buy. They included a line that I particularly liked: "After all, we don't just work here. We have to drink the coffee, too."

United even designed a funny and ingenious TV ad that captured what Starbucks meant to them. In it, a delivery man with a ripped bag of Starbucks coffee trails roasted beans through the airport to a plane door, attracting customers all along the way.

After so much careful preparation and quality control, the coffee should have been great from Day One. But we had not anticipated one major glitch. We had set February 1996 as the target date to start serving Starbucks on all United flights. By that date, United would have used up all supplies of coffee from its previous vendor. But as the Starbucks program began, only 30 or 40 percent of its 500-plus planes had the right brewing equipment. We had discovered that in the old machines, the hot water was passing through the grounds too quickly. To remedy that, United arranged for a brew cup with a metal plate at its bottom to be custom-built, but the supplier hadn't been able to produce all the new parts by February. On some flights, United had to use the old coffeemakers for the first month or so.

United got an earful, too. But with guts and determination, both companies decided to stay the course. We immediately threw a lot of people at the problem to fix it. Within four months, the new brewing equipment was built and delivered to all United planes, and the coffee started tasting flavorful and strong.

Today, United rates its decision to serve Starbucks as one of its best moves—right up there with the idea of offering Happy Meals to kids. A survey we conducted in April 1996 indicated that 71 percent of coffee drinkers on United described the coffee as excellent or good overall. About 14 percent had tasted their first Starbucks coffee on United. While some said the in-flight coffee was not quite as good as what they had bought at Starbucks stores, a large majority of passengers said that it was better than that of other airlines.

There's a metaphor Vincent Eades likes to use: "If you examine a butterfly according to the laws of aerodynamics, it shouldn't be able to fly. But the butterfly doesn't know that, so it flies." At Starbucks, we likewise do things we don't know we're not supposed to be able to do.

At both United and Starbucks, we think the risk has paid off. And 20 million people, on 2,200 flights a day to destinations on every continent around the globe, are drinking Starbucks coffee, at 35,000 feet.

• • •

You Are the Company You Keep

Many people are surprised at how many opportunities for partnerships we turn down—far more than we accept. At the time we were debating the United arrangement, for example, we nearly implemented another multimillion-dollar deal with a chain of stores that would have taken our coffee to towns across the United States. But that store's image and philosophy, we decided, were not consistent with ours.

While 87 percent of our sales are still generated through our own retail stores, we are besieged by inquiries to expand the distribution of our coffee to other venues. In assessing any of these ventures, Vincent's specialty sales group looks not for standard vendors but for strategic partners.

We have a fairly rigorous screening process. Companies we've turned down include those who compete too directly with our retail stores, those whose management does not have the same quality orientation, and those whose attitude toward customers is incompatible with ours. Sometimes, too, we aren't prepared, logistically, to service the business, often because of its geographic location. We also have to make sure we can build a long-term relationship that is beneficial to both parties, in terms of both profits and brand-building.

What began as Starbucks' restaurant division, supplying coffee to white-tablecloth restaurants in the Seattle area, has now formed alliances with an elite group of organizations. Instead of merely evaluating proposals that come across the transom, Vincent has turned the specialty sales group into a professional sales force that strategically approaches specific businesses that fit into our larger objectives.

Our goal is to make our coffee available where people shop, travel, play, and work. Strategic partnerships have made it possible to drink Starbucks coffee at Nordstrom stores, on Holland America cruise ships, at Sheraton and Westin hotels, and in Barnes & Noble and Chapters bookstores, as well as in offices supplied by U.S. Office Products. The list keeps growing.

But as our coffee becomes more widely available, the inherent contradictions between increasing sales and preserving brand integrity have intensified. Ideally, we want everybody to have access to Starbucks coffee. But every time we sign on another big account, we face the same worry we faced with United: Will we lose control over quality? And will the increased exposure help or hurt our retail stores?

The answer, we found, was picking the right partners, training their people thoroughly, and monitoring as closely and regularly as we can their adherence to our standards.

When we enter into any partnership, we first assess the quality of the candidate. We look for a company that has brand name recognition and a good reputation in its field, be it hotels or airlines or cruise ships. It must be committed to quality and customer service. We look for people who understand the value of Starbucks and promise to protect our brand and the quality of our coffee. All these factors are weighed before financial con-siderations.

Vincent Eades, who joined us from Hallmark Cards, has a quick way of weeding out inappropriate partners. He simply asks them: "If a pot of coffee had been sitting on a burner for one hour and a customer came in, would you serve them a cup right away?" If the answer is yes, we show them the door. If they're not willing to throw away half a pot and brew a fresh pot, they don't understand Starbucks' commitment to quality.

Another key determinant is how willing a potential partner is to train employees. Usually, the owner or manager is not the person who serves the coffee. While at the negotiating table, he may declare his appreciation for quality coffee, but is his company really willing to make the necessary investment of time and money to train his wait staff?

We start with one-year agreements and then extend the commitment to multiple years if the partnership seems successful. That arrangement gives us time to evaluate how well our strategic partners are living up to their promises, and it gives them time to see if the Starbucks connection enhances their business. So far, all our corporate partnerships are working.

The nail-biting moments with United highlighted for me the need to make risky decisions. Nothing truly great can ever be achieved without taking risks. For a brand-dependent company, it's vitally important to champion and elevate the brand, but you can't let that worthy goal prevent you from breaking new ground. When problems crop up, serious setbacks that might seem to threaten the image you have lovingly cultivated, you have to withhold judgment on the success of the venture until you've thrown all your resources into attempts to solve those difficulties.

Whatever you do, don't play it safe. Don't do things the way they've always been done. Don't try to fit the system. If you do what's expected of you, you'll never accomplish more than others expect.

20

You Can Grow Big and Stay Small

The fundamental task is to achieve
smallness within large organization.

—E. F. Schumacher,
Small Is Beautiful:
Economics as if People Mattered, *1973*

How to Be Everywhere without Being Faceless

Actress Janeane Garofalo recently joked about us on the *HBO Comedy Hour*: "They just opened a Starbucks—in my living room."

We liked that line so much that we adapted it for an ad that pictured a bottle of Frappuccino and a woman standing in an empty field, with the caption: "A great place to open a Starbucks."

Funny as those lines are, they do strike perilously close to the heart of Starbucks' greatest vulnerability. We're opening so many stores that people are starting to feel we're approaching ubiquity. The danger is that the bigger the company gets, the less personal it feels, to both partners and customers. If our competitive advantage has always been the relationship of trust we have with our partners, how can we maintain that as we grow from a company of 25,000 people to one of 50,000?

There is no doubt in my mind that Starbucks can realize its financial goals. A more fragile issue is whether our values and guiding principles will remain intact as we continue to expand. I for one would consider it a failure if we reached the $2 billion–plus level at the expense of our unique connection with our people.

How do we grow big but maintain intimacy with our people? This is the toughest dilemma I face as the leader of Starbucks.

Achieving that ideal may ultimately be impossible, a contradiction in terms. But we've got to try. If we don't, Starbucks will become just another soulless big chain. I'm determined never to allow that to happen.

CAN A BUSINESS GROW BIG
WITHOUT BECOMING "BIG BUSINESS"?

In America, small businesses are generally admired, yet Big Business is hated and feared. Perhaps the reason lies in our strong leaning toward individualism. Yet the more small business succeeds, the bigger it becomes. Does that make it suddenly worthy of scorn?

If you asked people in a focus group, "Tell me what Big Business means," you'd almost certainly get a series of negative statements. At one extreme they might mention the Exxon *Valdez* oil tanker crashing and ruining Alaska's waters. You'd get "asbestos." You'd get "Love Canal." You'd get "people who lie." You'd get Danny DeVito's movie *Other People's Money*. Big Business, the common thread would run, is capitalistic and therefore threatening.

And what's small business? Ask the same focus group, and they may well give you a set of completely opposite reactions. Small business means hard-working people struggling to earn a living. Small-business owners are often well-intentioned and care about their customers. Some have left jobs in big corporations and want to live life a different way.

Finally, if you ask: "How many big businesses act like small ones?" most people would answer: "Not very many." When we tell people that we're trying to build a big business on a foundation of small-business values, many don't believe it. Either they assume we're incurable optimists or they begin looking for hidden agendas that would explain our *real* intentions.

One of Starbucks' greatest challenges is to try to break the mindset that big can't be good. If we don't, we'll lose the very values that attracted people to us in the first place.

VALUES DON'T WITHER AS SALES GROW

Ever since Starbucks started on its trajectory of fast growth, we've faced skeptics who criticized that strategy. Most of us were so pumped about achieving our vision, however, that we just discounted them. Our customers were telling us, with their frequent return visits and enthusiastic comments, that they approved of us. Today, that approval is stronger than ever. More than five million customers a week visit our stores, and theirs are the votes that count.

But increasingly, we've also been hearing other voices. As Starbucks grows faster every year, opening hundreds of stores and entering locales ever more distant from Seattle, the chance for misunderstanding looms ever larger. One site location, mishandled, can damage a reputation we took years to build.

In a handful of places, we've gotten pushback from activists who don't want Starbucks in their town. A few times a local business owner, fearful that he can't compete, has gotten his customers to protest and keep us out. In a few cases, critics have made unfair charges that are hard for us to respond to without appearing defensive. How can we convince people who have no experience of our stores and our coffee that we're not "predatory" or "ruthless"?

It is painful to hear such words. Starbucks is not some faceless corporate entity. It's me, and Dave Olsen, and Howard Behar, and other individuals who have defied conventional wisdom and built a company based on passion and values. We set out to win, no doubt about that, but our goal is to win with integrity, as a talented and highly principled player in the free enterprise system. We channel our competitive energy against rivals far larger than ourselves, like the big packaged foods companies, not against local mom-and-pop coffeehouses. Our mission is to expand the number of people who appreciate great coffee, to make it ever more widely available and enjoyed.

The criticisms leveled against us, I think, crystallize a deeper issue: the growing fear about the homogenization of neighborhoods and towns. Most of the opposition we've encountered has been in close-knit urban areas or small towns, where people are highly protective of their distinctive character. They worry that national chains will displace locally owned stores and that fast-food restaurants will elbow out the corner diner. A few groups have even prevented us from opening a store, by passing some ordinance or claiming insufficient parking.

Some communities don't know what to make of Starbucks. We don't fit neatly into existing categories of retail, restaurant, or fast-food. Starbucks is not a restaurant but a high-end specialty retailer that serves coffee beverages. But because most retail stores don't serve food or drinks, we occasionally have to apply for a "change of use" permit because we provide seating, as restaurants do. Then there are people who expect a coffeehouse to be bohemian, with wood floors and fabric wall coverings and worn tables and mismatched chairs. When they see that Starbucks is clean and efficient with a complete line of coffee-related merchandise, they are baffled.

Clearly, there's room for many different styles of coffee stores and coffeehouses in a given neighborhood. We've noticed that whenever several coffee businesses locate near one another, customers flock there. When people know that an area has neigh-borhood gathering places, they make plans to go there, and then decide which coffeehouse to visit. They may vary their choice of establishments, depending on their need or mood. In the end, all of us benefit.

The way I see it, we've enhanced the coffee category. Coffee consumption in America has improved since Starbucks arrived, both in quantity and in quality, in large part because of the aware-ness and choices that the specialty coffee industry has provided. Some of our competitors have openly admitted that they wait for Starbucks to enter a market and educate customers before they go in. One of our Seattle rivals announced a deliberate strategy of opening a store across the street from every Starbucks. Does that make me happy? No. But we concentrate on our customers, not the competition.

Landlords occasionally exacerbate the problems we face in new markets. Good sites are hard to find, especially in small towns where the retail corridor is only two or three blocks long. Our real estate people have to act quickly when a site becomes available. Property owners sometimes use Starbucks as a bargaining chip, informing another coffee company or another prospective tenant that we are interested in the space and then jacking up the rent. Then Starbucks gets blamed for the rent increase when we were never even involved in the negotiation.

In a few cases, we have been deliberately misled. A landlord might call Starbucks up and ask: "Are you interested in leasing our space?" They don't mention that it's already occupied by another café, perhaps a tenant with whom they have not had a good rela-tionship, one they want to get rid of. We express interest, but before we have a chance to investigate, an outraged story in the local paper announces, "Starbucks is coming to town and is willing to pay higher rents because they want to kick somebody out of the market." We don't find out about the existing tenant until he starts a grassroots campaign against us. Once we've been painted as a heartless national chain, no one wants to hear our side of the story.

In two cases, when activists protested, we examined the situation closely and decided not to open a store in their community. We want people to feel delighted and excited that we're in their neighborhood, not put upon. Our goal is to find communities that eagerly welcome us.

An article in *Newsweek* particularly angered me by comparing Starbucks to Wal-Mart. The charge is unfair and inaccurate. First, we don't change the economics of a town. We don't undercut prices charged by other stores; in most cases, our prices are higher, not lower. We don't draw traffic out of town to warehouse locations; instead, we enhance downtown commercial districts and existing retail centers, increasing traffic for neighboring shops. In fact, Starbucks recently received the 1997 Stafford Award, an honor that Scenic America presents, in recognition of our "sensitive reuse of older spaces within cities" and our excellent design standards. Scenic America is the only national organization dedicated to preserving and enhancing the scenic character of America's countryside and communities. Many complementary retailers, such as bakeries and bagel shops, locate their stores near ours as a matter of strategy.

Many cafés are small, local businesses, and some of them accuse Starbucks of having abandoned its principles simply because it has grown large. They complain that we deliberately open up across the street from them to lure away their customers. In fact, though, if they weren't competing with Starbucks for locations, they would be competing with someone else. As tenants, we cannot control rental rates; rents are market-driven and set by landlords.

As an entrepreneur myself, I have great respect for anyone who goes out and creates a business, whether it's a coffeehouse or some other enterprise. A growing category like specialty coffee has proven large enough for many of us to succeed. Pleasing customers and thinking ahead of the curve are much more relevant to a company's success than who opens a store across the street.

From the beginning, we've executed our expansion plans according to our own real estate strategy—locating in sites we consider desirable—and not as a response to the competition. We carefully analyze the demographics of a given area, our human and financial resources, the level of coffee knowledge, and each market's ability to accommodate a cluster of stores.

Almost everywhere we open a store, we add value to the community. Our stores become an instant gathering spot, a Third Place that draws people together. That's what community should be all about, yet a few activists persist in arguing that we're damaging the character of their communities. I think it's more about misunderstanding than reality. Nevertheless, it's troubling.

What I've learned in the process of responding to these critics is that Starbucks has to increase its sensitivity to local issues and loyalties. In communities that are troubled about our entry, we have met with local leaders to understand local concerns. We also need to speak up more forcefully about our values and the contributions we have made. Starbucks managers have the power to allocate donations to local causes like ballet and opera companies, AIDS organizations, food banks, schools, and PTAs. In every city, all eight-day-old coffee beans are donated to food banks. Store managers also provide coffee for fund-raisers. One store in Seattle gives half its profits to the Zion Preparatory Academy, an African-American-run school for inner-city children. In fiscal 1996, we gave away more than $1.5 million in cash and kind, equaling about 4 percent of our net earnings. Since we don't exploit these actions for public relations, a lot of our customers don't even know about them.

Community giving is a policy to which we've been committed since we began in business. We do it because it's right and because it makes Starbucks partners proud to work here. At Starbucks, we're human, so we don't always hit the bull's-eye. But we strive to live our values. Our hope is that the public will judge us by our intentions and our actions, not by hearsay.

How Do You Grow Big and Stay Small?

Ultimately, the answer to this conundrum lies in the hands of our baristas. Once a store opens, it's the person behind the counter, making the espresso drinks and selling the coffee, who is the face of Starbucks. The customer won't care about ubiquity if the store manager is her neighbor or the barista is her son's friend or she gets to know the staff as cordial and welcoming.

But how can we make new baristas feel a sense of identity with Starbucks? We're hiring more than 500 people a month. It's a dilemma all retailers face if they expand to city after city. As Starbucks grows, how can each barista feel the same passion for the coffee, the same drive, the same heartfelt commitment to the company that our early baristas did?

If you ask people who were with Starbucks in its earlier years what motivated them, it was an intimacy and a sense of common purpose. In 1987, we had fewer than 100 employees, and the offices and roasting plant were in the same building. When a store manager needed something, he or she could call the plant and have it within a few hours. I had an open-door policy, and those who had a gripe felt free to come to my office and tell me about it. We celebrated the births of our children, mourned the deaths of our parents, and laughed at pie-throwing contests each Halloween. (I never caught one in the face, but Orin and Howard Behar did.) Dave Seymour, who has worked in distribution in the plant since 1982, became our unofficial photographer, and he has boxes of albums and home videos of those gatherings.

I used to think that marketing was the most important department at Starbucks. Today, I'd say, unequivocally, it's human resources. Our success depends entirely on the people we hire, retain, and promote. However outstanding our performance in marketing, design, real estate, manufacturing, store operations, new products, or R & D, it is ultimately interpreted and given life and meaning by the people of the company. How well each function is carried out depends entirely on how they feel about one another and how much they care about Starbucks.

But how can 25,000 people feel intimate with a corporation? I ponder this question all the time.

Giving stock options to all our employees was probably the best step we took toward keeping the company personal and caring. As a partner and part-owner, even the most remote barista senses a connection to the company.

We've always tried to keep hourly wages higher than the industry average and to offer benefits second to none. In addition, we have crafted a wide array of programs to ensure that we continue to recognize our partners as individuals. In addition to responding to our partners' Mission Review comments, we communicate directly through quarterly Open Forums.

Every fall we bring field management from all over the United States and Canada to Seattle for a leadership conference. We show them around the support center and talk with them in large- and small-group settings. We honor managers of the quarter in each region and invite them to an annual dinner in Seattle where we celebrate the achievements of our Managers of the Year.

Every store has E-mail, called Dateline Starbucks, and we try to keep retail partners up-to-date with voice-mail messages. I send out recorded messages to all partners whenever the company has important news. But disembodied voices can't do what real people can.

In mid-1994, when our total workforce reached 2,800, we recruited a senior human resources executive, Sharon Elliott, to help us deal with the "people issues" of growing big and staying personal. From her years at Macy's, Squibb, and Allied Signal, she understood the hazards faced by large companies. But she had never encountered a culture as fast-moving and caring as the one she found at Starbucks. "This isn't a mystique. This is the way Starbucks is," she said shortly after joining. "I feel like I'm home."

We handed Sharon two major assignments: to recruit a senior

management team that would take us through the year 2000 and to maintain the caring, small-company atmosphere that had for so long nurtured our values.

Within a year, the first task was complete. We had seven new senior managers, all with experience at companies far larger than Starbucks:

Michael Casey, our chief financial officer, had worked at Grace and Family Restaurants.

Vincent Eades, specialty sales and marketing, came from Hallmark.

Ted Garcia, head of distribution and manufacturing, had worked at Grand Met.

Shelley Lanza had been general counsel at Honda of America.

Scott Bedbury had headed advertising at Nike.

Wanda Herndon, communications and public affairs, brought experience from Du Pont and Dow Chemical.

Some people in the company felt threatened by the heavy dose of new talent, all arriving at the same time. But I was exhilarated by it, for it showed that Starbucks had grown to the point where executives would leave large, successful companies and move to Seattle to join our team.

In recruiting senior managers, we looked for people who shared our values and brought the skills and experience we needed. But we also deliberately aimed for diversity in our executive team. As a high-powered African-American herself, Sharon was especially conscientious about making sure we met this goal. Before she arrived in 1994, our senior management team consisted of eight white men and two white women. By 1996, it consisted of nine white men, three white women, two African-American women, and one African-American man—a group far more representative of the face of America in the 1990s.

But as a human-resources professional, Sharon had a far broader view of diversity than one considering only race and gender. She encouraged a broadening of the workforce in terms of age, handicaps, personality, and learning style. We had already decided to give benefits to same-sex domestic partners, not as a political stance but as a recognition of the needs of the wide variety of individuals who already worked at Starbucks. We also began to locate stores in a wider variety of neighborhoods, recognizing that people of different racial, ethnic, and age groups also want convenient access to high-quality coffee. And we began to offer diversity training for all partners, stressing tolerance as not only the right thing to do but also as a key to winning and going global.

In 1996, Sharon proposed adding a line about diversity to our Mission Statement, the first change made to it since its adoption in 1990. To us, it felt as momentous as changing the Constitution, but it was unanimously approved.

Sharon also encouraged greater directness and accountability in our relations with one another. After she arrived, she encountered too often what she calls "the Dark Side of the Force": an unspoken belief that being direct and open with co-workers is the equivalent of treating them with insufficient respect and dignity. Supervisors were reluctant to tell people honestly when they were underperforming, to the point that employees occasionally weren't even aware their supervisors were dissatisfied and were shocked when they were subsequently fired. It was the downside of niceness, and I was as guilty as anyone. Sharon relentlessly reminds us that it's more professional to be forthright with people about their shortcomings so they know how they can improve.

Another of Sharon's strategic moves was to hire Wanda Herndon, who plays a key role in our efforts to explain our values to an increasingly skeptical world. Wanda develops the strategies to shape our public image and communicate not only with our partners but also with communities, customers, and the media. She also plans shareholder meetings to make investors feel they are valued members of the Starbucks community. Wanda tends to disarm critics: As a smartly dressed African-American woman with close-cropped hair and an infectious laugh, she is far from most people's preconceived image of a stiff corporate executive. She raises eyebrows with her direct and frank style.

To ensure two-way communication with our store partners, we have undertaken frequent surveys and cultural audits. The results of one coordinated by ARC Consulting in October 1996 gave us a sobering wake-up call. ARC conducted fifteen focus groups in seven cities and surveyed 900 partners by telephone. Their overall findings confirmed my belief that we have managed to maintain an extraordinary culture that truly values people:

88 percent were satisfied with their jobs,

85 percent thought Starbucks showed concern for its employees,

89 percent were proud to work at Starbucks, and

100 percent thought "working for a company that you respect" was an important factor in job satisfaction.

The professionals at ARC, who survey many companies, told us that these marks were extraordinarily high.

The poll also revealed that a high percentage of our baristas were in their late teens or early twenties, and many saw working at Starbucks as an acceptable "way station" on the road to a meaningful career. Baristas took pride in the coffee skills they had learned and judged a Starbucks job as much higher in status than working at a fast-food outlet. That was the good news.

The worrisome findings were that their level of satisfaction seemed to be slipping. When store managers felt overworked or baristas worried about short-staffing, they tended to blame these problems on the company's rapid growth. They expressed concern that Starbucks would become just another huge, impersonal chain, losing its respect for the individual. Although still in the minority, other partners feared that Starbucks was beginning to care more about growth and profits than about its employees.

Fortunately, we have been able to provide an environment that makes people want to work for us. Even more than their stock options, baristas told us they cared about the emotional benefits they got from their jobs: the camaraderie among co-workers, interaction with customers, pride in a new skill and knowledge, respect from managers, and the fundamental satisfaction that came from working for a company that treated them well.

Clearly, we needed to find better ways to ensure that the quality of the Starbucks experience continued, both for partners and for customers.

When I heard these results, I knew that the company stood at a crossroads. The tension that accompanied our rapid expansion was a symptom of an underlying ailment that could have long-term consequences. If we were to put the brakes to our growth, even for just a year, we would disappoint shareholders, who expect continuous rapid earnings growth. It would also erode the momentum and pride our people take in working for a vibrant, successful company. The solution, it seemed to me, is to be continually diligent in our efforts to provide a great work environment for our partners and to offer them a range of opportunities to develop their skills. And we need to communicate our mission better, to help Starbucks people understand that our goal is not growth for growth's sake (or worse, for Wall Street's sake) but rather to bring our great coffee to the widest possible audience. We needed to reinvigorate their emotional connection to the company.

AS YOU GROW, YOU NEED TO GROW YOUR PEOPLE, TOO

Any company that has expanded as dramatically as Starbucks inevitably realizes that fast growth can be painful for the individuals involved. At Starbucks, we try to promote from within, but sometimes the sheer speed of growth outpaces the abilities of our early contributors. We also find that people who throw their hearts and energy into their work to the degree that we do are at an especially high risk for burnout. A company whose growth never stops accelerating seldom manages enough time to reward its employees for achievements other companies would celebrate.

For me, the most painful downside of growth has been those few occasions when we've had to let go caring, committed people who were not up to the next level needed. I'll never forget the day when one loyal, long-term partner came to my office in tears because his manager told him he didn't have the expertise to stay in his job. "This is *my* company, dammit!" he shouted. I was filled with sympathy, but not sure how much more we could do for him. Fortunately, he was able to find another position at Starbucks, but others have had to be let go. For me, this kind of experience is gut-wrenching. It forces me to consider the question: How far should we go to provide for an individual if he or she is not contributing as much as we need?

Almost as difficult have been those times when passionate, devoted partners come to my office to tell me they can't take the stress anymore. It's happened too often. I'm aware that the demands of the work and the level of intensity at Starbucks are too high for many people. It's harder for some than for others to sustain passion about work day after day, year after year. But when you've shared a dream and a goal with someone, it's hard to see him or her go.

In contrast, one of the most rewarding experiences for me has been to witness the development of gifted people who do grow with the company, however painful that maturing may sometimes be. At one board meeting not long ago, I watched with pride and respect as one of our executives made a highly professional and persuasive presentation. She was Christine Day, now Starbucks' vice president of operations services, responsible for strategic planning for our biggest division. She is the same Christine who joined Il Giornale as my office assistant when we had one store.

Christine's success is a good illustration of the opportunities to grow a career within a quickly expanding company. But her progress hasn't been without its moments of angst. When we bought Starbucks, the transition was hard for her. She had to let go of many of the things she had managed and carve out a new role with a narrower set of responsibilities. Her job eventually evolved into one of managing purchasing, traffic, and inventory, and coordinating new store construction until 1990. She had to transform herself from a generalist in an entrepreneurial company to a specialist in a professionally managed one.

In 1990, Christine became vice president for store planning, during a period when our store opening schedule was accelerating every year. In April 1995, she moved to retail operations. Gradually, she became more comfortable and more capable as she acquired the knowledge and experience she needed at each level. She had to learn to live with constant change and pressure, while some of her colleagues chose not to make the transition to working for a large company.

Christine adopted the Starbucks vision as her own, as have most of the other managers at the company. "We all believe," she says. "We believe because there's value and quality in the product and in the people we work with and in the work environment. That's what makes it special and why it works."

Although Christine is the only one who advanced from assistant to vice president, Starbucks is filled with individuals who, like her, chose to stay and grow with the company, despite the hurdles. Our longest-tenured partner, Gay Niven, started in 1979 answering phones for the merchandising manager, when the old Starbucks had only three stores. She later headed retail merchandise buying as we grew to the 50-store level. Since then, she has developed retail training programs and worked in several departments, becoming our chief storyteller and helping to pass on the legacy and culture to new people.

Deborah Tipp Hauck, whom I hired as a store manager in 1982, is today vice president for markets and products. Jennifer Ames-Karreman, who in 1986 was the first Il Giornale barista, later headed retail operations for the Northwest, and then became retail director for coffee. Countless others, still keeping alive the passion that brought them here, have found ways to develop fulfilling careers by gaining experience in a variety of departments. Many of those who helped refine our Mission Statement in 1990 have remained, whether in our roasting plants, in our warehouse, or in our retail stores.

It's hard, from the CEO's office, to assess how well our passion is taking root in newer markets. In December 1996, I racked up a lot of frequent-flyer miles by attending pre-Christmas sales meetings in California, New England, Wisconsin, and Canada. I was the keynote speaker at each. As I sat and listened to the opening speeches, I took note of the connections people had to one another, and to the coffee, and finally to the company itself.

One of these gatherings took place in Newport, Rhode Island, for partners from New York, New Jersey, Philadelphia, and New England. It was the one meeting I was most concerned about, because I was sensitive to the fact that the East Coast is a more difficult operating environment. Some have told me it's harder to find people there who are not cynical about employers and work. I was afraid that, at these meetings far from Seattle, I'd see a fracturing of the Starbucks culture.

But to my surprise, I found myself overwhelmed with the energy and passion I saw in every region, especially in New England. Going from city to city, I heard managers stress the same themes and I saw the same reactions from the audience. I saw laughter and enthusiasm at the same inflection points. Partners I had never met came up to me to say they had never worked for a company that cared so much.

That trip taught me that there are people in every city who want to believe that work can be more engaging and rewarding than punching a time clock. I can't know everyone's name anymore, and we can't be as familiar as we were in 1987, but Starbucks can still be an employer of choice by providing a work environment with more camaraderie and concern and emotional rewards than most.

Our partners know what's genuine and what's phony. When I speak to them from the heart, they relate to the Starbucks vision and the Starbucks experience. When management listens to their concerns and responds honestly, they realize that Starbucks is neither faceless nor impersonal. We are going to make mistakes. But if our people recognize that what we're trying to do, in our hearts, is build value for us all, they're more likely to forgive the mistakes. Many are already coming to understand the advantages our size brings, and are helping to ensure that we can grow big and still be the same kind of company. They *are* Starbucks, and its success reflects their achievements.

21

How Socially Responsible
Can a Company Be?

*The evidence seems clear that those businesses
which actively serve their many constituencies in
creative, morally thoughtful ways also, over the long
run, serve their shareholders best. Companies do,
in fact, do well by doing good.*

—NORMAN LEAR, FOUNDER
THE BUSINESS ENTERPRISE TRUST,
IN AIMING HIGHER, BY DAVID BOLLIER

As CEO, my primary responsibility is to the people of
Starbucks: partners, customers, and shareholders. I
also feel accountable to those who came before me, those who created the legacy of Starbucks and built it into what it is today.

To me, "corporate responsibility," the term President Clinton
used for a conference of CEOs in May 1996, means that management must take good care of the people who do the work and show
concern for the communities where they live.

So what about "social responsibility," the term used by companies that give a percentage of their earnings to charity, or sell
organic products, or try to save the rain forest? We don't use that
term to describe Starbucks' approach, in part because our company

doesn't have any political leanings, and we encourage a diversity of opinion among our people. On balance, though, I think it's a positive when others categorize us with such enterprises because "contributing positively to our communities and our environment" has long been part of our mission.

Still, as an employer and a public company, Starbucks needs to sustain and grow its business. We need to generate profits to demonstrate that the company is healthy and well-managed. Actually, we've never distributed dividends; all our profits go right back into the business.

Some shareholders think companies should not make any charitable contributions; they prefer to make these decisions directly, rather than through stocks they own. But I have a different view. To reflect the collective values of our partners, we believe Starbucks as a company should support worthy causes in both the communities where our stores are located and the countries where our coffee is grown.

Who should set the agenda to decide which causes to support and how? And how far can we take this responsibility if it seems to conflict with the needs of building our brand and our business? Those are questions that become increasingly troubling as we grow and become more capable of making a difference.

WHEN THE UNDERDOG BECOMES A WINNER, THE CHEERING STOPS

Before Starbucks went public in 1992, we were a struggling Seattle company trying to make it big. Once we made it, though, public attitudes toward us began to change. Some of the same people who once rooted for us began to snipe at us. Once they decided we were no longer an underdog, they looked for ways to knock us down.

When measured against five million satisfied customers a week, our detractors are few in number. But when you are sincerely trying to build an enterprise with high principles, you can't help feeling discouraged when your intentions are misunderstood, and at times even misrepresented.

Many of our customers and shareholders still view us as a beloved local coffee company, an inviting Third-Place café, a tenacious enterprise that's always trying out bold new ideas. But our very success tended to make others suspicious of us and eager to believe the worst they hear. I've been called a "coffee magnate" and accused of being arrogant and ungenerous. It's the downside of success, and it's hard to swallow.

Executives at big corporations grow accustomed to being magnets for attacks from cause-oriented groups. When Starbucks started being targeted, it caught us off-guard. We were so used to regarding ourselves as the good guys, as the struggling underdogs, that we couldn't believe others would want to attack us. At first, we were confused by what we perceived as simple misunderstandings. We responded honestly, and sometimes we got bitten.

WHOSE CODE OF CONDUCT SHOULD YOU FOLLOW?

When we set Starbucks' standards high, we never anticipated that we would be criticized *because* we set high standards. That's what happened in late 1994, when a network of Guatemala activist groups started a leaflet and letter-writing campaign against us.

Some background: In April 1989, Peter Blomquist, then Northwest regional director for CARE, the worldwide relief and development foundation, was standing in line at a Starbucks. While waiting to order his morning cappuccino, he picked up a Starbucks brochure entitled *A World of Coffee*, which included a picture of Dave Olsen and a map showing the countries around the world where we buy coffee. Almost all were locations where CARE sponsors health, education, and other humanitarian aid projects. "You could have laid that map over a map of countries helped by CARE," Peter recalls.

He approached Dave about donating to CARE, and both agreed it was a natural fit. After traveling to almost every coffee-growing region in the world, Dave knew only too well how poor the living conditions are in rural areas of the Third World. By paying a premium to farmers who grow high-quality coffee, he believes we are inherently supporting local economies while also providing incentives for better-quality coffee. Still, we depend on coffee growers for our livelihood, and he was enthusiastic about the idea of helping improve their lives through an organization with a proven track record.

Dave talked to me about CARE, and we both liked its approach. CARE programs don't just feed the hungry, they help improve basic living standards in poor countries by such efforts as educating people about basic health care and helping them get access to cleaner water. Although we were then a small, private company with annual sales of less than $20 million, we liked the idea of giving back to coffee-origin countries through CARE.

But at that point we were not in a position to give. Starbucks was growing fast in 1989, adding 20 stores on a base of 26, and we were still losing money—more than $1 million in that year alone. We had to make up our losses before we could even mention charitable contributions to the board. But Dave and I set a goal: Once the company became profitable, we would start donating to CARE.

In 1991, Dave Olsen took a trip to Africa to observe CARE projects in Kenya. He visited a school and saw hundreds of African kids using CARE's magazine, the *Pied Crow*, to learn about hygiene, family and community, land reclamation, environmental protection, and rural development. Two hundred of the young students sang Kenya's national anthem for him and his family, and tears came to his eyes. He came back fired up and ready to formalize our involvement.

In September of 1991, finally in the black, Starbucks launched a partnership with CARE, kicking it off with a benefit concert by Kenny G. We not only committed to annual donations of at least $100,000, but promised Peter Blomquist that we would integrate CARE into every aspect of Starbucks' business. We began offering CARE samplers of coffee and other CARE-related items such as mugs, backpacks, and T-shirts, in our mail-order catalogue and our stores. When customers buy these items, a portion of the price they pay is donated to CARE. We have featured CARE in in-store promotions, stand-alone informational kiosks, and articles in *Coffee Matters*, as well as supporting it by organizing benefit concerts with Kenny G and Mary Chapin Carpenter.

Each year we increased our donation to CARE, until by 1993 we were CARE's largest annual corporate donor in the United States. In 1996, for CARE's fiftieth anniversary we sent three partners, Dave Olsen, Don Valencia, and events specialist Vivian Poer, on a fund-raising climb to the summit of Africa's Mt. Kilimanjaro. Our contributions to CARE have supported programs in four coffee-producing countries—Indonesia, Guatemala, Kenya, and Ethiopia—including such projects as clean-water systems, health and sanitation training, a literacy effort, and a new project to help small farmers in Ethiopia's Zege Peninsula where, according to legend, coffee originated. We target programs where we can help develop lasting, life-saving solutions that will remain long after CARE has moved on to address other needs.

Because our relationship with CARE has become a source of pride for our partners, we were taken aback when, shortly before Christmas of 1994, a Chicago-based group of Guatemala labor activists began passing out leaflets at our stores. They contained claims that were misleading and highly inflammatory. They said that coffee workers in Guatemala worked under inhumane conditions to earn only two cents a pound, while Starbucks sells the beans for up to $9 a pound. The leaflet led people to believe, falsely, that these workers were on our payroll and that Starbucks was pocketing the difference. Finally, it called for people to write to me and to organize against Starbucks.

We were understandably dismayed, for we believed we not only had been behaving responsibly but in fact had taken initiatives that went far beyond what any other coffee company had done. We hadn't exploited our support of CARE's programs in these countries for public relations purposes, and now we wondered if we had erred in not being more vocal about it. It was clear that we had to respond to this attack, but how?

Over the next few months, we received dozens of phone calls and thousands of cards and impassioned letters. Well-meaning individuals wrote, asking us to triple the daily wages of coffee workers, while others dismissed our long-standing support of CARE as "a hand-out." Although we purchase less than 1/20th of 1 percent of all the world's coffee, and coffee prices are set on international commodity exchanges, people seemed convinced that we single-handedly had the power to change the coffee plantation system in Guatemala.

It quickly became clear that Starbucks was being targeted for a reason: because we have both a well-known national brand and a reputation as a principled company. Precisely because of our CARE donations, activist groups knew we were concerned about issues impacting Third World coffee-growing countries. They wanted us to use our purchasing power to promote social change according to their agendas. Some of our supporters even began asking: "Why not just stop buying coffee from Guatemala?" Yet we knew that a boycott—or even a threat to boycott—would hurt most directly the people who could least withstand it—the coffee workers.

What these protesters didn't understand was that, since we don't grow coffee ourselves, we cannot guarantee which farm produces it, whose hands pick it, or how much farm workers are paid. The Guatemalan coffee we sell comes from thousands of different farms. It is processed, bagged, and delivered to an exporter before it is shipped to us. We can inspect the quality, but we cannot easily determine, for any given shipment, exactly which farms it came from. We are one customer, and not even the largest customer. If we refused to buy from Guatemalan exporters, they would sell to someone else. Our customers would lose out, and the coffee workers would not be any better off.

We can't bow to pressure from every cause-oriented group that pickets our stores. But the working conditions of coffee workers is a matter close to our hearts, and we didn't want even one customer to think we weren't doing all we could to help them. So, after much internal discussion with Dave and the board, we decided to study the issues involved to see if it might make sense to establish a code of conduct for our suppliers.

At our next annual meeting, in February, I made a public commitment to establish a code of conduct, setting forth guidelines for our dealings with suppliers in coffee-origin countries. I also explained that the issues were far more complex than the picture presented by the protesters. Human-rights activists applauded the announcement, though I warned them that it wouldn't be easy. "I don't want to make an agreement I can't live up to," I said at the time.

Over the following six months, Dave led an intensive study of similar codes that had been adopted by such companies as Levi-Strauss, The Gap, J.C. Penney, and Reebok, as well as a close examination of our own beliefs, ethical values, and attitudes toward supplier countries. He held meetings with representatives from a variety of cause-oriented groups, as well as CARE and ANACAFE, the Guatemalan coffee producers' association. Dave tried to keep the tone of these discussions upbeat and constructive. One message he wanted to get across: An attack on Starbucks is an attack not on a faceless corporate entity, but on a group of people who, in fact, share many of the same values and goals as our critics.

By September 1995, Dave and his group had completed "Starbucks' Commitment to Do Our Part," a framework outlining our beliefs and aspirations as well as a set of specific short-term commitments for helping to improve the quality of life in coffee-origin countries. We used the term *framework* rather than *code of conduct* because our guidelines necessarily differed from the codes adopted by importers of manufactured goods like jeans and shoes. Levi's, for instance, buys from about 600 discrete factories worldwide; each factory has machinery contained within four walls, which makes it possible to inspect working conditions there. In contrast, Starbucks buys, indirectly, from thousands of farms in about twenty origin countries. We could never conduct meaningful inspections the way a manufacturer does.

We stopped short of threatening to impose penalties on Guatemalan plantations that didn't live up to our standards, as some had proposed, because of the practical difficulty of enforcing those standards. We did, however, outline a specific work plan for educating suppliers about our mission and values, communicating our goals to the coffee industry as a whole, and gathering further information during visits to selected origin countries. Our aim was to do our part in ways that we believed could have measurable effects, and for which we could be held accountable.

As far as I know, no American company importing agricultural products has ever attempted a code of conduct for foreign suppliers. But after we announced our framework, some still criticized us for failing to put teeth in it.

In early 1997, we followed up by forming an alliance with Appropriate Technology International to help poor, small-scale coffee farmers in Guatemala increase their income by improving the quality of their crops and market access. With a $75,000 first-year grant, we initiated a revolving fund to facilitate loans for producer cooperatives, starting with the funding of a wet-coffee processing facility designed to minimize environmental impact. Most of the growers we're helping are struggling to feed themselves and their families from the produce of a few acres of land, and they suffer from high rates of illness and malnutrition. We see this effort as just a first step, an innovative program that could be expanded to make a difference for coffee farmers in other countries, too.

The leafleting incident taught us the downside of being responsible and responsive. It makes you vulnerable to an ever-wider array of special interest groups and individuals with diverse and sometimes unclear agendas. In Vancouver, British Columbia, our stores were spray-painted and vandalized after another group leafletted us because Starbucks supports the Vancouver Aquarium, which keeps whales in captivity. Yet another group asked us to pressure Pepsi, our joint venture partner, to stop doing business in Burma because of human-rights abuses there. We don't even do business in Burma! Even the Audubon Society has petitioned us to protect migratory birds whose forest habitats are being cut down for coffee plantations.

As a company grows, its values will inevitably be challenged, but not in predictable ways. Big, successful enterprises can afford to be more generous and socially responsible than smaller ones, but they may also be held to impossibly high standards.

To be responsible to employees, communities, shareholders, and the greater good means to carefully balance a host of competing interests. You have to be very sure of your values and weigh them honestly against the need to sustain the enterprise. If you anger suppliers, if you alienate groups of customers, if you spend too much time and money on causes, you cannot build a strong, long-lasting company. If your company fails, or fails to grow, you can no longer afford to be socially responsible.

At Starbucks, we have to weigh what's affordable against what we think is right. That's why we keep giving to CARE even when profits are tight, as they were in early 1996. And that's why we set up the Starbucks Foundation in 1997, recruiting Peter Blomquist as its director. But we will take a stand and support causes according to our own agenda, acting on our beliefs and values and not those dictated to us by others.

"Don't say we're doing nothing," Dave says to our critics. "Say we are doing other than you would like us to do."

No matter how others judge us, we will continue to hold strong to the values that sustained us when we were underdogs—cheering or no cheering.

What to Do When Your Environmental Ethics Clash with Basic Business

Running a company while keeping to high ethical standards presents another dilemma: Sometimes you can't figure out how to live up to them.

Consider the case of the Starbucks cup.

For more than ten years, Starbucks has been selling coffee-to-go in a paper cup with a plastic lid. Yet that cup has been one of the most nagging issues we've dealt with, a brainteaser that seemed to pit our values against our brand image and our desire for customer service.

The problem is this: Hot coffee in a paper cup can be uncomfortable to hold. Espresso drinks like lattes are not as hot because they are tempered by the addition of steamed milk. But for regular drip coffee and *caffè Americano*, we have always had to put one paper cup inside another so the drinks will be easier to carry.

For customer convenience, double-cupping works fine. But every time we double-cup a serving of coffee, twice as many Starbucks cups end up in the trash—an apparent waste of material that runs counter to our environmental ethic. Living in an environmentally aware city like Seattle, I'm especially conscious of and bothered by the amount of waste we generate.

If you ask Starbucks retail partners—many of whom are in their twenties—what world issues concern them most, the overwhelming consensus is the environment. They hate to see disposable paper cups walking out of the store every minute, Starbucks napkins fluttering about the sidewalk, plastic lids that get used once and discarded. They love the coffee, but they don't want to add yet another piece of refuse to landfills that are already overloaded.

In response to these concerns, Starbucks set up an Environmental Committee, a high-level group that looked for systematic ways to reduce, reuse, and recycle waste, as well as to contribute to local community environmental efforts.

We developed what may be a unique approach to addressing environmental questions. To coordinate efforts for our retail stores, we created an all-company Green Team, which consists of store managers from all our regions. Three times a year they meet with senior management and representatives from departments such as marketing and retail operations, coordinate plans for Earth Day activities, conduct recycling audits, and champion new ideas, which they then take back to their regions. It's our way of trying to get the best thinking from our partners on how to become not only environmentally sensitive but a leader in this field.

Each district of around 10 stores has an environmental liaison, who coordinates efforts. Most stores appoint a partner to monitor recycling efforts and come up with innovative ways to cut waste. Stores often conduct Green Sweeps, sending people out into their neighborhoods, and even to nearby beaches, parks, parking lots, and other areas, to pick up trash. We encourage our customers to support our environmental efforts by offering them a discount if they bring their own cups for us to fill, selling commuter mugs, and serving drinks in porcelain cups if customers specify "for here" rather than "to go."

Our system is not always as effective as we'd like it to be, but it ensures that our operations people are always conscious of our environmental goals.

Often good ideas originate in the stores and percolate upward. One store removed plastic knives and spoons from the condiment bar, making them available only upon customer request. That initiative dramatically reduced the number of plastic utensils that are thrown away. One region negotiated with a local dairy to take back used milk cartons. We need to rely on local store initiative because recycling practices and services vary across the country.

In October 1994, we hired Sue Mecklenburg from the University of Washington business school to serve as director of environmental affairs. By the time she joined, we had already implemented numerous initiatives to reduce waste in packing and shipping. There wasn't, she recalls, much low-hanging fruit. So she set to work on the biggest environmental issue still facing us: double-cupping.

In 1995, we assembled a Hot Cup Team, with members from environmental affairs, purchasing, marketing, R & D, retail operations, and food and beverage. Their first step was to talk with suppliers. The primary alternative to paper cups, they discovered, is polystyrene, which insulates hot beverages far more effectively than paper.

We chose three kinds of polystyrene cups and conducted focus groups on their use with 250 customers. The favored alternative was a thin, pressed polystyrene, the kind used in convenience stores and gas stations. We produced a quantity with our logo and test-marketed them in Denver. While some customers thought these cups were an improvement over double-cupping, many disapproved. Polystyrene didn't reflect the quality people had come to expect from us, and the public perception is that plastic is even less environmentally friendly than paper. To dispose of used cups, we shipped them to a polystyrene recycling facility in California. In fact, while it's technically possible to recycle polystyrene, it's impractical in many cities.

We had to face another practical difficulty, too. Typically, our customers leave our stores with their cup. A collection bin placed by the door would be useless to someone who drank her coffee away from the store. Anyone planning to finish it in the store could have requested a porcelain cup in the first place. Realistically, there is no way most of our customers could recycle polystyrene cups independently.

Switching to polystyrene would have saved Starbucks $5 million a year at that point in time—and far more as the number of stores multiplied in future years. But we decided against it. It didn't solve the environmental issue, and it wasn't consistent with our image.

Back at Square One, we started looking for a better paper cup, but we couldn't find one that met our needs. So we decided to test market a paper sleeve. Instead of two cups, we would slip a ring of corrugated cardboard around the middle of each paper cup of regular coffee. The sleeve used only about half as much material as a second cup and even contained some recycled paper. By the time we printed our logo on it, we realized the sleeve wouldn't save us any money, but we decided to offer it anyway.

For a longer-range solution, though, we decided to look outside the company. In early 1996, Sue approached the Environmental Defense Fund, which had partnered with McDonald's to find an environmentally preferable alternative to the plastic clamshell in which they had been packaging their hamburgers. Eager to help companies develop innovative solutions to environmental problems, the Environmental Defense Fund had jointly established the Alliance for Environmental Innovation with The Pew Charitable Trusts. In August 1996, Starbucks and the Alliance agreed to work together to reduce the harmful environmental impacts of serving coffee. Our goal is to reduce the use of disposable cups both by increasing the use of reusable cups and by introducing a new, environmentally preferable single-use cup.

We contacted about forty-five parties—cup suppliers, industrial designers, and so on—who we thought might know of ways to solve our problem. We met with about twenty-five of them, reviewed their ideas and prototypes, developed a short list of eight cups that we presented to focus groups in three cities, and tested the three semifinalists in Seattle, Chicago, and Boston during the summer of 1997. Our goal was to identify a preferred alternative by the fall of 1997 and then move to production in 1998.

Holding yourself to a higher standard is expensive and time-consuming. It requires you to spend an enormous amount of time and money dealing with issues that many other companies would comfortably ignore. When the problems seem unsolvable, you have to keep after them.

It's an ongoing struggle. But we care how people feel, what our partners are thinking, what the customer believes. So we keep at it.

22

HOW NOT TO BE A COOKIE-CUTTER CHAIN

*Art is an adventure into an
unknown world, which can be explored
only by those willing to take risks.*

—MARK ROTHKO, IN THE NEW YORK TIMES,
JUNE 13, 1943

Nothing pains me more than hearing critics compare Starbucks to a chain of discount stores or fast-food operations. It's not that I don't admire the way Wal-Mart and McDonald's have grown their businesses, for there's much to learn from their success. But the image they project, in their products and design, is far removed from the tone we've cultivated at Starbucks, of style and elegance.

Perhaps I've set the bar too high. Like an overachieving parent, I want it all for Starbucks: success in all the conventional ways, plus an extraordinary level of innovation and style.

At Starbucks, we hold design to the same high standards that we demand of our coffee. It has to be best-of-class, top-quality, and express a personality that's sophisticated yet approachable. We want each store to reflect the character of its neighborhood, yet it must be clear that all belong to the same family. Our fast growth has pushed us to standardize design and purchasing, yet we create a variety of options so we are not producing a chain of clones. We want our style to be consistent without being pedestrian. From the beginning, we've struggled with this internal contradiction: How do we project a distinctive and individual style when we are opening stores so rapidly?

I would never allow Starbucks to sacrifice or downgrade its elegance and style for the sake of growth. In fact, we've been quietly heading in the opposite direction. As we grow bigger, we can afford to invest in the kind of creative, innovative design that pushes the envelope. That's how we'll maintain the edge of surprise and delight that has always been a hallmark of the Starbucks experience.

CREATING A DESIGN PERSONALITY

I've always loved the design aspects of Starbucks. I consider graphics and store design to be a differentiating factor, a way to show our customers that Starbucks is one step ahead. Many of our customers are sophisticated and discriminating, and they expect us to do everything with taste, not only our coffee preparation but also the esthetic design of our stores and packaging. When they come into our stores, they're after an affordable luxury, and if the setting doesn't feel luxurious, why come back?

Starting at Il Giornale, we tried to re-create the Italian espresso bar experience, using decor that was European and contemporary, well-lighted and friendly. I worked with an architect, Bernie Baker, to plan the layout of the store, the placement of the logo, the location of the stand-up bars by the windows, the fixtures for newspapers, and the menu board, which was designed to resemble an Italian newspaper. The espresso machine stood at center stage, with counters curving back from it.

Once we merged Il Giornale with Starbucks, we totally

redesigned the Starbucks stores to make sure they reflected a similar Italian look. In the new configuration, we placed the espresso bar at the back, so that the first thing customers would notice as they entered was the whole-bean displays. We dropped the brown mercantile look and added some chairs, no more than nine in each location at first. At the time this setup was unique.

Just after the merger, I came up with an idea that has since become one of the most distinctive elements in the Starbucks look: the use of graphics to highlight the uniqueness of each type of whole-bean coffee.

Until then, when you walked into a Starbucks store and asked for a pound of, say, House Blend, the person behind the counter would rubber-stamp the name of the coffee on a plain white and brown bag. But those plain words did little justice to the rich variety of flavors and the different cultures of the origin countries. To me, each coffee has a personality, based on where it was grown or why the blend was created. It was incumbent upon us, I figured, to find a visual way to reflect those distinctions to our customers.

I turned again to Terry Heckler, for both his sense of style and his linkage to the founding of Starbucks, and asked him to create images that captured the spirit of each coffee. After he designed our green Starbucks logo, which we put on our bags, he also designed a series of stick-on stamps for each type of coffee we sold. Each one evoked cultural elements of the origin country, local flora or fauna, or the mood that particular coffee created or elevated. To this day, if you order a half-pound of, say, Kenya coffee, the barista will put it in a standard Starbucks bag but identify it with a colorful stamp designed for that type of coffee—formerly an elephant, now an African drummer image. The Sumatra stamp for many years showed a tiger's head; New Guinea a brightly colored toucan; Costa Rica Tres Rios a woman balancing a fruit basket on her head. I wanted the graphics to become strong visual signals that would remain evocative even after the product was brought home.

Introducing the new stamps was expensive, adding 2 cents to the cost of each bag of coffee. Not only did we have to manufacture the stamps, but affixing them to bags took a little extra labor in our stores. My justification, of course, was: "Everything matters."

We used those original stamps for nearly ten years, updating them and adding ones only as needed. Then, in 1997, we refreshed our look with a newly designed set of stamps, with different images.

Many other companies have since copied our idea of stamps. But the stamps have become visible symbols of the style of Starbucks, vivid mementos of the Starbucks experience that resonate with people and keep them coming back.

Other coffee purveyors also started to copy our store design, once they saw the importance of its role in attracting customers. In fact, Starbucks has had to challenge several competitors to stop them from using images too similar to ours. One company went so far as to imitate not only our store design, colors, and logo but also our in-store brochures.

Over the years, our packaging evolved, as we tried to maintain a consistent style but still convey variety and depth. Beginning in 1987, our coffee bags, cups, napkins, and other materials all were white with the green logo. But by September 1992, we wanted to broaden and freshen the look, so we hired a design firm, Hornell Anderson, to redesign our packaging. Working with Myra Gose in our marketing department, they created a new graphic vocabulary, with natural earth tones. They also gave us the coffee steam pattern that we used on bags, walls, posters, and wrapping paper, a brand icon that became a visual cue for Starbucks. And they designed a distinctive coffee bag using a terra-cotta red and charcoal background with the same steam pattern. In 1992 we also asked Terry Heckler to revise our siren logo: She stayed mostly the same but lost her navel. Inside the company, Myra became the keeper of the look, the design conscience of Starbucks, making sure that any new packaging or product was consistent with the image we want to convey.

• • •

EARLY STORE DESIGN:
BALANCING CONSISTENCY WITH STYLE

Beginning in 1987, we developed a strong overall design theme that would ensure that our stores looked alike. My objective was to make each store in each new market reflect a mirror image of the early Starbucks stores in Seattle. When we moved to Chicago and Los Angeles and other cities, I wanted the new stores to project the values and style of the original Starbucks.

As the roll-out accelerated, we gradually realized the importance of designing our stores ourselves, for speed and efficiency as well as design integrity. We tried using outside designers and architects, but some of them didn't get it. They gave us what was "in" in retail that year, and we wanted a look that was unique and sustainable.

So we made a decision that was costly but also far-sighted: Starting in 1991, we built up our own team of architects and designers, to ensure that each of our stores would convey the right image. Most entrepreneurial companies can't afford to employ such skilled people at this stage of growth. At first, they worked under Christine Day, who was then vice president for store planning. We had, in effect, an in-house architecture and design firm.

The first 100 or so stores were designed by hand, on drafting tables, and I examined and approved the detailed plan for each, from signage to counter finishes. Once, when layout issues cropped up at our first three stores in Los Angeles, I flew there with our designers the next day to figure out how to make it right.

Ironically, though all our stores looked similar, they were never uniform in a cookie-cutter way. At first, in fact, we custom-designed every store because we had to. Unlike McDonald's, we don't own our real estate and build freestanding stores, but rather sign leases and move into existing spaces that differ in size and shape. To control costs, we had to use similar materials and furnishings, but no two stores were exactly alike. For example, depending on the setting—urban or suburban, formal or informal—we varied the type of wood finishes used (dark cherry, light cherry, or maple) within the larger design parameters.

To keep the look consistent and the expenses reasonable, two of our designers, Brooke McCurdy and Kathleen Morris, developed a series of palettes, each with six basic colors and multiple options, including choices of various light fixtures, countertops, and colors of hardwood veneers. Christine Day used the analogy of sisters— each with an individual appearance, but clearly from the same family. Our designers had a sense of ownership for each project, and often took calls from the field when construction managers uncovered a brick wall or other aspect that might affect design.

Still, as Starbucks expanded across the country, people began to complain that too many of our stores looked alike—a vulnerability that competitors were eager to exploit. In every city in America, small, independent coffeehouses opened up with original decor tailored to the local mood and sensibility. In college towns, they were funky and offbeat. In suburbs they were down-home and cozy. However the coffee tasted, if they created an atmosphere that felt comfortable and pleasant, they would attract customers. People began to say our design was hard-edged and institutional.

It's a criticism that cuts to the heart. We want to establish a personal connection with our customers, but we also want our stores to be accessible and convenient. How do you open 300 stores a year, each one of them distinctive and designed to fit the tone of the local neighborhood?

In 1994, under Arthur Rubinfeld, we began to experiment with different formats. We designed a handful of unique stores customized to fit specific needs. We experimented with a few drive-throughs in locations where commuters were in a rush to get somewhere. We designed kiosks in a few supermarkets and other public places.

But most important for those who wanted a Third Place, we added seating and introduced the concept of Grand Cafés, large flagship stores with fireplaces, leather chairs, newspapers, couches, attitude. Customers love them. There's something wonderfully satisfying about curling up with a cup of coffee in front of a fireplace.

At one location in Manhattan's Upper East Side, we created a bohemian living room on the second floor. Complete with tattered couches and easy chairs bought at garage sales, it quickly became an afternoon oasis and an evening gathering place in a city not known for safe places to kick back and relax.

But this approach led to a bigger problem. Our rapid growth into numerous new markets, coupled with our larger formats, was causing initial store investments to spiral out of control. Our average store-opening cost hit a peak of $350,000 in 1995, an impossibly high figure. The Grand Cafés we had custom-designed cost much more.

So we faced a new dilemma: how to cut costs drastically yet still compose a next-generation design scheme that would look fresh no matter how many stores we built.

TO STAY ONE STEP AHEAD, YOU HAVE TO INVEST IN CREATIVITY

That's the conundrum we handed Wright Massey when Arthur hired him in 1994 to be vice president of design. Wright doesn't fit the typical image of a designer. With his thick face and strong jaw, he looks as if he'd feel more at home on a football field than in a studio. Yet not only is he an experienced architect—he has designed some forty hotels—but he's also a watercolor artist. He's outspoken and direct, with a strong Carolina drawl, quick to criticize and quick to recognize a brilliant idea.

Wright forced our people to work together as a team in ways they never had before. He had them hammer out a plan for "synergistic rollout," laying out expectations for our people in each of the disciplines of real estate, construction, design, operations, purchasing, and contract management. Before that effort, our designers had kept most information in their heads, like tribal knowledge, and he pushed them to write it down and systematize it. The goal was to revamp the whole process of store planning to achieve quicker development, lower cost, and better designs.

Before we hired Wright, our people in the field had been trying to pare down our costs on a per-project basis. But Wright recognized that the big savings would come only if we took advantage of our size and scale. Building hundreds of stores a year gave us tremendous buying power that we had never really leveraged. So we centralized buying, developed standard contracts and fixed fees, and revised our relations with contractors, promising large volumes of work to those who kept costs under control.

But that wasn't enough. What we needed to do was to learn a few lessons from the cookie cutters. Our retail operations group outlined exactly the minimum amount of equipment each core store needed, and the design group worked with purchasing to pre-order and pre-stock standard items at 20 or 30 percent lower cost by getting volume discounts direct from the vendors. That meant finding warehouse space or implementing complex just-in-time delivery. For parts needed in every store, such as drawers for whole-bean coffee or the espresso bar, we were able to standardize the sizes and cuts, so that we could order in bulk. Any odd spaces could be covered with filler panels. The goal was to develop processes that didn't enslave designers but helped them be more creative.

Although modular case work is usually the kiss of death for good design, we found a way to make it work for us. In 1996, we revamped our computer system and developed new software that helped us fit in standard equipment and fixtures and estimate costs as the design evolved. By taking advantage of our size and coordinating our operations needs with our design goals, we were able to cut store development time from twenty-four to eighteen weeks and reduce the average store costs significantly. That freed up the resources we needed for a more fulfilling project: designing our Stores of the Future.

Wright's goal was to raise our store design to a higher level, leaping ahead of our competitors. He aimed to create a lyrical and esthetic new design, with richness and texture, strong enough to tell the Starbucks story, going beyond just a revised new color scheme, another kind of wood, or a new style of chairs, and trying to capture the essence of the Starbucks experience. He directed his creative team to draw from culture and mythology to weave a fantastic tale.

"Good design is not pretty colors," Wright likes to say. "It's putting something out of reach and making people go get it."

To get the creative juices flowing, we set up a "secret" studio, deep in the recesses of the Starbucks Center building in Seattle and hired a team of artists, architects, and designers to fashion our next generation of stores. Few knew of the studio's existence. Only a handful of people had keys, and others had to sign nondisclosure forms to be admitted. We kept the project hush-hush so we'd have a major impact when the new designs were released in late 1996.

Dave and I met with the Store-of-the-Future design team early on, explaining our vision for what Starbucks should be: an authentic coffee experience, an extension of the front porch, an enriching, rewarding environment that could accommodate both fast service and quiet moments. Then the designers took it further, doing research about sirens, as seductive and unpredictable as coffee itself, and about Starbuck, the level-headed first mate. They explored the mythology of the sea, the idea of the Third Place, and the art and literature of coffee culture throughout the ages. They learned about coffee blends and origin countries. The designs they created try to convey these themes subliminally, through murals and icons and other images.

They got rid of everything stiff and hard-edged, and brought in romance and mythology, mellowness and warmth, using contemporary production processes to capture an eclectic, handmade look. But they kept my original vision of the artistry of espresso-making, spotlighting it by placing the machine behind a rounded bar and creating a wooden "hand-off" plane where baristas could place finished drinks ready for customers.

Rather than opt for a simple, uniform look, they evolved complex variations on the four elements of earth, fire, water, and air, by relating them to the four stages of coffeemaking: grow, roast, brew, and aroma. That allowed for four different store designs, each with its own color palette, lighting scheme, and component materials, yet all unified by an overarching concept. *Grow*, for instance, highlights shades of green. *Roast* combines deep reds and rich browns. *Brew* emphasizes blue, for water, and brown, for the coffee. *Aroma* uses a light color palette with yellows, greens, and whites. All of the concepts incorporate natural textures, hand-blown light fixtures, and suspended ceiling elements based on organic shapes. Within these four basic templates, we can vary the materials and specific details to adapt them to different settings, from downtown buildings to suburban areas to college towns.

For the people involved, the process was gut-wrenching, with wide swings of morale, redefinition of roles, and reexamination of core values, like a rebirth of Starbucks. They were, after all, messing with the image I had carefully composed for Starbucks. Wright says he wondered, some days, if he was going to get fired or shot for the revolution he was trying to bring about. At times progress was slow and agonizing, and some early concepts either went too far or didn't have enough edge. But I made a point of stepping back from the team's work and letting their imaginations run.

I remember how I felt when I walked around the mock-up stores in our fifth-floor studio to see the final design concepts. Arthur and Wright were with me, but I didn't want to have any discussions or listen to any explanations. I simply wanted to immerse myself in the mood the team had created. What I saw reflected a level of creativity and artistry so far above what we had come from, that original Il Giornale design.

The artists showed me icons they had developed, using variations on the shape of the siren, for use in the stores, and an entirely redesigned set of stamps to identify our coffees. The end result was a series of images so original and imaginative that I felt a sense of awe at the kind of talent we were able to inspire. Some of these images appear in this book.

"This is great," I said. "Hurry up and get it into our new stores."

Once the new store prototypes were approved, we faced the challenge of finding ways to build them within the strict budget that had been set for existing stores. That meant negotiating contracts with a different set of vendors and suppliers. By June 1996 Wright and his team had figured a way to purchase more than 300 items directly from vendors, lowering our overall investment costs by 10 percent.

The final plans, rolled out in late 1996, included four formats and four palettes. Our typical 1,400-square-foot Core A stores, with flexible seating areas and a complete selection of merchandise, can use any of the four color palettes and designs. Core B stores, formatted for smaller spaces, emphasize spatial efficiency. They draw on the same four design palettes, but cost less to build.

We also introduced two new formats: the *breve bar* and the *doppio*. Breve bars are designed as a store-within-a-store in supermarkets or office building lobbies, and are compact enough to fit into sites previously considered too small for a full-sized Starbucks. Doppios, named for a double shot of espresso, are the smallest outlet, fitting into an approximately 8-foot-square space. They are self-contained and can be easily relocated. Both the smaller units use the same style and finishes as the larger stores.

Given the apparently contradictory tasks of lowering costs while creating a better design, Wright's team not only accomplished that but also a third: devising novel formats that would allow sales in locations we never could have considered before.

HOW NOT TO BE A COOKIE-CUTTER CHAIN

It wasn't just the "cookie-cutter" criticism that drove the Store-of-the-Future effort in 1995 and 1996. We were reaching higher than that. But this experience is typical of the way Starbucks reacts. If there's a problem, we try not only to fix it but to create something innovative and elegant in the process.

23

WHEN THEY TELL YOU TO FOCUS, DON'T GET MYOPIC

If you can keep your head when all about you
Are losing theirs and blaming it on you,
If you can trust yourself when all men doubt you,
But make allowance for their doubting too; . . .
If you can fill the unforgiving minute
With sixty seconds' worth of distance run,
Yours is the Earth and everything that's in it,
And—which is more—you'll be a Man, my son!

—RUDYARD KIPLING, "IF"

December 1995 was the holiday season from hell.
Every Christmas, we, like most retailers, prepare to be incredibly frenzied—in the roasting plant, in the stores, in the offices. At Starbucks, it's the one time of year when our retail merchandise—coffee beans, espresso machines, chocolates, mugs—become as important as the daily lattes and cappuccinos. Usually, the holiday spirit pervades the bustle, customers ooh and aah over the colorful products on the shelves, executives pitch in at the cash registers, and we collapse at the end of the month with contented smiles, promising ourselves that we will be better organized next year.

Christmas 1995, however, was a different story. Windstorms and heavy snows hit several different regions, forcing a number of stores to close for days at a time. The papers were filled with desperate quotes from retailers, trying to wish shoppers into their stores. Predictions for the shopping season got ever gloomier.

Each morning our retail sales team met in the conference room next to my office. These meetings were increasingly full of bitten nails and twitching ankles. Someone would hand out the computer reports of the previous day's sales, broken down by region, by product category, by sales dollars, by number of customers. It was like getting our test scores. We would compare actual versus budgeted figures, and would revise our forecast every week. If we didn't make plan one day, we would recalculate some numbers to figure out what we needed to make plan for the rest of the week, and then for the month and quarter and year.

The key figure was the daily comp, which measured sales growth for stores open a year or more. With more stores open, overall sales were obviously growing. But was each individual store selling more than the year before?

Monthly comps had been averaging about 5 percent growth over the same month in the previous year. Now the daily comp numbers were coming in at 2 percent, 1 percent, 0, sometimes even negative. It was a frightful trend.

Adding to the pressure was the fact that our stock kept breaking through record highs. If we didn't make our numbers for the month, we knew, investors would react dramatically and the stock would plummet.

To make things worse, we knew our profit targets would be hard to meet anyway, since Starbucks still had high-priced coffee inventories purchased during the summer of 1994. Orin expected some of his cost-saving measures would bear fruit, but it was too early to calculate just how much impact they would have on the bottom line. With Orin, I could be honest about how dejected I was. He felt the same way.

What could we do? Most of the key decisions that determined our sales had been made six months earlier, when we ordered merchandise, designed packaging, and bought coffees for our blends. We quickly discovered some mistakes that we couldn't fix. For Christmas 1995, we had rejected the traditional red-and-green packaging for playful pastels, and customers didn't take to it. We had ordered too many espresso machines and not enough affordable gift items. Our planning was off, so that we had prepared far too much inventory of certain coffees, including our Christmas blend. We had packaged our gift coffees in big one-pound bags, as usual, but also offered, for the first time, tiny quarter-pound samples of coffee as stocking stuffers. The small bags were a hit, but we had already prepackaged most of our coffee in the larger bags before December. People at the roasting plant had to work overtime, frantically emptying coffee from big bags and stuffing it into tiny ones. It was an added expense we could ill afford.

Still, in previous years we had always been able to boost holiday sales with special promotions or other last-minute tweaking. So Orin and I created a game plan. We'd check which products were selling ahead of plan, which behind, and refine our advertising message accordingly each week. Scott Bedbury had been eager to try some image-building slogans like Brew unto Others, but we ended up focusing on the more straightforward Great Gifts for under Twenty Dollars. At my suggestion, we even offered free coffee after 5 P.M., to encourage customers to stop by our stores after shopping. In a spending mood, they might notice and want to buy some of our merchandise.

Early in the month, it felt as though our business had become a high-stakes poker game. The chips were down, but I was sure we would win, one way or the other. But with each passing day, I felt less and less sanguine. I decided to cancel my family vacation to Hawaii. That was hard on Sheri and the kids, but I felt I needed to be in the bunker with the troops .

Every morning, I received a fax at home with the previous day's sales figures. Then I'd rush into the office for a 7:30 A.M. meeting with Orin. After that, we'd meet with the retail operations team. I began to dread these meetings. My stomach would be twitching, but I knew I had to appear optimistic. The people in our offices and stores were jittery, and I wanted to pump them full of optimism. The worst thing I could do, I thought, was to start spreading the word that I was terrified about the holiday season. That would just exacerbate the problem.

One of the fundamental aspects of leadership, I realized more and more, is the ability to instill confidence in others when you yourself are feeling insecure.

Finally, in mid-December, I came to a conclusion that was both painful and liberating. Because of the size and scale of the company, I no longer am able to make the singular difference in solving crucial problems. In the old days, Starbucks was like a speedboat, nimble and easy to steer around obstacles in its path. Whatever the issue was, I could get involved and, with concentration and effort, help bring about a solution. If sales were lagging, we could change sales tactics with a day's notice, responding quickly and intuitively. I could turn the steering wheel one inch or a half-inch, and the entire boat would turn. The results were immediate.

By 1995, Starbucks had become more like an aircraft carrier. Once it was set in a given direction, its course couldn't easily be altered. No matter how much I jerked the wheel at the last minute, the ship ploughed ahead. It had grown too big for quick handling.

As a large company, we needed to rely more and more on planning and discipline, rather than on our instincts and last-minute fine-tuning. That's an ability we should have developed long before December 1995, but unfortunately, it took a major problem to make us all understand that we needed to find more accurate forecasting methods and plan for longer lead times. And I was beginning to accept what management consultants have advised me since: To be an enduring, great company, you have to build a mechanism for pre-

venting and solving problems that will long outlast any one individual leader.

Once I realized this, I changed tactics. I decided to communicate my worries openly, not only with my managers, but with
everybody inside the company. I called a big meeting of all the
people who worked at our offices in Seattle. Since our commons
area wasn't finished yet, we gathered in a cafeteria on the third
floor, everyone standing in a crowd, with me at the center.

The cafeteria was decorated with Christmas trimmings, but
there was no holiday spirit in the room. I was surrounded by long
faces and somber eyes. Although most partners didn't see the daily
numbers, rumors had been circulating that we were not going to hit
our targets.

What I did then was uncharacteristic, for I've always been
known for delivering upbeat, rousing talks. But on this day, I knew,
a speech like that would have simply stuck in my throat.

"Perhaps for the first time in the tenure of many of your years at
Starbucks," I began, "we're having a disappointing holiday season.
We're not performing as well as we had hoped for. There's no
excuse. It's no one's fault. But I'm worried." I explained my concerns
and what the ramifications would be if our sales and earnings numbers fell short of plan.

"Success," I told them, "is not an entitlement." We had to earn it,
every day. Just because Starbucks had achieved all its goals in the
past didn't mean that we were immune to mistakes. We had to be in
a mode of constant renewal and recognize that the future of our
company was not based on what we achieved yesterday. We had to
persevere, even when our near-term targets seemed out of reach.

For a bunch of overachievers, that message was hard to swallow.
I could see eyes glancing downward and feet shifting weight.

"I hope we'll make our numbers," I concluded. "But if we don't,
we're still the same company we were a month ago." I tried to get
them to focus on the long-term issues: what the company stands
for, not to allow a disappointing season to get in the way of the

great enterprise we had built, and to learn from our mistakes.

People came up to me later on, saying, "I've worked for other companies, and I've never heard a CEO speak so honestly and emotionally about a difficult situation. I appreciate how directly you explained what we're dealing with."

But I also heard others tell me they wished I hadn't been so straightforward. They had viewed me as the conquering hero, the star hitter who could turn even the worst game around, and they didn't like it when I stepped off my pedestal and admitted I wasn't invincible. They thought I should have hidden my personal vulnerabilities and concerns. A few fellow managers came to my office later that day, saying, "Howard, I really don't think you should have done that. What's the point? Why add more fear?"

It took a few months before my inner circle came to the same conclusion about the company that I had reached. Going through adversity like that together helped hone the senior management team—fully one-third of whom had been with the company less than six months.

One problem all of us in management had was dealing with the guilt. Unlike the coffee-price crisis, this was a disaster we felt we could have prevented. We felt personally responsible, that we had let each other down. The magic had always started with us, and this was the first time we couldn't sprinkle stardust and wipe the problem away.

Today, with hindsight, I'm convinced that speaking frankly was the right course of action. The head of a company can't, and shouldn't, always be the cheerleader. He has to be willing to let his people see the weaknesses and the pain, as long as they understand them in the context of the company's greater accomplishments.

When the chips are down, it's wrong to give a rah-rah Knute Rockne speech. People want guidance, not rhetoric. They need to know what the plan of action is, and how it will be implemented. They want to be given responsibility to help solve the problem and the authority to act on it.

A lot of managers find it hard to admit their fears to those who depend on their decisions. But I believe that if you level with your employees in bad times, they will trust you more when you say things are going well. I think our people came away from the experience of Christmas 1995 with a higher degree of faith in me and, more importantly, in what Starbucks stands for.

DON'T LET THE FUTURE SLIP AWAY, SLICE BY SLICE

Other insights struck me that Christmas, too. One is how easy it is to lose sight of the long term when short-term problems scream for attention. When times are tense, it's easy for people in the ranks to make bad decisions because they don't understand the larger implications.

In the early days, the business was easier to understand, and each manager could quickly see what impact his choices would have on the company as a whole. As we grew, we hired more experts with specialized functions, but many of these people—because they came from larger, more risk-averse companies and because they had observed only a thin slice of the business—had narrow viewpoints.

One of my most gnawing fears is what I call *incrementalization*. What may look right for each specialist's slice of the business could be a disaster for the company as a whole.

It was eggnog latte that drove the point home to me during that holiday season. That's a drink that Dave and I had introduced back at Il Giornale in 1986. It has since become a great seasonal favorite for Starbucks customers.

In 1994, someone in the food and beverage group found a great way to save money and time. Rather than going to all the trouble of opening carton after carton of eggnog to make these drinks, went the reasoning, why not use a premixed, eggnog-flavored syrup? It could be dispensed by pressing a button on a lever, holding the caffè latte underneath. It was simple and elegant. We tested the new version of the drink at our Portland stores during the 1994 holiday season, and it was well-received. But when we went to roll it out nationally for Christmas 1995, somehow the syrup did not taste the same, and no one caught the error. Because of the size and scale of the company, I was never informed of the change.

So in the middle of this lousy Christmas season, I was reading customer comment cards, as I always do, and I began to notice many of them making the same complaint: "Your eggnog tastes bad" and "What happened to the fresh eggnog?"

I strode into a food and beverage meeting and said: "What is going on with the eggnog latte?" The members of the department looked at one another sheepishly. On paper, the syrup made a lot of sense, and Portland customers hadn't complained during the test. But when eggnog latte sales started falling sharply, they realized what a blunder it was. Here was an example of the business being sliced so narrow that no one was paying attention to the overall effect.

We learned our lesson. The following Christmas, we brought back the real dairy version of eggnog latte.

A good chief executive keeps the broader picture in mind when everyone else is focusing on the details. But management also should strongly urge department heads to consult one another and examine the wider implications of policy changes. A decision to cut costs or raise efficiency will add value only if it is consistent with the overall long-term goals the company is trying to achieve.

GETTING ABOVE THE NOISE IN AN OVER-RETAILED NATION

Whatever mistakes we may have made internally, the major reason for our weak Christmas sales was external. As December went on, we began to hear alarming reports from other retailers. Gymboree, a great company, had negative 19 percent growth at comparable stores for the month of December. Computer City's comps were off 8 percent. Mervyn's fell 1.4 percent. For all U.S. retailers, same-store sales for December fell 4.1 percent, according to Telecheck Services.

By comparison, our troubles looked minor league. We ended the month with positive same-store sales growth of 1 percent.

Clearly the problem was bigger than Starbucks.

The United States has become an over-retailed nation in which too many stores are chasing too few customer dollars. Consumers simply face too many choices in the marketplace to be able to wisely decide how to spend their disposable income.

By the time Starbucks entered the national arena in the early 1990s, over-retailing had become a serious problem. Every year we find it harder to get our message out. We don't have a huge national advertising budget as large companies do. People are busier and less inclined to shop around and try out new places.

Yet over-retailing creates tremendous opportunity for Starbucks. Unlike packaged food brands, we are able to connect with people, one at a time, through our stores. And because we strive to consistently deliver a quality product and a quality experience, when other retailers are falling into mediocrity, we stand out.

But surprising and delighting our customers gets harder every year. We've led our customers to expect a high standard of service. Like every good retailer, we continually have to differentiate ourselves by offering products or experiences they can't get elsewhere. We have to work to provide more depth, more variety and richness in store design. Rather than driving down the highway exactly between the dotted lines, we may have to bounce off the guard rails a few times.

Customers are always looking for something fresh and interesting, especially at Christmastime. That demand necessitates continuous self-renewal and reinvention from retailers across America, and for us specifically. We have to keep on trying to create new categories and new products that will capture customers' imaginations.

Every retailer dreams of a blockbuster product that will fly off the shelves. That's what the *Blue Note Blend* CD was for us in March 1995, and Frappuccino in the summers of 1995 and 1996. But you can't expect to develop that kind of a hit every four weeks.

That's why, even in the face of heart-rending Christmas sales numbers, I kept pushing our R & D and marketing teams to continue their efforts for new product development. We need those farsighted projects to retain customers' interest and loyalty.

Even though we could identify obvious external trends that explained our disappointing sales, it would have been wrong to just sit back and say, "Everybody's having a bad year. It's not our fault." We have to keep looking for a way to rise above the noise in an over-retailed nation.

THE BEST CEOS ARE BOTH FARSIGHTED AND NEARSIGHTED

In the end, we didn't figure it out that year. In early January, when we announced our same-store sales numbers, the stock price sank. Later that month, we calculated that we had missed our profit-growth target by only one percentage point, thanks to Orin's backroom improvements. Starbucks was still very profitable, but earnings were not growing as quickly as we had predicted.

Still, Wall Street analysts were merciless. A few blamed me and my product innovations for distracting the company from its core business. History, one of them said, shows that the biggest danger for retail and restaurant operators is a loss of focus. "When this occurs, any brand equity the company has built up begins to dilute," he said. "We would prefer to see more attention paid to store-level execution."

That burned me up. It's precisely this short-term orientation that annoys many CEOs about Wall Street. A company whose management is not planning for the distant future can never grow beyond the latest faddish concept.

Even inside Starbucks during those months, some people groused that I was putting too much pressure on them, demanding work on longer-term projects when our core businesses needed urgent repair. I heard resentment in some voices. While they were mopping up the post-Christmas mess, I was playing with my new toys: ice cream, bottled Frappuccino, a big new contract with United Airlines.

Was my eye off the ball?

No. My eyes were focused on the long-term future. I was looking around the corner, to see what would hit us next. Procter & Gamble had just bought one of the largest suppliers of whole-bean coffee to the supermarkets, Millstone Coffee of Everett, Washington. Were the majors coming after us? Should we reconsider our early decision not to sell our coffee in supermarkets? What products could we create that would be proprietary, that would give us an unassailable niche in an ever-more competitive marketplace? How could we leverage the Starbucks brand, keeping its elegance and style but reaching more customers? We needed to pursue a long-term vision of building the Starbucks brand by creating new products. To be ready by the year 2000, we had to start experimenting immediately.

With improvements in manufacturing, retail operations, and planning, Starbucks also got better at handling the short-term future. During Christmas 1996 we avoided many of the problems that beset us in the previous year. Once again, the overall retail climate was weak, and weather was bad, especially in the Pacific Northwest. Our same-store sales growth, at 2 percent, was not as good as we would have liked. But our cost containment efforts had worked well, and earnings came in right at Wall Street's consensus estimate. As managers, we knew what to expect, and the stock market did not overreact.

We did everything we could to ensure strong sales during the holiday season in 1996. We did our homework. We executed according to a well-crafted plan, and, with far more accurate forecasts, packaged almost exactly the right amount of coffee to meet demand. What's more, I was more sanguine and could put it in context. I didn't expect a last-minute Christmas miracle, and I could focus on the outlook for the new year. With a new vice president for merchandising, Peter Gibbons, hired from Disney, and a larger staff in Don Valencia's labs, we had new products in the pipeline for summer.

That second year, we were all calmer. I realized it wouldn't be the end of the world if we weren't able to knock the cover off the ball for Christmas. Why? Because we all knew the value that we were creating, over the long term, for the brand and for the company. Christmas sales do not determine the fate of Starbucks.

Wall Street, too, understood, and the stock began to rise in January, reflecting the positive outlook for 1997.

Like the captain of that aircraft carrier, I set my eyes on the horizon and steamed ahead. This time I didn't even miss the old speedboat.

24

LEAD WITH YOUR HEART

Leadership is discovering the company's
destiny and having the courage to follow it. . . .
Companies that endure have a noble purpose.

—*JOE JAWORSKI,*
ORGANIZATIONAL LEARNING CENTER, MIT

A VISION FOR THE LONG-TERM

On the bookshelf in my office, I have a small crystal ball. It was given to me by the local chapter of the Young Presidents Organization, as a symbol of their Merlin award.

According to legend, Merlin was born in the future and lived backward in time, moving toward the past. He must have often felt out of step with his contemporaries, filled as he was with unconventional notions of what might be. I'm no sage, but sometimes I think I know how he must have felt. My vision for the future, my aspirations of what kind of company Starbucks should be, are so easily misunderstood by people both inside and outside the company.

A Santa Fe, New Mexico, management consultant, Charles E.

Smith, has compared visionary executives to the famous wizard. "Exceptional leaders," he wrote in 1991, "cultivate the Merlin-like habit of acting in the present moment as ambassadors of a radically different future, in order to imbue their organizations with a breakthrough vision of what it is possible to achieve."

Back in the early 1980s, and even more so today, I had a pretty clear idea of what Starbucks could become. I knew the look I wanted, the feeling the stores would convey, the pace of growth, and the connection with our people.

Today, when I look ahead, I see a future extending far longer than the twenty-five years Starbucks has lived so far. In annual strategic planning sessions, our senior management team has been refining that vision to make sure it is both audacious and achievable. We've been clarifying our values and trying to articulate our long-term goals. Even though many of our executives are relatively new, I'm amazed at how similar our beliefs and goals are.

The company we envision is a great, enduring one, still zealous about its mission of bringing great coffee to everyone everywhere. Its stores will provide a rewarding experience and enrich people's lives in communities around the world, one cup at a time. But we want our boldness and defiance of conventional wisdom to take it in new directions, too, leveraging the strength of the brand, inventing new products that surprise and delight, selling through many channels of distribution, possibly moving beyond coffee to other items that touch people's daily lives.

The opportunities are exciting. In most countries, average adult consumption of coffee is two cups a day, yet the quality of that coffee is, for the most part, pretty bad. Starbucks is well on its way to doubling the number of its stores in North America by the year 2000, and I'm convinced that we could eventually have more stores in Asia than we will have in North America. Within a few years, we expect our joint venture with Pepsi, by selling bottled Frappuccino and other products, to produce revenues in excess of $1 billion, a sum larger than Starbucks' total annual sales today.

But our plans go far beyond the numbers. The underlying foundation of this company is not about growth. It is about the passionate, soulful connection we have with our people, our customers, and our shareholders.

No matter now many avenues Starbucks pursues, and no matter how much we grow, our fundamental core values and purpose won't change. I want Starbucks to be admired not only for *what* we have achieved but for *how* we achieved it. I believe we can defy conventional wisdom by maintaining our passion, style, entrepreneurial drive, and personal connection even as we become a global company. It's imperative that Starbucks people at all levels share in the success of the company, in terms of both pride and financial rewards. And if by our conduct and principles we could inspire individuals and leaders of other companies to aim higher, that would be cause for rejoicing.

I'm convinced, more than ever, that we can both do well and do good. We can be extremely profitable and competitive, with a highly regarded brand, and also be respected for treating our people well. In the end, it's not only possible to do both, but you can't really do one without the other.

We have to lead with our hearts. In business, as in life, we each should have an internal compass that guides our decisions, an instinctive understanding of what matters most in this world. For me, it's not profits, or sales, or number of stores, but the passion, commitment, and enthusiasm of a dedicated group of people. It's not about money, it's about pursuing a dream others think you can't achieve and finding a way to give something back, to the employees, to the customers, to the community. I would hope that if you examine Starbucks, every time you focus on any part of the image, instead of a fracturing of values you get a close-up of the guiding principles of the company. As you look deeper, what you see is honest and authentic and respectful and dignified.

In their book *Built to Last*, authors James Collins and Jerry Porras talk of "Big Hairy Audacious Goals." For Starbucks, our ambitious long-term goal is to become an enduring great company with the most recognized and respected brand in the world, known for inspiring and nurturing the human spirit.

The Starbucks of today falls short of these high aspirations. We make a lot of mistakes. No company can ever be a utopia. But if you don't aim high, if you aim for only "good enough" or "above average," that's precisely what you'll get. If you reach for excellence, you'll inspire your team to work for a higher goal. When you encounter difficulties and shortcomings, you should deal with them in a way that is forthright and consistent with doing better in the future. Your people will be more forgiving if they understand the common mission you are working together to achieve.

The problems that Starbucks has faced in recent years—the flak we've gotten about our ubiquity, volatile coffee prices, disappointing Christmas sales, complaints and protests —haven't blinded us to the larger picture, the long-term value we've created. No enterprise can be built, no dream achieved, without confronting challenges, surprises, disappointments along the way. The more heartfelt our commitment, the more these setbacks will hurt, but the more we'll be capable of devising solutions that reflect our values.

Starbucks still fights hard to succeed, and we will face many hurdles in the future, some far more serious than any we've overcome to date. We can't keep increasing our revenues and earnings at a rate of 50 percent a year indefinitely. All great companies have passed through bad years that forced soul-searching and rethinking of priorities. How we deal with them will be the litmus test. I hope we in management have learned enough from our small troubles to manage through the bigger ones to come.

I suspect that many of the extraordinary ideas that will shape Starbucks' future will percolate up from within. By emphasizing a strong commitment to reinvention and self-renewal, by keeping the entrepreneurial spirit alive, we're doing all we can to foster an atmosphere that encourages innovation.

• • •

KEEP LISTENING FOR THE MUSIC

The music of the Beatles resonates with me, as with many members of my generation, because it reminds me of people and places and times when I was growing up. So I was eager to watch the Beatles anthology special on TV and hear the Beatles themselves talk about the history of the band. In an interview during one of the programs, Paul McCartney said something that really hit home with me.

It was after they had drawn a crowd of "only" 50,000 at Shea Stadium, and they were getting fed up with touring. Their final tour ended at Candlestick Park in San Francisco on August 29, 1966.

On the TV program, Paul, George, and Ringo were sitting around a table, recalling the reasons they had decided to quit touring. "We were getting worse and worse as a band while all those people were screaming," Paul said. "It was lovely that they liked us, but we couldn't hear to play."

That one quote struck me as profoundly relevant. They could no longer hear the music. When that happened, they lost their meaning. They had to go back to the studio to find their sound again.

At Starbucks—as in any business, in any life—there are so many hectic moments during the day when we are simply trying to do the job, trying to put out the fires, trying to solve any number of small problems, that we often lose sight of what it is we're really here to do.

I would be devastated if, twenty years from now, Starbucks achieved the penetration, the presence, and the recognition we aim for at the expense of our core values. If we lose our sensitivity and our responsibility, if we start thinking it's acceptable to leave people behind on our climb to the top, I will feel we've somehow failed.

No matter how much clamor surrounds us, we have to make sure we can still hear the music. As one of my favorite authors, Noah benShea, wrote in *Jacob the Baker*, "It is the silence in between the notes that makes the music." Sometimes we have to stop and listen for it.

Some newer partners at Starbucks hear us talk about the numbers and don't yet appreciate the foundation of values and principles that mean so much to those of us who built the company. For them and for our customers, we need to make it human and personal. We need to speak with our own voice and show our personality, so others don't misjudge us based on lack of knowledge.

We need to make Starbucks into a global enterprise while maintaining the culture, the heart, and the soul of a small company in Seattle, Washington.

What's Hope Got to Do with It?

My kind of unfettered idealism is, I realize, out of sync with the cynicism of the 1990s. Skepticism has come to be synonymous with sophistication, and glibness is mistaken for intelligence. The pundits regard idealists as either naive or calculating. And even if someone is doing right 90 percent of the time, the critics will inevitably focus on the other 10 percent. If a company sets high standards, it's easier to judge it as wanting.

In such an atmosphere, why bother aiming high?

Far too many people don't. So mediocrity is far too common in America and throughout the world. As we approach the end of the millennium, we find ourselves confronting an ever deepening fracturing of values.

Over the last few years, as my two children have been growing up, I've tried to guide them and make sure they mature into responsible and caring adults. I want to pass on to them the values that I've found meaningful in my life.

One night we rented the movie *Forrest Gump* and watched it as a family. My kids loved it, and for a week they kept quoting the line, "Life is like a box of chocolates." I began to think about why that film, which wasn't especially profound, produced such a powerful, emotional effect on so many people. Its hero was a man who, though obviously slow, proved to have more insight than anyone else because he hadn't let the world's negative values muddle his understanding of what really matters about life.

A few weeks later, I took my son to see *Hoop Dreams*. That film had a similar effect on him, for he shares my love for basketball. Here was a lengthy documentary set in the inner city, center of despair, yet its subjects were relentlessly shooting hoops in an effort to beat the odds.

What struck me about both movies was that they inspired strong feelings of hope. We're all so hungry for a hero, for a story that rings true, that everyone can relate to. We're all eager for something upbeat, something honest, something authentic.

That heartfelt need again became apparent a few weeks later, when Cal Ripken broke the all-time record for number of baseball games played. As my son and I watched Ripken deliver his speech on television, my eyes misted. Standing near him, in his shadow, was a teary-eyed Joe DiMaggio, hero of all heroes for the last fifty years, a guy who had actually played with Lou Gehrig. Then Cal Ripken says, "I can't even say my name in the same breath as Lou Gehrig." You could see Ripken's mother and father and his wife and his kids, ordinary people, caught in an inspiring moment.

Why were so many fans so invested in Cal Ripken's success? It was not simply about cheering him on for breaking the record, but a genuine response to his humbleness. Day in and day out, as he said, all he's done is his job, but he's done it selflessly and better than anyone else. In an era when half a season of baseball can be canceled because of a strike over money, our hearts go out to a player who just gets out and plays ball, again and again, and ends up breaking an all-time record.

In the ethical vacuum of this era, people long to be inspired. Even if it's just a movie, or a TV program, or a great cup of coffee, they want a break from the negative noise that inundates us all.

When you step into a theater or pick up a good novel, you just need some time out.

When five million people a week seek out a Starbucks store and wait in line for an espresso drink, when customers return several times each week, they're not just coming for the coffee. They're coming for the feeling they get when they're there. And that feeling is directly related to the fact that we refuse to do things the way others do. We won't give up hope that there's a better way.

When You Get to the Finish Line, Be Surrounded by Winners

As a kid in Brooklyn, I was afraid to look into the crystal ball. After half a lifetime, I have come to realize that we all have it in our power to shape the image we see in that ball. If we envision it, plan it, are smart about acting on it, we can will amazing feats to happen. But we need to make sure it's a vision worth bringing to life. If it has a noble purpose, the rewards are far greater.

Success should not be measured in dollars: It's about how you conduct the journey, and how big your heart is at the end of it.

Business can teach us a lot about what people can achieve when they work together. One person can do only so much. But if he gathers a company of people around him who are committed to the same goals, if he galvanizes them and inspires them and taps into their inner drive, they can perform miracles together.

It takes courage. A lot of people will try to tell you it's impractical or impossible. They'll tell you to lower your sights. They'll tell you business can't be benevolent.

Remember: You'll be left with an empty feeling if you hit the finish line alone. When you run a race as a team, though, you'll discover that much of the reward comes from hitting the tape together. You want to be surrounded not just by cheering onlookers but by a crowd of winners, celebrating as one.

Victory is much more meaningful when it comes not just from the efforts of one person, but from the joint achievements of many. The euphoria is lasting when all participants lead with their hearts, winning not just for themselves but for one another.

Success is sweetest when it's shared.

ACKNOWLEDGMENTS

Collaborating on a book about something as personal as a life story and the internal struggles involved in building a company requires a high degree of mutual respect and trust. Dori Jones Yang and I were fortunate to develop that early in the writing process, which proved to have lower lows and higher highs than we could have anticipated. What kept us centered during the two-year experience was a strong, shared belief that others could benefit from, and perhaps be inspired by, the stories and insights behind Starbucks' success.

Dori and I both would like to thank the seventy individuals, inside and outside Starbucks, who agreed to be interviewed during the research for this book, as well as the fifty people who read and commented upon early drafts of the manuscript. Without their memories, stories, insights, and suggestions, this book could not have been nearly as lively or complete. In my office, Georgette Essad, Nancy Kent, and Christina Prather helped us in innumerable ways with this book over the course of two years.

Although many Starbucks partners are named in this book, many others who are not named here have made invaluable contributions to the company and have shown by example what it means to "pour your heart into it." My thanks to them for their efforts and for their commitment.

We are also profoundly grateful to Joel Fishman of Bedford Book Works, our literary agent, who sprinkled stardust on this project and transformed it forever. And we'd like to express our appreciation to Rick Kot, our editor at Hyperion, who embodies the balance described in this book: meticulous and professional as an editor, sensitive and thoughtful in human relations.

Most important, I would like to express my deepest appreciation to Sheri, for being there every step of the way and for showing me the way to create the perfect balance in life between work and family.

And from the co-author, Dori Jones Yang:

In addition to the above, I would like to extend my personal thanks to my parents, William B. Jones and Margaretta H. Jones, who nurtured a love of writing in me at an early age; Bruce Nussbaum, my valued and trusted mentor; Lew Young and Steve Shepard, editors-in-chief of *Business Week*, who believed in me over fifteen years; Lynn Tonglao, who transcribed many of the interviews; Paul Yang, who lived through every stage of this book and provided vital sustenance and inspiration to "get it done"; Emily Yang, my confidante, helper, and beloved daughter; and Howard Schultz, who really is what he says he is.

INDEX

Adams, Marcia, 194
AEI Music Network, 210
Africa, 295, 296
AIDS programs, 256
Aiming Higher (Bollier), 292
airlines:
    Horizon, 269
    United, 267–71, 272, 273,
        274
airports, 173–74
Alex. Brown & Sons, 184
Alliance for Environmental
    Innovation, 304
Ames-Karreman, Jennifer,
    88, 289–90
Appropriate Technology
    International, 299
ARC Consulting, 286
Audubon Society, 300

Baker, Bernie, 307
Baldwin, Gerald (Jerry), 27–30,
    32–35, 38–44, 47, 63
    espresso drinks and, 58,
        60–62

Peet's acquisition and,
    55–57, 58
Schultz's coffee bar enter-
    prise supported by, 66, 67
Starbucks' expansion and, 116
Starbucks sold by, 90–95, 99
baristas:
    at Il Giornale, 87
    in Italy, 50, 53, 59, 62
    at Starbucks, 5–6, 59, 173,
        194, 246, 249, 250–51,
        262, 282, 286–87
Barnes, Brenda, 224
Bass, Barbara, 152
Bayview Projects, 4, 12–13,
    15, 16, 18–19
Bean, Curt, 193
Bean Stock, 132, 133–37
Beatles, 334
Bedbury, Scott, 261–64, 284,
    320
beer, 169, 226
Behar, Howard, 113, 154–60,
    166, 175, 194, 196, 203–4,
    207, 211, 226, 227, 244,
    250, 278, 282